Distributed by:
South Asia Books
P.O. Box 502
Columbia, MO 65205

S0-FBB-149

BOEINGS AND BULLOCK - CARTS
Studies in Change and Continuity
in Indian Civilization

(ESSAYS IN HONOUR OF K. ISHWARAN)

Volume 3
LAW, POLITICS AND SOCIETY IN INDIA

General Editors

YOGENDRA K. MALIK
DHIRENDRA K. VAJPEYI

Editorial Committee

JAYANT LELE
(Queen's University, Kingston, Canada)

YOGENDRA K. MALIK
(University of Akron, Akron, U.S.A.)

K. RAGHAVENDRA RAO
(Mangalore University, Konaje, India)

DHIRENDRA VAJPEYI
(University of Northern Iowa, Cedar Falls, U.S.A.)

BOEINGS AND BULLOCK - CARTS
Studies in Change and Continuity in Indian Civilization
(ESSAYS IN HONOUR OF K. ISHWARAN)

Volume 3
LAW, POLITICS AND SOCIETY IN INDIA

Edited by
YOGENDRA K. MALIK
DHIRENDRA K. VAJPEYI

Chanakya Publications,
Delhi

5 VOLUME SET
ISBN: 81-7001-062-4

Volume 3
ISBN: 81-7001-065-9

BOEINGS AND BULLOCK-CARTS, Volume 3
LAW, POLITICS AND SOCIETY IN INDIA

Edited by
YOGENDRA K. MALIK
DHIRENDRA K. VAJPEYI

Copyright © 1990 Yogendra K. Malik & Dhirendra Vajpeyi

First Published 1990
by
CHANAKYA PUBLICATIONS
F 10/14 Model Town Delhi 110009

Laser - typeset
by
QUICK PRINTS
103 Kundan Bhawan Azadpur Delhi 110033

Printed in India
at
Presswork, 1813 Chandrawal Road, Delhi 110007

Notes on Contributors

George H. Gadbois, Ph.D. is a Professor of Political Science at the University of Kentucky. Professor Gadbois has published several articles on the Indian legal system in many internationally known journals including, the *Journal of Indian Law Institute, Economic and Political Weekly*, and *Journal of Asian and African Studies*.

George C. Kozlowski, Ph.D. is an Associate Professor of Islamic and South Asian History at DePaul University, Chicago. He is the author of the book, *Muslim Endowments and Society in British India*. His articles and reviews have appeared in *Indian Economic and Social History Review, South Asia, Journal of Asian Studies*, and other journals.

Yogendra K. Malik, Ph.D. is a Professor of Political Science at the University of Akron. He is author of several books including, *East Indians in Trinidad: A Study in Minority Politics, North Indian Intellectuals*, and co-author of *Government and Politics in South Asia*. Professor Malik has edited several books and published articles in internationally known journals including, *Journal of Politics, Asian Survey, Western Political Quarterly, Comparative Education Review, Political Quarterly*, and *Journal of Asian and African Studies*, and several others.

Aradhana Parmar, Ph.D. teaches political science at the College of Delhi University and she is presently serving as a visiting fellow at the University of Calgary, Alberta. She has published a book on Kautlya.

John J. Paul. Ph.D. is an Assistant Professor of History at the University of Wisconsin-La Cross. He has published articles in various journals including *Journal of Asian Studies* and *Fides et Historia*.

V. Narayana Rao, Ph. D. is an Associate Professor in the Department of South Asian Studies, University of Wisconsin, Madison. Professor Rao (with Professor Heifetz) has recently published a book, *For the Lords of the Animals-Poems from the Telugu*. He has contributed articles to *Contributions to Asian Studies* and *South Asian Intellectuals and Social Change*.

Chhatrapati Singh, Ph.D. taught Philosophy at the University of Ottawa for several years before joining the Government of India, Department of Science and Technology, as a Social Scientist. At present he is a Professor of Jurisprudence at the Indian Law

Institute, New Delhi, and Legal Advisor to the Ministry of Environment and Forests. Professor Singh is author of several books, including *Law from Anarchy to Utopia* and *Common Property and Common Poverty*.

Dhirendra K. Vajpeyi, Ph.D. is a Professor and Chairman of the Department of Political Science at the University of Northern Iowa. He is author of several books including, *Modernization and Social Change in India* and co-author of *Government and Politics in India*. He has recently edited with Professor Malik, *India: the Years of Indira Gandhi*. He has published several articles in internationally known journals including, *Journal of Asian and African Studies, Indian Journal of Public Administration, Journal of Local Administration Overseas*, and several others.

Dedication

PROFESSOR K. ISHWARAN

This volume is one of the series honouring Dr. K. Ishwaran. The series has brought together scholarly contributions from an array of social scientists around the globe. We have tried to produce a reasonably balanced mix of works by established scholars and researchers along with essays by somewhat less senior and less established scholars who have shown the promise of making new and insightful contributions that diverge from and at times challenge the established, collective wisdom of contemporary social science. While the contributors of the former bear testimony to Professor Ishwaran's membership in an international community of distinguished scholars and the high status he occupies in it, those of the latter are a tribute to his tireless efforts and dedication to the encouragement of independent, innovative scholarship through his role as a teacher, author and editor of numerous journals and monographs. Although the contributors to these volumes bring a variety of disciplinary and philosophical perspectives, we are all united in our respect, admiration and gratitude to Professor Ishwaran for his service to a better understanding of the social world in general and of Indian society in particular. I should also add that given the limitations of time, space and other commitments, which have affected our planning of these volumes, we have been able to bring together only a small fraction of a large global circle of Dr. Ishwaran's friends, peers and students.

The common theme of these volumes, an assessment of the ongoing restructuring of Indian society, was chosen because it reflects some of the major preoccupations of Professor Ishwaran's most recent work. Those who are familiar with his writings also know that for the past several years Dr. Ishwaran has been showing, through his diverse, well-documented studies how the contemporary Indian society is gradually transforming itself in response to emerging challenges and opportunities. In the assessment of these changes, Ishwaran insists, the values of freedom, equality and rationality have universal validity. These and a conscious evolution of an integrated national community based on these values, must be kept at the centre of any sociology of change and development. We have made an effort to focus on these criteria while planning this series. The volumes, therefore, range over a wide substantive spectrum. Starting with an overview of the past in terms of centuries of gradual and dramatic shifts in Indian civilization and culture, at local, regional and national levels, we wanted to bring into focus the present and the potential for the future in terms of more contemporary changes, often consciously planned and implemented from above, in the various religious, social political and legal institutions. Trying to do anything less would have meant ignoring the magnitude of Ishwaran's own contributions. Whether all of these changes do in fact contribute to "modernity" is a question that we are all, implicitly or explicitly, concerned with. Needless to say, we are guided not by the usual ethnocentric definitions of modernity but by an enlightened and humanistic view of modernity which Ishwaran has put forward in much of his work.

In none of the volumes have we tried to summarize or assess Ishwaran's own work. That is a task which should not be undertaken lightly. I can only point to some of its more salient features, as I see them. His career, spanning a period of over three decades, has produced outstanding scholarship in such diverse domains of social studies as religious ethnicity, family, urban life, politics, socialization and modernization. The most noticeable feature of his work is its grounding in history and its adherence to the comparative method. His work is methodological sophisticated and reveals a sensitive understanding of the basic conceptual problems and preoccupations in social anthropology, sociology and history. His contributions as a scholar and his value to the sociological profession are amply demonstrated by the popularity of his work among teachers and students and by the frequent citations in the works of young as well as established scholars.

During the fifties much of the Western academic practice, inherited from the colonial days, was to investigate forms of rural social life in Third World societies as esoteric and hence as a useful, contrasting backdrop to their understanding of their own societies as rational and modern. Many Indian scholars had come to share this mode of reasoning because of their training and their consequent alienation from their own folk heritage. Going against this mainstream, Ishwaran in fact 'turned the tables' as it were, by means of a courageous venture to study the Dutch family. He did this in his *Family Life in the Netherlands* (1959) with a remarkable thoroughness, openness and sensitivity towards an alien milieu. Thus, according to an eminent Dutch sociologist, Professor Groenman, Ishwaran drew the attention of the Dutch sociologist to the traits in Dutch family life that they had neglected. Many Westerners had delved into non-Western communities for comparison "not all with the same grace and same success", says Professor Conrad Arensberg.

Ishwaran's insights about the Dutch family were attributed to his 'foreigner's vision' of the unfamiliar. His subsequent study of a totally familiar Karnataka village showed that what is unique about Ishwaran's work is his keen sensitivity to the essentially human dimension of all social relations. In his *Tradition and Economy in an Indian Village* (1968) Ishwaran develops the theme of continuity and change which has highlighted his work on the Dutch family. It was, once again, an eye opener for those who tend to take their own people for granted. Professor Arensberg saw in it a plea to administrators and planners to bridge the gap of understanding, perhaps even a failure of empathy. At the same time, Arensberg concludes, "the book adds significantly to the roster of comparable studies of modern Indian villages and sharpens our understanding of the universalities shared by them in highlighting the variant peculiarities proper to each region." The theme of change and continuity which is central to Ishwaran's work in Sociology and is thus the appropriate theme of these volumes that seek to honour him, was carefully outlined by Ishwaran in his editor's introduction to *Change and Continuity in India's Villages* (1970). Here Ishwaran offers a reasoned critique of the origins and popularity of the concept of Sanskritization. Ishwaran's work on Shivapur was, in fact, an early example of 'sociology from below', it pointed put the enormous gap between the Brahmanic varna model of Hindu Society and the actual life-world of the rural people. He also contrasted the notion of Westernization, as far too narrow, with a more sophisticated version of the concept of modernization. He points to the global diffusion, and hence the universal validity, of the underlying values of such modernity, equality, rationality, freedom and progress. These early reflections on the inherent modernity of the Indian folk matured into his description of Shivapur as an example of what he calls the "populistic community".

A sophisticated conceptual apparatus, thus developed from a systematic scholarly understanding of East and West, continues to characterize Iswaran's forays into a number of interesting sociological phenomena. He has written on family and kinship, childhood and adolescence in Canada with equal ease. His latest and continuing work, the trilogy on the sociology of the Lingayat religion, is guided by the same sympathetic understanding, a prerequisite for a thorough scholarship about any social-human phenomenon. Ishwaran is exploring in these three volumes, two of which are already available in English, the historic origins, the social organization and the aspects of continuity and change in one of the most fascinating religious-social communities, grounded in a six hundred year old heritage of egalitarianism.

Even a cursory look at Prof. Ishwaran's publications will show that he has the vision of a society as a totality. Functional specialization in sociology has not made him blind to this essential unity of human social relations Thus his work touches on all major dimensions that have been artificially fragmented into disciplines such as archaeology, anthropology, religious studies, sociology, political studies or legal studies. Our purpose in presenting him with these five volumes as a *Festschrift* is to acknowledge this unity in his sociological perspective. Many of the contributors to these independent volumes do share this perspective even though they concentrate their scholarly activity in one or the other discipline. Thus for those who know much of Ishwaran's work, the appropriateness of these five volumes on; 1) Indian Civilization; 2) Religious Movements; 3) Social Organization; 4) Political Development; 5) law and Social Transformation, will be obvious. For those who are not familiar with all of his work, we hope these volumes will propel them into discovering the unfamiliar insights embedded in his various writings.

Much of what I have said about Ishwaran's scholarship is fairly well known. What is far less known, however, is the uniquely integrated nature of Ishwaran's professional work and his everyday life. In the Western World today, the nineteenth century ideal of science as a fearless commitment to truth and thus to the abolition of ignorance, suffering and dogma, has become a matter of either nostalgia or ridicule. In the universities that have come to resemble business enterprises in terms of their administrative thinking, such traditional commitments are being subjugated to financial expediency. The conviction that commitment to truth must enter the conduct of our life through reflexive education and rational reinterpretation of our cultural traditions is becoming more and more difficult to maintain. Ishwaran, in my view, has successfully resisted such pressures and has not allowed the atmosphere of fractured world views and atomistic individualisation to distort the relationship between his life and his work. Instead, he has appropriated the best in his own tradition so as to confront and battle these tendencies. He displays in his writing and in his life an integrated world view that combines the best of classical Hinduism and revolutionary *veera-saivism*, both of which have their roots in the universalistic and communal social relations of the rural folk. The essential modernity of these traditions Ishwaran once tried to capture in his insightful concept of a 'populist community'.

The cognitive, normative and aesthetic unity of that tradition, rationally reconstructed and adapted to a new cultural context and consciously practised in everyday life, allows Ishwaran to feel at home in the professional culture of European and North American Universities. His success as a professional is grounded, not in the easy entrepreneurial opportunism of some of the academic enterprises, but in the deeply felt and fiercely practised commitment to work. In a way he epitomizes the Lingayat tenet: work is a heavenly activity. That undoubtedly is the secret of his 'methodically rational conduct', his enviable energy and his monumental productivity. But his family and friends also know that his zest and enthusiasm for what some people mistakenly treat separately as 'the things of life' is just as irrepressible and as highly contagious.

Ishwaran began his career as a student of Kannada literature. In that field he is known as an authority on the major medieval poet, Harihara. His sensitivity and imagination have distinguished him as a humanist. They also constitute the subterranean life force of his sociological enterprise. All of Ishwaran's sociological work has been recognized as theoretically and methodologically respectable by the canons of contemporary social science. But its real strength lies, in my view, in its philosophical underpinnings, for as Agnes Heller points out, in philosophy one can rely on one's good intuition as the final resort. The basis for such an intuition is the knowledge of the lives, concerns, ideas and actions of everyday actors and of one's philosophical tradition. In his sociological research Ishwaran approaches the problems of truth and correctness simultaneously as a humanist and a scientist. He does it with a sympathy and sharpness that enhance rather than detract from each other. Awareness of this unity has moved Professor Raghavandra Rao, who probably knows Ishwaran longer and more closely than many of us, to describe it as "humanistic imagination minus the arrogant homo-centrism of the post-renaissance and post-reformation Western tradition." Ishwaran has tackled the nuances of the family and socialization in East and West, the virtues and vagaries of urban and rural life and has presented a reasoned critique of ehtnocentric abridgement of the concept of modernization. The humane and the rational constitute a unity in the perspective from which these diverse analyses flow.

From a small village in Karnataka to the centres of education in Europe and North America, Ishwaran's has been a journey full of struggles and challenges as well as innovative accomplishments and lasting comradeships. In a Kannada narrative, *Valasehoda Kannadiga* (A Kannadiga in Exile), Ishwaran tells us how and why he went from Karnataka to Oxford and then on to the Hague and Leiden to finally arrive in Canada, after having played a pioneering role in the establishment of the Social Sciences at Karnataka University at Dharwar. What is most fascinating and inspiring about this journey is the final transformation of a life in a new land into a dynamic and courageous pursuit of values, adherence to which seemed to have been threatened at various points. This, I believe, is Ishwaran's greatest accomplishment and contribution. Along the way he has created a community of friends that includes professional associates, students and a host of others whom he encounters in various walks of life. Whether they know much about his biography or not, they all share a sense of affection and admiration for the kind of human being he is.

In a sense, the creation of a community that is physically dispersed around the globe and extends beyond the usual circle of colleagues locally, has had its price. Despite his stellar scholarly achievements and his standing in the academic community, he has chosen to live somewhat aloof. He seldom attends conferences and is not part of the network of European and North American scholars of South Asia. And yet, when it seemed as if the interest of scholarship on South Asia was in jeopardy, when many scholars, in search of grants, drifted towards the more fertile fields of research such as China and the Pacific Rim, Ishwaran rose to the challenge. As usual, through his tireless efforts, including the founding of an Association of South Asian Studies, he finally succeeded in restoring a healthy balance in the professional preoccupations of the organization that represents the Canadian community of scholars working on Asia.

Ishwaran's lasting contribution to institution-building in social sciences and to the production and transmission of sociological knowledge as well as to an ongoing reasoned discourse between social scientists is represented by his editorship of various journals and monographs. My respect for Ishwaran in this regard has grown enormously since I took on this editorial assignment. Despite the massive goodwill and dedicated effort by the editors of these various volumes and despite the willing cooperation of all individual contributors that has been an uphill task. But I am ashamed to have to admit this because I know that in the last couple of decades Ishwaran has faced these kinds of difficulties many times over, on a continuing basis and has succeeded admirably.

This, then, is a rather modest tribute to a man who rarely talks about his own work, yet all the time is encouraging others to pursue their own. These volumes try to reflect the intellectual preoccupations that are characteristic of Ishwaran's work but they are also an avenue for scholars, young and old, to bring their discoveries and insights into an arena of reasoned intellectual discourse. Together they are an affectionate offering by over fifty scholars whose lives have been touched in one way or another by a modest man who has always preferred to remain actively in the background. This isn't much when one considers what Ishwaran has done, but anything less would not have done justice to our gratitude and affection for Ishwaran.

Jayant Lele

Contents

Notes on Contributors   v

Dedication to K. Ishwaran   vii
by Jayant Lele

1. **Yogendra K. Malik**
   Law, Politics and Society in India   1

2. **George H. Gadbois, Jr.**
   The Indian Superior Judiciary: Help Wanted:
   Any Good People Willing to be Judges?   16

3. **Yogendra K. Malik**
   Electoral Laws and Campaign and Party
   Finances: Implications for Polity and Society   52

4. **George C. Kozlowski**
   Shah Banu's Case, Britain's Legacy
   and Muslim Politics in Modern India   88

5. **Chhatrapati Singh**
   Law, Poverty and Welfarism:
   The Basis of Anti-Poverty Programmes   112

6. **Aradhana Parmar**
   Women and the Law   153

7. **Dhirendra K. Vajpeyi**
   Freedom of the Press, Court and the
   Indian Constitution   177

8. **Velcheru Narayana Rao**
   Courts and Lawyers in India: Images from
   Literature and Folklore   196

9. **John J. Paul**
   Authority and Professional Control of the
   Subordinate Legal Profession in the
   Madras Presidency during the
   Late Nineteenth Century   215

Index   245

1

YOGENDRA K. MALIK

LAW, POLITICS AND SOCIETY IN INDIA

An Overview

Law as an Instrument of Social Change

All major changes including political take place either on account of official initiative and as a matter of deliberate policy or as a reaction and response to government policies. In this process, law works as a catalytic agent for reflecting and transmitting the said ideals into a reality through extra political, i.e, the legislative, the executive and the judicial mechanism."[1] Ralph Brabanti, who looks upon the legal system as an instrument of political development, contends that the strengthening of the legal institutions is a "precondition for economic change, ... crucial to the viability of the new political system," and is an "agent of social change" having a "modernizing and innovative impact on the social order."[2] These may sound like sweeping statements. However, there is little doubt that those who believe in social engineering, in the deliberate rational organization of the society, and in the role of the elites in the conscious control of human environment, look upon law as a tool of social transformation.[3]

The centrality of the legal system in the modernization and the development of the countries of the Third World, particularly, became the major theme of the literature dealing with development theories in the early 1960s. Believing in the unilinear development process— societies moving from simple to complex, from traditional to modern — the exponents of the developmental theories held that legal and administrative system would become instrumental in initiating social change. The consequent development is defined as "progressive social change" and from this perspective "law and development" is an aspect of "law and social change."[4]

Although colonial administrations in the countries of the Third World sometimes used law as an instrument of social reform and creation of a new order, the colonialists soon discovered that merely introducing a modern legal system was not enough to change the traditional societies. There was a realization that

> "if the social and economic intercourse were to be conducted in an orderly fashion, if life was to be made more predictable and if disputes were to be more effectively managed — that is, if the beneficial effects of rule of law were to be realized—it would be necessary to supplement legal systems with the powers and authority of rational administration. Law requires order, and a legal system needs to backing of a civil administrative system."[5]

Despite the introduction of modern legal and administrative systems in the colonies, the colonial powers lacked the will and the capacity to use law as an instrument to initiate extensive social reforms.

In India, the rulers introduced the populace not only to the British systems of administration and law but also to the representative institutions and various schools of liberalism of Europe. It was the combination of these developments which enabled the leaders of the nationalist movement in India to perceive that the legislative process, conducted through representative institutions, can open a way for an orderly transformation of the traditional social order. Therefore, it was not surprising that reform-oriented sectors of societies like that of India saw the law as a primary means of accomplishing major changes in the social and economic order which they had inherited from the colonial period.

Interdependence Between Law and Society

Scholars have recognized that the legal system alone cannot become an instrument of social change. In fact, some argue that "it is society that controls law and not the reverse."[6] But a more realistic view is that there is an interdependence between the two. Selznick correctly stresses that there is no longer any need to "argue the general interdependence of law and society."[7] Law is the product of the society and its culture. According to this school, "The most common and basic assumption is that the legal system is a part of or aspect of society: events that occur outside the legal system may have legal consequences, and events that occur within the legal system may have social consequences."[8]

Particularly referring to the countries of the Third World, where customary and traditional practices abound, Lawrence Rosen holds that it is easy to overstate the impact of law on social change, and at the same time it would be unrealistic to say that law is simply the product of the social and cultural milieu.[9] This position appears to meet the realities of social organizations of the new nations because, whereas on the one hand, the ancient societies of many of he countries of Asia and Africa maintain their links with their historic past and thus keep influencing the formation of legal codes, on the other hand, political elites, eager to change the socio-political conditions of their societies, look upon the legal system as one of the important methods to bring about certain radical transformation in their societies.

One should not forget, however, that the effectiveness of a law is dependent upon the support it receives from such critical segments of the society as the intellectuals, the leaders of social reform groups and of course, religious and social organizations which are able to mobilise the masses for or against the laws.

In plural societies, where many religious, ethnic, and occupational groups maintain their own codes of conduct, the penetrative role of the legal system becomes all the more limited. In fact, even in more advanced and industrialized societies, various professional and occupational organizations developed their own self-regulating and self-enforcing codes of conduct within the broad framework of the state-created legal system. The state authorities are unable to alter such systems unilaterally.

To be more precise Lawrence Rosen, therefore, delineates three specific areas where law plays a significant role in the socio-political systems of the new nations:

(1) Definition and interpretation of the particular concept of social order.
(2) Limiting the exercise of arbitrary executive power
(3) The use of the legal system as an "instrument for encouraging and precipitating social and economic change."[10]

Interdependence Between Law, Politics, and Society In India

Accepting Rosen's basic proposition about the functions of law in the new nations, we will look briefly at the interactions between law, politics, and society in India. First of all we will look at the philosophical and ideological value premises of the elites who wish to use law to define the concept of a new social order. I must stress, however, that I have no intention of discussing the detailed historical evolution of the basis of such value premises.

As is well-known, India's freedom struggle was rooted in a cultural revival and social reform movement. Despite the presence of many of the traditionalists like Madan Mohan Malaviya, Dr. Rajinder Prasad, Purushottam Das Tandon and many others in the Indian National Congress, the organization which led India's freedom movement eventually came to be dominated by the modernists like Jawaharlal Nehru. Steeped in the traditions of British liberalism and Fabian Socialism, the founders of the modern state system in India were committed to two contradictory goals, namely, the preservation of individual rights and freedoms and the creation of an egalitarian society. They also perceived law as an important instrument of social change.

Many politicians and some legal scholars believe that the Directive Principles of State Policy, adopted in the constitution of India, were a kind of wish list of the founders of the Republic of India. For many others, however, they represent the value premises that reflect the various shades of opinion among the nationalist elites of India. The Directive Principles visualize an activist and reformist role for the state. They direct the authorities at both the national and the state level "to promote the welfare of the people by securing and promoting as effectively as it may a social order in which justice, social, economic and political, shall inform all the institutions of the national life."[11] This is, indeed, a tall order for any state let alone a liberal state, which is hemmed in by various constitutional restraints. But there is little doubt the Principles provide the image of the kind of social order which the elites sought to create through a legal system.

On several occasions constitutional experts have questioned the wisdom of incorporating the Directive Principles of State Policy in the constitution while making them non-justifiable. Granville Austin, however, is right when he says that, "The Directive Principles of State Policy set forth humanitarian socialist precepts that were, and are, the aims of the Indian social revolution."[12] And he further adds that they represent the "two streams of socialist and nationalist sentiment in India that had been flowing ever faster since the late twenties. It is not unreasonable to conjecture also that the placing on the government major responsibility for the welfare of Indians has even deeper grounding in Indian history."[13] In other words, the activist and reformist role of the state is not simply the product of the nationalist movement, due to historical experience; rather, Austin holds that such a role is, indeed, imbedded in the Indian psyche.

Rosen's second concern, in relation to the role of law in the countries of the Third World, is with restraining the exercise of executive power. India has established a cabinet system of government with responsibility to parliament. It has also provided a list of fundamental rights and a Supreme Court, empowered to enforce the fundamental rights.

The Supreme Court in India possesses the power of the judicial review enabling it to declare the executive and legislative decisions unconstitutional. In other words, under the classical liberal model of government, the constitutional law and the system of judicial review serve to restrain the powers of both the executive and the legislature.

Theoretically, furthermore, the creation of a federal system is expected to dilute the powers of national government, whatever the intentions of the founding fathers might have been. In this way, the constitution of India created what Karl Lowenstein has called a system of vertical and horizontal control over the exercise of power in India.[14]

Finally, according to Rosen and as we have noted above, the function of law in the new nations is to serve as a tool to initiate and encourage socio-economic changes. Within the framework of the ideological orientation of the national elite, the state was to undertake systematic economic planning and to direct the course of the industrialization process. Given the complexity of the legal and institutional system created and the ideological goals set by the elites in India, the

Law, Politics and Society in India: An Overview

development of conflict between the two sets of systems was to become inevitable.

The Legal system Under Stress: Social and Political Constraints

Contradictions between the ideological goals set in terms of the social and economic transformation of the society and the concept of a liberal state committed to protecting the rights and freedoms of the citizens, were apparent. The founders of the Indian republic were quite conscious of this. Jawaharlal Nehru, speaking before the Constituent Assembly, declared that

> "No Supreme Court and no judiciary can stand in judgement over the sovereign will of Parliament representing the will of the entire community. If we go wrong here or there it can point it out but, in the ultimate analysis, where the future of the community is concerned, no judiciary can come in the way. And if it comes in the way, ultimately, the whole Constitution is a creature of Parliament. But we must respect the judiciary, the Supreme Court and the other High Courts in the land. A wise people, their duty is to see that in a moment of passion, in a moment of excitement, even the representatives of the people do not go wrong: they might. In the detached atmosphere of the courts, they should see to it that nothing is done that may be against the good of the country, that may be against the community in the larger sense of the term.... (but) no system of judiciary can function in the nature of a Third House, as a kind of Third House of correction. So, it is important that with this limitation the judiciary should function."[15]

In other words, Nehru had already issued a warning to the courts that it is only the parliament which has the power to legislate and to bring about socio-economic changes. The courts are not expected either to assume the role of law makers or to obstruct the will of law-making bodies. He did not want the courts, consisting of activist justices, to incorporate their political philosophies in their judgements.

It was not surprising, therefore, that "during India's first decade as an independent state, successive Congress governments bent on carrying on social and economic reforms, particularly land reform confronted successive supreme courts bent on upholding fundamental rights, particularly property rights."[16] This led to what Lloyd and Susanne Rudolph describe as a struggle over the issue of the system of judicial review versus parliamentary sovereignty.[17]

With the rise of Indira Gandhi to the position of undisputed leader of the Congress party in the early 1970s, the conflict between the national executive, with an absolute majority in parliament, and the Supreme Court became further accentuated.

Since the creation of a socialist society has been the declared goal of the Congress party, its leaders looked upon the judiciary, particularly the Supreme Court, as a hurdle in that process. H.R. Gokhale, Indira Gandhi's Law Minister in 1976, asserted that "There is a general feeling that the fundamental right to property has stood as a stumbling block in the path of realizing the socio-economic justice."[18]

Indira Gandhi went a step further and denounced the Anglo-Saxon juridical system which she thought "often equates liberty with property, and which has not made adequate provision for the needs of the poor and the weak."[19] There might have been some valid ideological reasons for the expression of dissatisfaction with the role of the judiciary in reaction to the elites' efforts at creating an egalitarian society. And subsequently, even though the conflict took the familiar guise of parliamentary sovereignty vs. judicial review, it was really an effort on the part of Indira Gandhi, supported by a rump parliament, to assert her authoritarian rule in the country.

Political and social realities further inhibited the political elites' use of law as an instrument of social change. In a multi-cultural society like India's, ethnic, religious and cultural groups use their votes, organizations and ability to mobilize their supporters to sometimes block the reformative role of law. Even when reform-oriented laws exist, public officials and law enforcement officers lack the will to enforce them effectively.[20]

The essays presented in this volume discuss the elites' value premises in reference to the role of law, their actual behaviour patterns as well as the implications for the society and the polity (see Table 1).

These essays demonstrate how interaction between the political institutions, political process, electoral politics and social forces help or hinder the role of law in the transformation of a traditional social order. Also, these case studies show that despite the best intentions of the founders of the Indian political system, the elites' power motivation and their political behaviour are likely to transform both the nature of laws and the agencies which are entrusted to enforce them.

Steeped in British traditions of judicial independence, Indian justices and the courts enjoyed both the trust and high prestige within the society. However, George Gadbois in his essay, demonstrates that the national executive of India, under powerful and charismatic leaders like Indira Gandhi, employed various pressure tactics to bend the courts to its wishes and thus undermined the morale of the justices. Today, it has become hard to find upright and qualified persons to fill the positions on the courts.

Electoral laws are enacted to ensure the purity of the electoral process and to guarantee the legitimacy of the authority of the ruling elites. Malik in his essay demonstrates how the parties and the candidates for electoral positions in

Table 1
Laws, Politics and Society
Summary Classification of Major Themes

Themes

Author	Elites Value Premises	Elites' Actual Behaviour Pattern	Implications for Society	Systemic Implications
Gadbois	independence of judiciary/restraint on executive powers	politicization of judiciary undermining judicial independence	gradual decline of public trust in legal institutions	decline of authority/independence of courts
Malik	legal restraint on the influence of money in electoral politics	intentional flouting of electoral laws	increased corruption/decline of political/public morality	contamination of electoral process/decline of respect for law/authority
Kozlowski	judiciary as an instrument of social reform	judicial activism	enhanced tension between minority/majority	inability of the political system to withstand political pressure

Author	Elites' Value Premises	Elites' Actual Behaviour Pattern	Implications for Society	Systemic Implications
Singh	amelioration of conditions of scheduled castes/tribes/poor	politicization of social divisions/state-supported exploitation	aggravation of social inequality	increased political alienation among the poor/low castes
Parmar	improvement in women's conditions	half-hearted implementation of laws	increased women's mobilization	increase in political pressure
Vajpeyi	freedom of expression	suppression/intimidation	control of information	authoritarianism
Rao	rise of an independent class of lawyers	manipulation of law and witnesses to win the cases	satirizing of lawyers in literature	decline of respect for lawyers
Paul	independence of legal profession	resistance by a section of colonial authorities	rise of indigenous class of professionals	political mobilization of lawyers

India violate these laws by resorting to illegal collection and spending of campaign money. Such illegal practices have led to the development of a black economy, undermining the health of both the economy and the polity.

Kozlowski's essay on the well-known Shah Banu case and subsequent passage of *The Muslim Women's (Protection of Rights and Divorce) Bill* demonstrates how a centralized state system, beginning with the British period, offered an opportunity to the *ulma* to influence the formulation of Muslim personal law, in both the pre-and post-independence periods of India. Muslim religious scholars, he argues, had developed close relations with the leaders of the nationalist movement and thus they could influence the so-called reform orientation of the Congress party. Without having the historic perspective of the power of *ulma* and the development of a centralized state system, one cannot understand the controversy surrounding the contemporary policies of the ruling elites of India.

Poverty and rigid social stratification are some of the undesirable features of India's social structure. The Directive Principles of States Policy, as noted above, instruct the political authorities to use legal remedies to change these inequities. Chhatrapati Singh, in his essay, shows that the state has singularly failed in improving the lot of members of both the Scheduled Castes and Schedules Tribes. The Harijans in rural areas are still subjected to atrocities at the hands of high caste Hindus. The lifestyle and the properties of the tribal population of India are being endangered. The state authority, controlled by the westernized upper caste, is both ineffective and inefficient and thus unable to protect the poorer sectors of the society.

The social status of women and their ill-treatment by different types of religious authorities have been a major concern of the leaders of the independence movement. Parmar traces both the historical developments leading to the decline in their status and efforts by the elites to improve women's status within the society through legal instruments in recent

Law, Politics and Society in India: An Overview

years. Despite these efforts, Parmar points out, women in Indian society still suffer from social and cultural restraints.

Singh, Kozlowski, and Parmar show how the traditional social forces are able to block the changes initiated by law. Also they demonstrate that despite the best intentions of the legislators, due to public apathy the ineffective enforcement of the laws renders them incapable of achieving the desired social goals.

Freedom of speech and expression are considered essential to the survival of a liberal state. The leaders of the nationalist movement in India recognized the value of such freedoms and provided a constitutional warranty. Vajpayee, however, documents in his case study the struggle between the press and the ruling elites. Although the Supreme Court has sided with the press, the political elites, in violation of the spirit of the constitution of India, have devised various ways to intimidate, suppress, and control the press in India. The ongoing struggle between the journalists, the reporters, and the press on the one hand and the political authorities on the other demonstrates the low level of commitment of the elites to the values of a liberal state and the rule of law.

The rise of lawyers as an independent professional group is an important development in societies like that of India. lawyers not only played a significant role in India's independence movement but also were responsible for the new institutional set-up in the post-independence period. Lawyers have been, therefore closely associated with the modernization and development process in India. Writing about the legal profession in India, Marc Galanter says that lawyers serve as "intermediary, 'linking higher law' promulgated at the upper reaches of the system with the law as applied at the local level,"[21] Lawyers also are the "carrier of nationwide legal culture."[22] The essay by Paul John traces the struggle which took place between the central and provincial authorities in the development of lawyers as a professional group, while Rao describes the poor image of the legal profession in the world of letters. The two essays give both the historical and the literary images of the lawyers both of which are less than flattering. But as L. Michel Heger points out, "Lawyers in the poor countries do not enjoy a favourable public image. Too often they are associated in the popular mind with personal ambition and self-interest."[23] Despite this image problem of the legal profession, lawyers in India enjoy a prominent and influential position which is matched by only a handful of other professions.

NOTES AND REFERENCES

1. S.N. Dhyani," Political Change and Law: Development and Dimensions," *Political Science Review* (October – December, 1980), p . 34

2. Quoted in L. Michael Hager, "The Role of Lawyers in Developing Countries," *American Bar Association Journal*, vol 58 (1972), p. 35.

3. Rosco Pound, "Contemporary Juristic Theory," in Dennis Lloyd (ed.), *Introduction to Jurisprudence* (London, Stevens and Sons, 1965), pp. 247 – 52.

4. John Merryman et. al. (eds.,), *Law and Social Change in Mediterranean Europe and Latin America* (Stanford, Stanford Studies in Law and Development, 1979), p. 7.

5. Lucian Pye, "Law and the Dilemma of Stability and Change in the Modernization Process", *Vanderbelt Law Review*, Vol. 17 (1963 – 64), p. 18.

6. Glynn Cochrane, *Development Anthropology* (New York, Oxford University Press, 1971), p. 93.

7. Quoted in Sally Falk Moore, "Law and Social Change: The Semi-Autonomous Social Field as An Appropriate Subject of Study," *Law and Society Review* (1973), p. 719.

8. Merryman, *op. cit.,* p. 5

9. Lawrence Rosen, "Law and Social Change in the New Nations," *Comparative Studies in Society and History*, Vol. 20 (1978), p.3. For a detailed case study of the limits Massell,

"Law as an Instrument of Revolutionary Change in Traditional Milieu: The Case of Soviet Central Asia," *Law and Society Review*, Vol. 2 (1967-68), pp. 179–228. also, See Joel F. Handler, Social Movement and The Legal System (New York, Academic Press, 1978), pp. 1 - 34.

10. *Ibid.*, p. 4.
11. Constitution of India, Article 38. For further elaboration see M. V. Pyle, *Constitutional Government in India* (Bombay, Asia Publishing House, 1968), Chapter 23.
12. Granville Austin, *The Constitution of India: the Cornerstone of a Nation* (Oxford, Clarendon Press, 1966), p. 75.
13. *Ibid.*, p. 76.
14. Karl Lowenstein, *Political Power and the Governmental Process* (Chicago, the University of Chicago Press, 1965), p. 123-344.
15. G.G. Mirchandani, *Subverting the Constitution* (New Delhi, Abhinav Publications, 1977), p. 15.
16. Lloyd I. Rudolph and Susanne H. Rudolph, "Judicial Review *versus* Parliamentary Sovereignty: The Struggle over Stateness in India," *Journal of Commonwealth and Comparative Politics*, November 1981, p. 231.
17. *Ibid.*, pp. 231-255.
18. Mirchandani, *op.cit.*, p. 58.
19. *Ibid*.
20. Gail Minault, "Legal and Scholarly Activism" Recent Women's Studies in India—A Review Article," *The Journal of Asian Studies* (November 1988), pp. 814– 820.
21. Marc Gallanter, "The Study of the Indian Legal Profession," *Law and Society* 1868, p. 202.
22. *Ibid.*, p. 215.
23. Hager, *op. cit.*, p. 33

2

GEORGE H. GADBOIS, JR.

THE INDIAN SUPERIOR JUDICIARY

Help Wanted: Any Good people Willing to be Judges ?

Forty-one years ago when India became independent, the offer of a judgeship on one of India's superior courts was the highest honor a leading lawyer could receive. A seat on the bench brought financial security, and meant high status, immense prestige, respect, dignity, and considerable authority and power. The bench at that time was the main attraction to most of the best in the legal profession. An invitation to join the bench was a great honor, proof that one had earned a preeminent position in the profession. And there was convention, inherited from England, that no member of the bar, no matter how high his income was or how highly placed he might in the profession, was at liberty to refuse an offer of judgeship. It was very rare for a distinguished lawyer to decline such an offer. The higher judiciary was highly respected — courts were referred to by some as "temples of justice," and judges viewed as virtually representatives of God.

By the late 1980s, there is increasing concern about the quality and integrity of those who wear judicial robes. The prevailing view now is that the best lawyers—"best" meaning leaders of the bar who are competent, honest and independent — if offered judgeships at all, are reluctant to serve on the superior judiciary. The then Chief Justice of India, P.N. Bhagwati, said in 1985 that those being appointed to the High Courts[1] "are not fit and competent" (Mahajan, 1988). A few years earlier, Bhagwati told the Law Teachers Conference at Varanasi that "during the last few years....., [because of] the unattractive conditions of service of High Court Judges, it has not been possible to persuade really good members in the bar to accept appointments on the High Court Bench" (1979:11). S.H. Sheth, a retired Gujarat High Court judge, recently wrote of "the meteoric fall in the quality of High Court Judges," and "a steep deterioration in the quality of judges from top to bottom" (1983). Soli J. Sorabjee, one of the India's most prominent lawyers, said a few years ago that because of the increasing politicization of the judiciary, the dignity of judgeships has been eroded, and "this has discouraged many talented people from joining the bench" (Intolerant Executive, 1981). Editorially, *The Hindustan Times* expressed the view that because of some new political decisions affecting judges, "a large number of second raters have been elevated to the Benches of different High Courts" (Judicial Appointment, 1980; cf. The Judicial Jungle, 1986).

This paper deals with several of the reasons, the major ones I believe, why the best legal talent is increasingly turning away from the bench. Although the focus here is on the High Courts, because 85 of the 87 Supreme Court Judges since 1950 have been promoted from the High Courts, the quality of Supreme Court judges over time is affected by High Courts increasingly populated by less than the best legal talent available. Supreme Court judges may be recruited directly from the bar, but of the eight eminent lawyers known to have been offered Supreme Court appointments since 1950, only two (S.M. Sikri in 1964, and S.C. Roy in 1971) have accepted.[2]

Salary Disincentive

The first authoritative statement that the bench was losing its attractiveness to leading lawyers[3] is found in the frequently cited Fourteenth Report of the Law Commission of India. Here it is stated that because of the salaries offered, eminent lawyers would not accept judicial appointments (1958, I: 81). Later, M.C. Chagla, who was a member of that Commission and the first Indian Chief Justice of the Bombay High Court, wrote in his autobiography that even in the 1940s, some Bombay lawyers offered High Court judgeships declined for financial reasons (1973: 143: cf. Beaumont, 1946). Discussing some of the particular lawyers he recruited from the bar, Chagla writes:

> I had to press every one of them to accept the judgeship, pointing out unless some at least of the best men came to the Bench, the reputation and traditions of the High Courts could not be maintained. I knew it entailed a sacrifice on their part ..... I .... sometimes even [had to] beg them to accept a judgeship (1973: 166– 167).[4]

Many others have commented upon the unattractiveness of the salaries of judges (Seervai, 1970: 31-39; Tulzapurkar, 1984: 1984: 2456–2460; 1986: 22). Indeed, it is quite clear that at least until 1976, when for the firsttime High Court judges were transferred to High Courts in other states without their consent, financial considerations were the main reason why leading lawyers refused to accept judgeships. Although no records are kept of how many have declined High Court judgeships, the problem seems to have arisen first at Bombay and Calcutta in the 1940s and 1950s, when the gap between judges' salaries and the earnings of leading lawyers began to widen. By the 1960s, if not a little earlier, salaries became a deterrent at some of the other High Courts also, and since then at least some leading lawyers have turned down judgeships at virtually all the High Courts. The number who have turned down Bombay and Calcutta High Court judgeships (mainly because these are large cities and major commercial centers, lawyers, earnings are higher than at other High Courts) since 1950 must be in the range of 100 to 125; at the other 16 High Courts, perhaps another 50 to 100.[5] According to Seervai (1978: 122), a Bombay High Court Chief Justice once stated publicly that 27 lawyers offered judgeships had declined. V.M. Tarkunde, who served on the Bombay High Court from 1957-1969, has said that because of the poor emoluments offered judges, "14 eminent persons" had refused Bombay judgeships during his own tenure at Bombay (Conflicting Views, 1970).

There are two distinct facets to the salary disincentive. The first is that the salaries of the judges were fixed by the Constitution in 1950 at Rs. 4000 per month for High Court Chief Justices, and Rs. 3500 for the associate judges, and remained at that level until 1986, despite the ravages of inflation and the quantum leaps in the earnings of top lawyers. Supreme Court salaries were fixed at Rs. 5000 for the Chief Justice, and Rs. 4000 for the associate judges.[6] Some perquisites were added over the years, and in the 1970s judges began receiving a cost - of - living adjustment. By 1984, according to the calculations of former Supreme Court Justice Tulzapurkar:

> Inclusive of all allowances, the Chief Justice of India and a puisne Judge of the Supreme Court receive, subject to tax deductions, total monthly emoluments of Rs. 7,675 and Rs. 6,475 respectively; while the corresponding figures for the Chief Justice and a puisne Judge of a High Court are Rs. 6,475 and Rs. 5,675 (1984:49).

Tulzapurkar observed that with such salaries, "not even the most average legal brain will be attracted to the Bench" (1984:49).

The salaries fixed in 1950, although lower than the colonial regime had been paying judges (Seervai, 1970: 31-39; 1984: 2456; 1986: 22 Gadbois, 1987: 124- 125) were not wholly unattractive, for except in Bombay and Calcutta, even leading lawyers seldom earned more. But soon they became increasingly less attractive. The income tax reduced the gross income and other emoluments by approximately 50 percent. Inflation, and the steady erosion of the purchasing power of the rupee, has taken an even greater toll. According to recently announced official figures, using 1949 as the base year, the value of the rupee has plummeted from 100 paise then to 10.929 paise in January 1988 (Rupee, 1988). So the Rs. 5675 in total monthly emoluments of a High Court judge of whom Tulzapurkar spoke was the equivalent in 1988 of about Rs. 620 per month in 1949 terms.

The other facet of the financial disincentive, and no doubt far more of a negative factor than the steady erosion of the value of the currency, is the fact that the gap between the judicial salaries and the earnings of leading lawyers has widened enormously. A few years ago, a retired Supreme Court judge wrote that some lawyers earn more in one day than a judge does in a month (Jaganmohan Reddy, 1984: 141). Other Supreme Court judges say that this judge understated the hiatus between judge and lawyer incomes, and that by the 1980s the more successful lawyers on some single days earned more than a Supreme Court judge did in six months or even a year (Interviews, 1983, 1988). When he was Chief Justice of India, Y.V. Chandrachud was quoted as saying that some lawyers earned 25,000 to 30,000 rupees per day (Mahajan, 1984). One of the senior lawyers who declined a Supreme Court offer told me in 1983 that "a junior of four years standing at the High Court bar makes as much as a Supreme Court judge." S. Sahay, a retired editor of *The Statesman*, and a recognized expert on courts, judges and law, wrote recently of a "not very senior lawyer" of his acquaintance who charged Rs. 11,000 per day to appear in a district court in a neighboring state, and of others who charge Rs. 5000 or more for brief consultations (The State, 1986: 60). Back in 1972, as Chandrachud left the Bombay High Court for the Supreme Court, he said that judicial salaries and other conditions of service, when compared with the earnings of successful lawyers, were "wholly unattractive and scare away even the marginal lawyers" (1972: 72).

As mentioned above, some peripheral emoluments have been added over the years, particularly since 1974. But until 1986, the Government periodically announced that it had no intention of raising the salaries of judges. Finally, in 1986, salaries were doubled or slightly more so for Supreme Court and High Court judges. The Chief Justice of India now receives Rs. 10,000 per month, and associate judges Rs. 9000 per month. A High Court Chief Justice Rs. 8000 per month (Constitution, 1988). And by the High Court and Supreme Court Judges (Conditions of Service) Amendment Act of 1986, certain other benefits apart from salaries have been enhanced or added. These include conveyance and petrol allowance, "sumptuary" allowance and, most significantly, an enhanced pension. According to the data published by the Ministry of Law in 1980, most retired Supreme Court judges were then receiving a before-taxes pension in the range of Rs. 1600–1700 per month (Ministry of Law, 1980), and retired High Court considerably less. The 1986 legislation raised the amount of pension to 50 percent of the enhanced salaries.

These improvements in salary and other conditions of service are substantial, but few believe that given the wide gulf which remains between the salaries of successful lawyers and the judges, and because of other disincentives, the bench will become more attractive to the best legal talent. And a top lawyer offered a High Court Judgeship at age 40-45 must wonder whether another 36 years will pass before there is another increase in salaries.

Transfer Disincentive

Another deterrent to attracting good people to the bench was introduced by the Government in 1976, and today, after the recent improvement in salaries, is, according to Chandrachud, the major factor discouraging the best lawyers from accepting High Court judgeships (1988). This is the policy of transferring High Court judges from their home High Courts to any other High Courts in the country, without their consent.

The transfer of a High Court judge, with his consent, was not unknown during the colonial period. And from 1950-1976, about 25 High Court judges were transferred, but per the convention of first securing the consent of the judge, almost all of these transfers were both consensus and either initiated by the Chief Justice of India, or approved by him (Nariman, 1981). The few exceptions were initiated by the Chief Justice of India (Not the Government) in an effort to resolve problems at particular High Courts (Gajendragadkar, 1983: 165–172). Most of these 1950–1976 transfers resulted in the promotion of an associate judge of his home High Court to the Chief Justiceship of another. Several of these transferred judges were later promoted to the Supreme Court, e.g., S. R. Das, B.P. Sinha, K.N. Pathak. There was little controversy about these transfers, and no evidence that they alarmed prospective judges.

Since mid-1976, however, the whole context and atmosphere concerning transfers have changed. At that time, which was during the darkest days of the 1975–1977 Emergency, Mrs. Indira Gandhi's Government summarily punished 16 High Court judges by transferring them to other states. Their consent was not sought, and the Government also made it known by a calculated leak that it had compiled a list of another 40 judges who were to be transferred (Seervai, 1983: 892). These 16 transferred judges, who were given just a few days to pack, had, in various ways, mainly by handing down decisions that went against the Government, angered the then authoritarian regime. These transfers were clearly punitive in nature. They were an attempt to terrorize independent judges and to make them more conducive to toeing the line. After the Congress Party was defeated in the March 1977 national election, and the emergency lifted, the new Janata Government offered these transferred judges the opportunity to return to their home High Courts. All availed themselves of this opportunity.

Mrs. Gandhi returned to power in 1980, and in January 1981 the Government suddenly ordered the transfers of Patna Chief Justice K.B.N. Singh to the Madras High Court, and Madras Chief Justice M.M. Ismail to the Kerala High Court. These transfers, and those that followed, provoked a loud and continuing controversy which focuses on the obvious threat that transfers pose to the much - valued independence of the judiciary. Ismail, who had an excellent reputation as an independent judge, and who was offered a Supreme Court judgeship by the Janata Government, resigned rather than accept this compulsory, non-consensual transfer (Ismail, 1981). Singh went south to Madras, but took his objections to court.

The controversy escalated on march 18, 1981, when the Union Law Minister, P. Shiv Shankar, sent a letter to the State Chief Ministers and High Court Chief Justices, informing them that they should obtain from all "additional" judges their written consent to be appointed as permanent judges of any other High Court, and obtain the same consent from all High Court nominees "in the pipeline." and from all future nominees. The Government's rationale, contained in this circular letter, was as follows:

> It has repeatedly been suggested to Government over the years by several bodies and forums including the States Reorganization Commission, the Law Commission, and various Bar associations that to further national integration and to combat narrow parochial tendencies bred by caste, kinship, and other local links and affiliations, one-third of the Judges of a High Court should as far as possible be from outside the State in which that High Court is situated (Seervai, 1984: 2275: Noorani, 1982: 22).

The idea of some one-third of High Court judges being from other states is indeed not a new one, and it has been recommended since 1955 by a variety of eminent and trusted national figures as a means of promoting national integration and reducing parochial behaviour (States Reorganization, 1955; Fourteenth Report, 1958: I, 100; Administrative Reforms, 1963: Eightieth Report, 1980: 25). But after the punitive transfers of 1976, the transfer of judges, like family planning, became "dirty words". The attentive public, especially the press and the large lawyer community, but also High Court and Supreme Court judges, fear that the Government will again use the transfer sword to punish independent judges. The fear is that although the Government talks in terms of promoting national integration, the real motive is the disintegration of an independence judiciary. The executive is simply not trusted to carry out an otherwise salutary policy in a fair manner (Judicial Reform, 1983). The concern is that the Government is trying to weaken the judiciary, denigrate, humiliate and demoralize the judges, and reward pro-Government judges and punish those whose opinions go against the Government in effect, to coerce and capture the judiciary, to make it compliant (Jit, 1981; Sahay, 1981; Judging Transfers, 1983; Rajagopal, 1983; Nariman, 1983; Bar Panel, 1983; Nayar, 1986b; Jurists criticize, 1988; Abdi, 1988).

Adding fuel to the controversy was the fact that earlier in March 1981, the Government had granted three Delhi High Court "additional" judges extensions of just three months instead of the customary one or two years. An additional judge is one appointed to a High Court initially for a two-year period, the reason being that the increasing backlog of cases required a temporary increase in the number of judges, a practice introduced by the British. The Indian Constitution - makers made no provision for the appointment of additional judges in the 1950 Constitution, but the Seventh Amendment (1956) to the Constitution made such appointments possible. Such appointments were not a matter of controversy until recently because a convention quickly developed that once a permanent, i.e., regular vacancy occurred on a High Court, the additional judge would be confirmed as a permanent judge. Certainly those appointed as additional judges in the 1950s, 1960s, and 1970s expected that their confirmation as permanent judges would be routine. With but a few exceptions, this is what happened.[7] So additional judges, prior to 1981, were not considered to be on probation and enjoyed security of tenure.

The ominously brief and eleventh-hour extensions of the three Delhi High Court additional judges, and of some other additional judges on other High Courts, took a nastier turn in June 1981 when two of the Delhi judges were not given another extension (Judges denied, 1981). Permanent slots were vacant, so these men were fired. The Government refused to provide any reasons for their non-extension (Nayar, 1982). Short and last-minute extensions keep additional judges on a very short leash, and non-extensions simply terminate their services (Judges on the leash, 1981).

Since 1981, an additional judge cannot afford to decide too many cases against the Government and must be hesitant about issuing writs in cases of alleged corruption involving Congress(I) figures. When an additional judge is not extended, it is not because the backlog of cases has eased, for the arrears continue to mount. As retired Supreme Court Justice V.R. Krishna Iyer has said, "to say that an additional judge is independent is a contradiction in terms" (CJ for body, 1983; Cf. Additional judge, 1981).

Very recently, the Government added another weapon to its arsenal for the taming of additional judges, a new punitive twist to the policy of keeping additional judges on tenterhooks. Justice B.M. Lal, who was appointed an additional judge of the Madhya Pradesh High Court in May 1984 for two years, and then reappointed through May 13, 1988 received another extension on May 15, i.e, there was a one day break in service. Because seniority largely determines who will become Chief Justice, and because seniority is calculated from the date of continuous initial appointment as an additional or permanent judge, Lal's date of continuous service is now May 15, 1988. Had there been no break in service, Lal would have been in line to become the Chief Justice of Madhya Pradesh some years hence. The one day interruption "has ended the chances of Justice Lal's becoming Chief Justice" (Justice Lal, 1988), because it dropped him to the bottom of the seniority list, junior even to two judges appointed two weeks earlier. Surely not coincidentally, it was Justice Lal who delivered a much-publicized judgement in a corruption scandal against then (and again now) Madhya Pradesh Congress (I) Chief Minister Arjun Singh in 1986 (Nayar, 1986a; Cf. Quit?, 1986). [8]

The Supreme Court's decision in transferred Chief Justice Singh's case, which was joined by one of the two dismissed Delhi High Judges, S.N. Kumar (the other non-extended judge, O.N. Vohra, simply gave up and did not join this litigation. Vohra, not coincidentally, had delivered, during the Janata years, the judgment in the notorious *Kissa Kursi Ka* case, which committed Mrs. Gandhi's son Sanjay to prison), was handed down on December 31, 1981. It is the longest in the Supreme Court's history (956 pages of text, plus another 134 pages of headnotes), one of the most controversial ever (certainly the most controversial of this decade), and among the most fractured (each of the seven judges wrote separate judgments, and there were changing majorities dealing with the several issues raised). Usually referred to as the Judges' Case, or the Judges' Transfer Case (S.P. Gupta 1982), the various majorities ruled that Singh's transfer was valid, that any High Court judge can be transferred without his or her[9] consent, that the non-extension of Kumar's term as additional judge was valid, that the Law Minister's letter of March 18th was fine also, and that although the Chief Justice of India must be consulted about appointments and transfers, his recommendations are just that, and the Council of Minister (Cabinet) can do as it pleases concerning the hiring, firing, and transfer of judges. There is much more to this decision, including evidence of serious personal and professional differences among the brethren, but for my purposes, this summary is sufficient (Cf. Shourie, 1982; Dua, 1983; Seervai, 1984; Baxi, 1985; Sorabjee, 1987).

Nineteen eighty-one was not a good year for Indian judges. But there is an articulate and still influential constituency in India which vigorously defends judges and an independent judiciary. This constituency loudly criticized the transfer policy in particular, and probably for that reason the Government decided to proceed slowly, cautiously, and with remarkable subtlety. There were apparently were no transfers in 1982, but of the 49 additional judges on the High Courts in 1981, 32 quite promptly gave their consent for appointment as permanent judges at High Courts other than the ones to which they had been appointed (32 judges, 1981).

In late 1982 and early 1983, the Government reiterated its policy of transferring judges, but announced that it was particularly interested in having the Chief Justice of each High Court coming, by way of transfer, from another High Court (CJs to be, 1983). By May 1988, each of the 18 High Courts has been headed by at least one Chief Justice brought in from another state. Some of the most senior judges have become permanent Chief Justices of their own High Courts, but often after a menacingly long period as Acting Chief Justice. The Government's strategy seems to be that such Acting Chief Justices, who would much rather become permanent Chief of their home High Court, will be more agreeable to accepting the Government's nominees for permanent or additional judgeships (Malhotra, 1985). G.P. Singh, the permanent Chief Justice of the Madhya Pradesh High Court from 1978 to 1984, for years resisted what he considered to be not entirely meritorious nominees for the High Court pressed upon him by the Congress (I) state government. When he retired in January 1984 (retirement is mandatory for High Court judges at age 62; it is 65 for Supreme Court judges), there were ten or more vacancies on that High Court as a result of the long stand-off. The seniormost associate judge immediately moved into the center chair, but as Acting Chief Justice. On May 14, 1984, nine new judges were sworn in on that High Court. A few months later, G.L. Oza, the Acting Chief, was made permanent Chief of his home High Court, and the next year he was promoted to the Supreme Court. According to journalist N.K. Singh, former Chief Justice G.P. Singh, whose own credentials and reputation were superb, had his own list of names for the vacancies, and it "reportedly contains top names in the profession." The Chief Minister's list contained mainly patronage choice, "not all ... said to be professionally competent" (Singh, 1983). At least some of the latter are said to be among the crowd sworn in on May 14th (Nayar, 1984). Of course, perhaps all these new appointees were first class people in the judgment of then Acting Chief Oza. It is possible that G.P. Singh's principled stand cost him a promotion to the Supreme Court.

If an Acting Chief Justice is insufficiently agreeable to the Government's nominees, he runs the risk of being transferred, or superseded by a Chief Justice brought in from another state. It is widely believed that when a transfer of a Chief Justice occurs, there is an element of punishment somewhere. Respected journalist Inder Malhotra sees a "patent selectivity" in the transfers so far (1985). This can be very subtle. A Chief Justice may be brought in from the outside to block the chance a senior associate judge may have had to become Chief Justice according to the still viable, but somewhat eroding, seniority convention, i.e., the convention of the senior-most associate judge becoming Chief. There could also be an element of reward and promotion, as in the case of a judge who would reach retirement age before seniority would entitle him to the center chair on his own High Court, but becomes Chief of another Court via transfer. R.N. Pyne, e.g., who became the Chief Justice of the Delhi High Court in May 1988, was not senior enough to become Chief Justice of Calcutta, his home High Court. A Chief Justice commands much more status and prestige than an ordinary judgeship, and these are prized posts. So the Government now dangles the carrot of promotion before senior judges, while also swinging the stick of supersession or transfer. According to Kuldip Nayar, another of India's top journalists, "the threat of being transferred, a sword that hangs over the judges' heads, has made cowards of them" (1985 : 11; Cf. Injudicious, 1983).

At least two more Chief Justices, M.B. Farooqe of Jammu and Kashmir, and D.S. Tewatia of Punjab and Haryana, have resigned rather than accept transfers to Sikkim and Calcutta, respectively (Sikkim, 1983; Self-Inflicted, 1988; Abdi, 1988).

While the policy of having outsiders as Chief Justice of all High Courts is in full bloom, the policy of having one-third of the judges of each High Court from outside the state is being implemented very slowly. The Government has said that it would prefer to accomplish the latter via initial appointments rather than transfers, and it may be having difficulty finding people willing to accept an initial appointment far away from home. Although reliable and up-to-date information is not readily available, it looks as if no more than a dozen such fresh appointments or transfers of junior High Court Judges have occurred so far. If fully implemented, about 150 associate judges of the 18 High Courts would be from out-of-state. But additional judges and fresh permanent judge appointees are expected to sign the transfer agreement. Whether all who have refused to do so have not been extended or not appointed at all is not certain. But of the 15 additional judges of the Allahabad High Court in 1982, 14 were confirmed as permanent judges on the same day in December in 1982, 14 were confirmed as permanent judges on the same day in December 1982. The one who was not confirmed, K.M. Dayal, was the only one of this group who had not given his consent for transfer (Justice Dayal, 1983). Dayal resigned his not yet expired additional judgeship in protest (Allahabad advocates, 1983).

Clearly, these recent changes in government policy affecting the higher judiciary make a judgeship less attractive to competent lawyers of distinction and integrity. Former Supreme Court Justice Tulzapurkar says the transfer fear "has deterred many a competent advocate from accepting judgeship on the High Court bench" (1984 : 51). No one knows how many of those offered judgeships have declined because of the transfer policy. Tulzapurkar, when he was the Acting Chief Justice at Bombay, and just a few months after the transfer of the 16 judges during the Emergency, said that since those transfers

> on every occasion I have sounded a member of the Bar for accepting the Judgeship on the High Court Bench, he has politely declined the offer on the ground that

he did not want to get himself uprooted from its hometown and his moorings, which he would if he were to be transferred (1977 : 10).

The recently released 121st Report of the Law Commission reports that of the 18 Chief Justice polled, three said the possibility of transfer had caused some members of the bar to be unwilling to accept a judgeship, and other Chief Justices believed that the transfer policy had a "marginal effect" (1988 : 45). But given the carelessness and factual errors found in this report, one has to wonder about its veracity.

What is clear is that virtually all dimensions of the transfer policy cause apprehension and fear among those now on the Bench, and among those offered judgeships. Over the years, suspension, denial of promotion, and transfer are the three powers that have been employed to bend civil servants to a Minister's will. The latter two now apply to High Court Judges also, and the first is closely akin to denying a permanent judgeship to an additional judge. High Court judges are increasingly being treated as ordinary bureaucrats.

Why would a first class lawyer, enjoying a lucrative practice at his home state High Court, find a judgeship today an attractive proposition ? Most fresh High Court appointments are made after about 20 years of experience in private practice, so the lawyer to whom the offer is extended would be in his or her 40s. This archetypal lawyer would still have children to educate, daughters to be married, and probably elderly parents and in-laws to look after. To be transferred from Bangalore to Allahabad, from Gujarat to Himachal Pradesh, from Andhra Pradesh to Assam, even from Calcutta to Bombay (these are all transfers that have in fact taken place), is a major dislocation for the transferred judge and their families. Transfer entails a language problem, difficulties with the children's education, and often major adjustments to a new and unfamiliar culture. Knowing that the possibility is very real, surely more than a few good people are preferring to remain in private practice at home. As the *Times of India* said editorially, the transfer policy will

> make the working conditions of high court judges more irksome than they already are. This is bound to reduce the number of persons of distinction who would be prepared to accept judicial appointments. There is no surfeit of such persons at the moment and clearly it cannot afford to do without them (Transfer, 1981).

The Government's efforts periodically to justify the transfer policy in the face of widespread criticism are simply not accepted by an attentive public. As *The Statesman* said in a lead editorial commending Ismail's resignation in protest of his transfer, "the Prime Minister's and the Union Minister's disclaimers of any intention to threaten the independence of the judiciary have convinced none expect those who have found it expedient to be converted to their view" (An Example, 1981). The government's case becomes even more suspect, and its real motives more sinister, when it tells lies, e.g., in 1981 when the Union Law Minister "refuted the charge that political consideration had led to transfer of high Court judges during the emergency " (Note, 1981; Cf. Move on, 1981; Govt defends, 1983). There is also evidence of the Government violating its own professed transfer policy guidelines (Chawla, 1985 : 78-79).

Enough is already clearly spelled out and implemented concerning the transfer policy to frighten away prospective judges. Unknown, of course, is how much worse the situation might become after a courageous lawyer accepts a judgeship. At this time, only strong public opinion, voiced by individuals the Government still considers effective opinion leaders, seems to be causing the Government to proceed slowly. At any time, however, this could change, and 150 judges could be moved willy-nilly around the 18 High Court checkerboard.

Resignation, of course, is always an option. But it is important to be aware that resignation does not mean the judge can resume practice before his home High Court, if that is the

High Court he has served on. Once appointment as a permanent judge is accepted, one is constitutionally prohibited (Article 220, 1950) from ever practising again at that High Court. So a judge who resigns in disgust or protest must move to Delhi and practise before Supreme Court, or pack up and shift to another High Court in another state. An additional judge denied a permanent appointment may resume practice, but knowing that some upstanding additional judges have been "sacked" or otherwise kept on a short leash, why would a good person accept an additional judgeship?

Other Disincentives

Although I have stressed the salary situation and the transfer policy as major factors discouraging the best people from accepting judgeships, there are other disincentives which for some individuals may be even more compelling.

An absurd workload. The backlog of cases pending resolution by the superior judiciary is absolutely overwhelming and is crushing the institutions and the judges. The number of cases in arrears in the High Courts has risen from 480,000 in 1980 to 675,000 in 1983, and to nearly 1,500,000 in 1988. There were about 80,000 cases in arrears at the Supreme Court in 1980; the recently announced 1988 tally is over 175,000. At one time, an attractive feature of the bench was that it provided more leisure when compared with the long hours of private practice. Even the most conscientious, workhorse judges are increasingly discouraged by this literally out-of-control escalation of the workload. And the judges have no law clerks, in the American sense, to assist them in summarizing briefs and drafting opinions. Some judges have told me that they are ashamed of the poor quality of their hastily dictated published opinions. Others report having time to skim the daily newspaper, but no time to read professional journals.

Delays in filling vacancies. Related to the backlog of cases are the long delays in filling vacancies on the Supreme Court and the High Courts. With retirement mandatory for Supreme

Court judges at 65, and for High Court judges at 62, all involved in the selection and appointment process obviously know well in advance when vacancies will occur. However, during recent years, at any point in time, about 20 percent of the more than 400 High Court judgeships are vacant, and some of these vacancies are not filled for many years. According to the figures supplied by the Patna High Court, no less than 13,305 judge-days were lost between 1980-1986 on account of delays in filling vacancies (121st Report, 1988 : 149). The inherited tradition was that a retired judge was replaced the day after his retirement.

Four times the size of the Supreme Court has been increased, each time the rationale being the increasing size of the backlog. In mid-1986, its strength was raised from 18 to 26, but as of May 1988 the strength remains at 18; the new judges just have not yet been appointed; and no one seems to be in any hurry to make the appointments. The Union Law Minister announced in September 1980 that "very soon" seven vacancies on the Supreme Court would be filled (Seven, 1980); the seventh was in fact appointed in March 1983, two and one-half years later. When pressed in Parliament to make the filling of vacancies a higher priority, the Minister of State for Law, H.R.Bhardwaj, recently said, "it is not possible to indicate any definite time for filling up the vacancies" (No time, 1988). It is evidence of this nature that provokes judges to say "the Government really doesn't care about judges."

But more of a disincentive is what follows word or rumor that a particular person has been nominated or is under consideration for a Supreme Court or High Court judgeship. According to the recent Law Commission report, "a spate of letters start pouring in making all sorts of real or imaginary allegations against the recommended" (121st Report, 1988:46). These are "filthy and dirty allegations" amounting to "crass vilification" emanating from individuals or groups opposed to the nominee. Recently it was reported that the Delhi High Court Chief Justice has been running from pillar to post trying to persuade some eminent members of the Bar to accept High Court judgeships. But he has met with little success. People don't want their reputation sullied and nobody wants to get involved in a controversy (Judge's Impass, 1986).

Moreover, some nominees are in suspense for literally years before those involved in the appointment process ultimately decide to award or deny the judgeship. Understandably, some high quality people are simply unwilling to subject themselves to the abuse, intrigue, and delays which are part of the clandestine appointment process.

Denigration of the judiciary by government leaders. Increasingly, individuals holding high public office criticize, castigate, and denigrate the judges. As a recent illustration, no less a figure than the Law Minister, P. Shiv Shankar, delivered a speech in late 1987 in which he said that the Supreme Court was "composed of elements from elite class [with] unconcealed sympathy for the haves, i.e., zamindars,"and that the "anti-social" elements, that is, Foreign Exchange Regulation Act violators, bride-burners, and a whole horde of reactionaries have found their haven in the Supreme Court" (Contempt. 1988; Cf. SC's clean chit, 1988). Maligning the superior judiciary and bashing the judges are hardly conducive to attracting high quality judicial personnel (Nayar, 1986b).

Closely related to verbal assaults on the superior judiciary is the widely-held perception that the Government is trying to reduce the judiciary's autonomy, if not make it simply a captive of the ruling party. Upendra Baxi, regarded by most as India's premier contemporary legal scholar, wrote recently that "In reality, not a single section of the governing elite cares much for the independence of the judiciary" (1985: 33). Concern that the Government would like to weaken the judiciary was first expressed in earnest about two decades ago and increased in 1970 when the Government, enraged by the Supreme Court's decision invalidating the banks nationalization ordinance (R.C. Cooper, 1970), began talking menacingly about the need for "committed" judges.[10] Court supporters believe that meant commitment to the policies of the ruling party and accused the Government of launching a campaign to destroy the independence of the judiciary. In 1973 the Government violated the convention of promoting the senior most associate judge to the center chair upon the incumbent's retirement. This was done to punish three senior judges for decisions that went against the Government, and to reward the fourth-in-line, A.N. Ray, for his pro-Government decisions. This, too, was criticized as a blatant attack on an independent judiciary and provoked a national debate (Palkhivala, 1973: Nayar, 1973: Kumaramangalam, 1973). Again in 1977, H.R. Khanna, the most visibly heroic Supreme Court judge during the Emergency, was denied the Chief Justiceship as punishment for standing up to the Government.

The seniority convention was restored by the Janata Government in 1978 and has been honored by the Congress (I) Government when the center chair fell vacant in 1985 and 1986. But the transfer policy, which is almost always criticized as an assault on an independent judiciary, has resulted in a number of supersessions of judges in line for Chief Justiceships at various High Courts. The seniority convention is just that, a convention. The Government can violate it to reward what Indians term "convenient" judges, and to punish independent judges whose decisions go against the Government in important cases. Since some advocates accept judicial appointments because they know that given the workings of the seniority convention, they will at a predictable future date become Chief Justice (providing they are relatively young when appointed, and their seniors on the bench will reach retirement age before them), recent violations of this convention at the level of the High Courts probably has discouraged some from accepting judgeship offers.[11]

In sum, the best legal talent is unlikely to want to serve on courts which are losing their autonomy. A competent and proud lawyer, accustomed to the autonomy of the Bar, is unlikely to be attracted to a post in which behaviour pleasing to the powers that be is the price one has to pay in order to get promoted to the Chief Justiceship. Why not just remain at the Bar and get richer?

Abuse from the Bar. In recent years there have been several incidents of senior lawyers verbally abusing Supreme Court judges in court. A few years ago, lawyer N.C. Dey faced a contempt charge for "thumping the desk and making remarks such as 'You are judges, not auctioneers.'" (SC and Bar, 1983). During the same year, the Chairman of the Bar Council of India lashed out at judges "who draw the paltry sum of a few thousand attacking the Bar for corruption" (Mahajan, 1983). Apparently he was responding to a speech made earlier by Chief Justice Chandrachud in which the latter had talked of the gross incompetence that prevailed in the profession, which was reflected in appointments to the bench from the Bar, and asked whether any corruption in the judiciary could by possible without the existence of corrupt lawyers (Mahajan, 1983; Cf. Mahajan, 1984). Indian judges value status, prestige and dignity, and insolent or otherwise discourteous treatment by lawyers as a signal of declining status, dignity, and prestige. Some judges told me that they fear some senior members of the Supreme Court Bar — fear in the sense that they do not want to become targets of a vilification campaign. A current senior Supreme Court judge said, "the bar today is insolent towards the judges, has contempt for the bench. Leading lawyers look down on judges; they find our meager pay packet laughable" (Interviews, 1983). Where status is highly prized, the erosion of it makes judgeships less attractive to leading lawyers.

Conclusions

In 1949, during the late stages of the drafting of the Constitution, Prime Minister Jawaharlal Nehru said that independent India wants as judges "the best material from the Bar," and added that

> It is important that these Judges should be not only first-rate, but should be acknowledged to be first-rate in the country, and of the highest integrity, if necessary, people who can stand up against the executive Government, and whoever may come in their way (CAD, 1949, VIII, May 24 : 247).

Although Nehru occasionally carped about what he believed were unduly conservative Supreme Court and High Court decisions (Jacob, 1977 : 169-181), he also did much to institutionalize a strong and independent judiciary. The vast majority of those appointed to the higher judiciary during Nehru's long tenure as Prime Minister met the criteria he set forth in 1949.

Although this paper has drawn attention to factors which deter the best available talent from accepting judgeships, the superior judiciary, despite some deterioration, is for the most part qualitatively sound, and remains a bedrock of integrity which stands out in a political system awash with corruption. While without doubt some good people, perhaps by now too many of the very best, are refusing to serve as judges, anyone who has met a representative sample of India's Supreme Court and High Court judges would find them, in the main, an impressive lot. Despite the various disincentives, a number of individuals with superb credentials do accept, and some of these would distinguish the superior judiciary of any country.

In many nations where the legal profession is part of the free-market economy, the most talented and successful lawyers will earn incomes far in excess of what the top judges are paid. This gap is immensely more complicated in India because of the sad per capita income situation, and because all on the government payroll receive what would be considered in most countries as low salaries. According to official figures, the national annual per capita income in 1985-1986 (the latest available) was Rs. 2595. But at what is termed "constant prices," i.e., 1960 as the base year, that figure converts to Rs.

797 (Dhar, 1988). Moreover, "about 300 million of India's 800 million people live below the poverty line. The norm for determining the line is a per capita monthly income of Rs. 41 for the rural people and Rs. 46 for those living in urban areas" (Hair, 1988). Judges are poorly paid compared to what leaders of the Bar earn, but extraordinarily well compensated when compared with these per capita income figures, and well-paid when compared with virtually all others on the government payroll.[12] Union and State Ministers, Members of Parliament and the State Assemblies, and senior bureaucrats receive less, but they are able to amass great fortunes through corrupt means, plundering state exchequers, and extracting bribes from the private sector.[13]

If the integrity of the superior judiciary is to continue, the judges cannot afford to be corrupt. Of the 87 judges who have served on the Supreme Court since 1950, not a single one has been exposed as involved in any form of corrupt behaviour. At the level of the High Courts, there are whispers of some corrupt judges, especially during the past dozen years (Gupta, 1985 : 42-44). The tradition of an incorruptible is a very strong and valued one in India, but a poorly paid judge is more likely to succumb to various forms of bribery and unethical behaviour than a well remunerated one. Even after the recent improvement in salaries and fringe benefits, some Supreme Court judges have told me that it probably will not be long before a member of the Supreme Court is found to have been partaking of illegal financial gratification. The honest judge is still the norm, but all who speak on this issue express concern that the higher judiciary is gradually sinking to the level of the other major institutions. One can only hope that if lesser people are increasingly populating the superior judiciary, the hoary tradition of an incorruptible judiciary will make them better than they are.

In sum, the recent salary, pension, and fringe benefit increases probably have not made a judgeship a financially attractive proposition, but there are limits to what can be paid even to top judges in a poor country. Under these constraints, what needs to be carefully preserved, if not increased, is the psychic income that attaches to a judgeship. By psychic income, I mean compensations that money cannot purchase, e.g., prestige, esteem, honor, dignity, security of tenure, a greater sense of fulfillment in dispensing justice than in making money, a sense of pride in serving one's state and nation.

Sadly, the transfer policy and the other disincentives have had the effect of reducing this psychic income. If the government "doesn't care about judges," this psychic income is devalued. If a prospective new judge fears that he will have to cooperate with the powers that be, or be transferred (or fired, if he is appointed initially as an additional judge), or otherwise punished, these fears also sharply reduce psychic income, and clearly discourage the best from joining the bench. Perhaps a partial corrective to the disincentives associated with the appointment process and the transfer policy would be for the government, which simply is not trusted to be fair and honest,[14] to share the power associated with the transfer and appointment matters with an impeccably up-right national commission, composed of individuals well-known for rectitude and national-mindedness. This is not an entirely original thought and would reduce only some of the existing disincentives. However, there is no reason to expect that the government will be willing to share the great powers it possesses and which keep the judges on a short leash.

Just after the transfer policy was announced, the *Times of India* said editorially that if the entire (Chief Justices and one -third of associate judges) transfer policy is implemented,

> it will be a tragedy of the first order. The country is passing through a grave crisis. All the institutions which are expected to hold it together are run down and are unable to bear the terrible strains on them. At such a time to undermine the prestige, authority, and morale of the judiciary or the public's faith in its independence—which is what mass transfer will do—is an invitation to further trouble (A Bad Move, 1981).

The author of this editorial was right on target, for even the incomplete implementation of the policy during the past several years has indeed demoralized the judges and scared away many of the types of individuals who once graced the higher judiciary.

The erosion of the higher judiciary will markedly change the nature of Indian democracy. Because judges in the past earned a well- deserved reputation for honesty and integrity, the courts are perceived as having much more legitimacy than the other branches. Judges have become virtually the conscience of the nation, and they are increasingly being called upon to adjudicate or otherwise investigate a wide variety of major issues. One can only hope that good people will be offered, and will accept judgeship, and after joining the bench will be steadfast in preserving the fine traditions of their predecessors.

NOTES

1. There are 18 High courts in the country, and they are the second tier of the pyramidal judicial system.

2. The decliners are a distinguished lot -- H.M. Seervai, N.A. Palkhivala, L.N. Sinha, F.S. Nariman, S.N. Kacker, and K. Parasaran.

3. Approximately two-thirds of the 364 High Court judges in 1985 were recruited directly from the bar (63 judicial posts were vacant then).The other one-third were members of the state judicial service (Ministry of Law, 1986). My focus is upon recruitment from the bar. For members of the state judicial services, a High Court judgeship is a vary attractive promotion.

4. Chagla was Chief Justice from 1947 to 1958. The largely clandestine process of appointment is beyond the scope of

this paper. A useful introduction to the selection and appointment process is Dhavan and Jacob (1978). High Court Chief Justices in Chagla's time, and still today, are major participants in the selection of their colleagues.

5. These estimates are compiled from the interviews I conducted in 1983 and 1988 with more than 50 serving and retired Supreme Court judges and about two dozen serving retired High Court judges. About half of Supreme Court judges earlier were High Chief Justices and, as such, were involved in identifying prospective judges, and offering them judgeship.

6. Conversion of the rupee to the dollar equivalent poses problems that no one has ever resolved satisfactorily. Until the mid-1960s, Rs. 4000 was officially worth about $800. Today, with the market rate of exchange at about Rs. 13 to the dollar, Rs. 4000 would purchase about $300.

7. At least two additional judges were not given extensions during the 1975-1977 Emergency. One of these was H.R. Lalit of the Bombay High Court (Seervai, 1983: 980: Siwach, 1986: 50, 78-79). The other, R.N. Aggarwal of the Delhi High Court was also not extended and, because he was a memberd of the judicial service, non-extension meant reversion (demotion) to his farmer post of Sessions Judge (Seervai, 1984: 2293 - 2299). After the Janata Government came to power, Aggarwal was appointed a permanent judge of the Delhi High Court and, in 1987, by virtue of being then the senior-most associate judge, completed his career on the bench with a five day (the shortest tenure on record) stint as Chief Justice at Delhi.

8. For a slightly different account of this incident, see Naidu (1988), and "Stand up, speak out" (1988). The Supreme Court later cleared Arjun Singh of all corruption charges (Arjun Singh cleared, 1986).

9. Ten of the 364 High Court judge in 1985 were women (Ministry of Law, 1986). The first woman was appointed to a High Court in 1959. None have yet been promoted to the Supreme Court, but one is likely to be promoted shortly. Cf. Keshwaar, 1988: 69-74.

10. The author of the adjective "committed" is unknown. Most attribute it, incorrectly I think, to Mohan Kumaramangalam, a former communist and classmate of Mrs. Gandhi's at Cambridge, who became Union Minister of steel and mines in Mrs. Gandhi's Government after the 1971 national election, and who was the chief architect of the policy of trying to locate judges who would treat the Government kindly. The term "committed" entered the vocabulary of Indian politics not later than February 1970, i.e., just after the Banks Nationalization decision. It is referred to in an editorial by C.K. Dapthary in *The Indian Advocate* dated February 18th, although the journal itself is dated January-June 1969 (2-3). The term is also mentioned in a 1970 number of the *Supreme Court Cases* (Honorary Editor, 1970).

11. Both of the lawyers who came to the Supreme Court directly from the bar were in line to become Chief Justice of India. Sikri did serve as Chief Justice (1971-1973), but S.C. Roy died shortly after coming to Delhi.

12. Candor compels me to point out that one retired Supreme Court judge is on record as strongly opposing the raising of judicial salaries and perquisites. This is the sincere, irrepressible, articulate, brilliant maverick, V.R. Krishna Iyer (1973-1980). The first, and one of the very few genuine socialists to serve as a Supreme Court judge in this socialist republic, Krishna Iyer writes that Indian judges already enjoy too many benefits. About these "robed Maharajas" he asks the reader: "Do you know that the brethren in the Supreme Court already have unlimited telephone calls *ad libitum*, free furnished bungalows, free cars (for some) and car allowance, free water and electricity, five free peons and security men, free invitations for high functions, and state guest privileges in every state?" (1987: 29).

13. That corruption is rampant hardly needs documentation any more. In the August 1987 *India Today* -MARG public opinion poll, the nationwide sample of respondents identified corruption as the country's main problem (Opinion Poll, 1988: 31). Two years earlier, at the centennial session of the Congress at Bombay, none other than Prime Minister Rajiv

Gandhi told the delegates: "We [the Congress - I] obey no discipline, no rule, follow no principal of public morality, display no sense of social awareness, show no concern for the public weal. Corruption is not only tolerated but even regarded as the hallmark of leadership" (AICC(I), 1988: 22).

14. An alarming recent indication of the magnitude of distrust of the Government is found in the results of a non-scientific but otherwise random survey carried out by the Hindustani Andolan, a non political voluntary organization. The survey asked respondents if they believed the recent Joint Parliamentary Committee report dealing with the Bofors scandal. This scandal involving alleged kickback received by Indians after India awarded a large gun contract to Bofors, a Swedish arms company, has been front page news for the past year. The JPC report found no evidence of any wrong-doing by any one. Of the 519 respondents, only *two* agreed with, i.e., believed the report (People unhappy, 1988)

REFERENCES[*]

"A Bad Move" (1981) *Times of India*, January 21.

Abdi, S.N.M. (1988) "Justice Denied." *Illustrated Weekly of India*, May 15 : 30-31.

"Additional judge is not a servant" (1981) *Hindustan Times*, August 28.

"*Administrative Reforms Commission Study Team Report on Centre-State Relations* (1963). Delhi : Manager of Publications.

"Allahabad advocates boycott courts" (1983) *Times of India*, January 4.

"An Example Well Set" (1981) *Statesman*, July 20.

---

[*] all newspaper citations are New Delhi editions, unless otherwise indicated.

"Arjun Singh cleared in liquor case" (1986) *Overseas Hindustan Times*, November 8.

"Bar assails transfers of Chief Justices" (1983) *Hindustan Times*, October 20.

"Bar panel assails judges' transfer" (1983) *Hindustan Times*, April 5.

Baxi, Upendra (1985) *Courage Craft and Contention : The Indian Supreme Court in the Eighties*. Bombay : N.M. Tripathi.

Beaumont, Sir John (1946) "The Indian Judicial System : Some Suggested Reforms." *Bombay Law Reporter (Journal)* XLVIII : 12-18.

Bhagwati, P.N. (1979) Speech before All India Law Teachers Conference, Varanasi. Untitled, Unpublished, December 27.

Chagla, M.C. (1973) *Roses in December : An Autobiography*. Bombay : Bharatiya Vidya Bhavan.

Chandrachud, Y.V. (1972) *Bombay Law Reporter (Journal)* LXXIV : 71-73.

_____ (1988) Remarks made at a book review session, Indian International Centre, February 6.

Chawla, Prabhu (1985) "Appointments : Flouted Guidelines." *India Today*, June 15 : 78-79.

_____ and S.H. Venkataramia (1988) "AICC (I) Session : Follow the Leader." *India Today*, May 15 : 22.

"CJs for body to clear judges' appointment" (1983) *Indian Express* February 27.

"CJs to be from outside states: (1983) *Indian Express*, January 29.

"Conflicting views on role of judiciary" (1970) *Times of India*, July 5.

Constituent Assembly Debates (1946-1950) 12 volumes. Delhi : Government of India Press.

Constitution of India (1950) As amended to 1988. Lucknow : Eastern Book Company.

"Contempt Notice to Shiv Shankar" (1988) *Times of India*, February 11.

Daphtary, C.K. (1969) "Editorial."*The Indian Advocate* IX (January-June) : 2-3.

Dhar, M.K. (1988) "Steady fall in per capita income" *Hindustan Times*, January 28.

Dhavan, Rajeev and Alice Jacob (1978) *Selection and Appointment of Supreme Court Judges : A Case Study*. Bombay N.M. Tripathi.

Dua, Bhagwan D. (1983) "A Study in Executive-Judicial Conflict : The Indian Case. "*Asian Survey* XXIII (April) : 463-483.

Eightieth Report (1980) Law Commission of India. *The Method of Appointment of Judges*. Delhi : Government of India Press.

Fourteenth Report (1958) Law Commission of India. *Reform of Judicial Administration*. 2 volumes. New Delhi : Government of India Press.

Gadbois, George H. Jr. (1987) "The Institutionalization of the Supreme Court of India" in John R. Schmidhauser (ed.) *Comparative Judicial Systems : Challenging Frontiers in Conceptual and Empirical Analysis*. London : Butterworth.

Gajendragadkar, P.B. (1983) *To the Best of My Memory*. Bombay : Bharatiya Vidya Bhavan.

"Govt defends procedure for appointing judges" (1983) *Times of India*, February 23.

Gupta, Shekhar (1985) "Y.V. Chandrachud : 'We are not spineless'." *India Today*, July 31 : 42-44.

"Hair-Splitting" (1988) *Hindustan Times*, March 23.

Honorary Editor (1970) "The Re-Shaping of the Supreme Court." *Supreme Court Cases* (Journal) I : 79-83.

"Injudicious Moves" (1983) *India Today*, December 15 : 102-103. Interviews (1983, 1988) conducted by the author with Supreme Court and High Court Judges.

"Intolerant executive threat of judiciary" (1981) *Indian Express*, April 17.

"Ismail Quits in Protest" (1981) *Times of India* (Bombay), January 24.

Jacob, Alice (1977) "Nehru and the Judiciary." *Journal of the Indian Law Institute* 19 (April-June) : 169-181.

Jaganmohan Reddy, P. (1984) *We have a Republic—Can we keep it ?* Tirupati : Sri Venkateswara University.

Jit, Inder (1981) "Fresh Assault on Judiciary." *The Tribune* (Chandigarh), January 28.

"Judges Denied Term" (1981) *India Abroad* (New York) June 26.

"Judges on the leash" (1981) *Indian Express*, March 25.

"Judge's impasse : 'PM was misled'" (1986) *Overseas Hindustan Times*, July 26.

"Judging Transfers" (1983) *Hindustan Times*, January 31.

"Judicial Appointments" (1980) *Hindustan Times*, October 27.

"Judicial Reform" (1983) *Indian Express*, February 14.

"Jurists criticize transfer policy" (1988) *Hindustan Times*, February 23.

"Justice Dayal did not consent to transfer" (1983) *Indian Express*, January 1.

"Justice Lal given appointment" (1988) *Hindustan Times*, May 16.

Keshwaar, Sanober (1988) "Your Ladyship." *Sunday*, April 3-9.

Krishna Iyer, V.R. (1987) *Our Courts on Trial*. Delhi. Delhi : B.R. Publishing Corporation.

Kumaramangalam, S. Mohan (1973) *Judicial Appointments : An Analysis of the Recent Controversy over the Appointment of the Chief Justice of India*. New Delhi : Oxford & IBH Publishing Company.

Mahajan, Krishan (1983) "Legal Perspectives : Ahmedabad Signal." *Hindustan Times*, November 14.

_____ (1984) "Legal Perspectives : End of the Road. "*Overseas Hindustan Times*, January 21.

_____ (1988) "Arrears and CJs Meet." *Hindustan Times*, February 16.

Malhotra, Inder (1985) "State of the Judiciary : Erosion Must be Ended." *Times of India*, May 9.

"Minister's letter 'an attempt to put additional judges in fear' " (1981) *Hindustan Times*, August 13.

Ministry of Law and Justice (1986) *Judges of the Supreme Court and the High Courts*. New Delhi : Controller of Publications.

Ministry of Law, Justice and Company Affairs (1980) *Judges of the Supreme Court and the High Courts.* New Delhi : Government of India Press.

"Move on judges to fight parochialism" (1981) *Times of India,* July 16. Naidu, Chandra Kant (1988) "Judge pays for adverse verdict." *Indian Express,* May 25.

Nariman, F.S. (1981) "Guarding the guardians : Removal and transfer of judges." *Indian Express,* March 10.

_____ (1983) "Packing the Judiciary ?" *Indian Express,* July 20.

Nayar, Kuldip (1973) (ed.) *Supersession of Judges.* New Delhi : Indian Book Company.

_____ (1982) "Ruling on Judges Disquiets Many." *India Abroad* (New York), January 15.

_____ (1984) "Chief Justice of States Need Their Day in court." *India A road* (New York) December 14.

_____ (1985) "Prestige of the Judiciary Should be Restored." *Sunday,* March 10-16 : 11.

_____ (1986a) "Gandhi's Party Politics Lowers Standards." *India Aborad* (New York), May 2.

_____ (1986b) "Judiciary Takes Pounding by Privileged Politicians." *India Abroad* (New York), March 28.

Noorani, A.G. (1982) "The Twilight of the Judiciary." *Debonair* (February) : 19-23.

"No time frame for filling SC, HC vacancies" (1981) *Indian Express,* March 11.

"Note on Judges defended" (1981) *Times of India* (Bombay), April 17. One Hundred Twenty-First Report (1988) Law Commission of India.

A New Forum for Judicial Appointments. Cyclostyled.

"Opinion Poll : Rajiv's 'TINA' Factor" (1988) *India Today*, February 29 : 29-35.

Palkhivala, N.A. (ed.) (1973) *A Judiciary Made to Measure.* Bombay : M.R. Pai.

"People unhappy with JPC report : Survey" (1988), *Indian Express*, May 25.

"Quit ? Not Me, Says Arjun Singh" (1986) *India Abroad* (New York), April 25.

R.C. *Cooper* v. *Union of India* (1970) 3 S.C.R. 530.

Rajagopaul, G.R. (1983) "Protecting judicial independence." *Indian Express*, May 11.

"Rupee is worth 10.929 paise" (1988) *Hindustan Times*, March 19. S.P. *Gupta* v. *Union of India* (1982) 2 S.C.R. 265.

Sahay, S. (1981) "A Close Look : Shiv Shankar's Grand Design." *Statement*, April 17.

_____ (1986) "The State of the Judiciary" in "India 1985." *Seminar* 317 (January) : 60-62.

"SC and Bar in for confrontation" (1983) *Indian Express*, February 8.

"SC Bar panel to defend lawyers on contempt charge" (1983) *Times of India*, February 4.

"SC's clean chit to Shiv Shankar" (1988) *Times of India*, April 21.

Seervai, H.M. (1970) *The Position of the Judiciary under the Constitution of India*. Bombay : Bombay University Press.

———— (1978) *The Emergency, Future Safeguards and the Habeas Corpus Case : A Criticism*. Bombay : N.M. Tripathi.

———— (1983) *Constitutional Law of India* I. Third edition. Bombay : N.M. Tripathi.

———— (1984) *Constitutional Law of India* II. Third edition. Bombay: N.M. Tripathi.

———— (1986) " Cobwebs" in "The Judicial Jungle." *Seminar* 325 (September) : 21-25.

"Self-Inflicted Wounds" (1988) *Indian Express.*, February 19.

"Seven new Supreme Court judges soon" (1980) *Sunday Standard*, September 28.

Sheth, S.H. (1983) "Judicial Reforms." *Indian Express*, February 24.

Shourie, Arun (1982) "By what are judges bribed ?" *Indian Express*, January 24, 25, 26.

"Sikkim Chief Justice Resigns" (1983) *Statesman Weekly*. September 10.

Singh, N.K. (1983) "MP Govt. CJ row over new judges." *Indian Express*, January 14.

Siwach, J.R. (1986) *Sinking Indian Judicial Pyramid*. Delhi : Chinta Prakashan, Pilani.

Sorabjee, Soli J. (1987) "The Supreme Court of India : I-Erosion of Judicial Collectivism." *Times of India* (Bombay), January 6.

"Stand up, Speak out" (1988) *Indian Express*, May 27.

States Reorganization Commission Report (1955) Delhi : Manager of Publications.

"The Judicial Jungle" (1986) *Seminar* 325 (September).

"32 judges agree to appointment outside" (1981) *Hindustan Times* August 19.

"Transfer of Judges" (1981) *Times of India* (Bombay), April 3.

Tulzapurkar, V.D. (1977) "Our Judicial System : An Inaugural Address." *Bombay Law Reporter (Journal)* LXXIX : 6-14.

———— (1984) " Threats to the Independence of the Judiciary." *All India Reporter (Journal)* : 49-53.

3

YOGENDRA K. MALIK

ELECTORAL LAWS AND CAMPAIGN AND PARTY FINANCES

Implications for Polity and Society

Introduction

For a long time scholars have debated the relationship between the nature of the economy, the society, the level of wealth and the operation of stable democracies. Some assert that democracies can operate only in societies having a free market or capitalist economy, others say that it is possible only in wealthy societies, while a third group of scholars stresses that democracies can work only in societies with well-established traditions of political accommodation.[1]

Whatever the theoretical positions of different schools, there seems to be a scholarly consensus that democracies exist only in those societies which besides having freedom of expression and association and competing political parties also observe certain sets of rules which enable the peaceful transference of power from one set of leaders to another. Thus "Democracy ... may be defined as a political system which supplies regular constitutional opportunities for changing the governing officials, and a social mechanism which permits the largest possible part of the population to influence major decisions by choosing among contenders for political office."[2]

A successful liberal democracy is possible when the societies are able to create a balance between individual rights and citizens' obligations, between participation and respect for authority and law. The observance of such a balance is expected on the part of both the elites and the non-elites. John Locke was right when he asserted that "in all states of created beings, capable to laws, where there is no law there is no freedom."

The legitimacy of a democratic regime is dependent upon the degree of trust which it enjoys among its citizens. In turn, political regimes enjoy citizens' trust to the extent that the ruling elites' conduct is in conformity with the law of the land.

Laws, Elections, and Campaign Financing

Elections and citizens' participation constitute one of the most conspicuous aspects of modern democratic societies. The underlying assumption of the democratic system is the equality of all citizens, both in the value of their votes and in access to elective positions. It is no overstatement to say that "the legitimacy of the political regime depends, to a large extent, on the proper functioning of the electoral mechanism. If the verdict of the people, which forms the basis of the legitimacy of the political authority, is vitiated by unsalutary methods, the faith of the people in the political system is bound to be shaken. To the extent that this happens, the moral basis of state power shrinks irreparably."[4]

Societies are, however, asymmetrical organizations, with inequality of status, money, and resources. Winning elections requires enormous efforts and mobilization of human and material resources. There is little doubt that "in vitually all societies, money is a significant medium by which command over both energies and resources can be achieved."[5] In other words, since there is no equal distribution of money, those persons seeking political offices who have more money are better able to harvest votes than their rivals. This is perhaps the reason that led Oswald Spengler to declare that "money organizes elections in the interests of those who possess it; and the elections themselves are a rigged game as though the people were making decisions."[6] To ensure the legitimacy of the electoral process and the political authority, therefore, it becomes imperative to regulate the role of money in politics.

In this paper we will examine the nature of the electoral laws which govern the role of money in the electoral politics in India. We will also assess their impact on the nature of Indian democracy and society.

Laws Governing the Role of Money in Indian Politics

Money is used to undertake various types of political activities. Besides spending money on local, state, and national elections, politicians also collect funds for maintaining and managing political parties. Money can also be used for political subversion, to influence public opinion or to influence the political process in general. Although there exist several laws in India to deal with various aspects of political finance, our focus in this paper is mainly on the laws dealing with the electoral campaign and party financing.

Regulation of Campaign Spending

With the introduction of universal suffrage and the enlargement of electoral constituencies in the post-independence period, campaigning for election became expensive. In 1951, the Government adopted certain rules in order to control the use of money in electoral politics. Under Article 77 of the Representation of the People Act of 1951, a candidate for parliamentary and legislative elections was required "either by himself or by his election agent [to] keep a separate and correct account of all expenditure in connection with the election incurred or authorized by him or by his election agent between the date of his nomination and the date of declaration of the result thereof, both dates inclusive."[7]

One may note two important aspects of this rule : first, it sets a short time frame (from the day his nomination papers are filed to the day when the election results are declared) for which the candidate has to maintain the records. This excludes all those expenses which he might incur before his nomination papers are filed. The actual campaigning period in India is short—around six to eight weeks. Furthermore, this rule is applicable to the elections for the House of the People and the legislative assemblies of the states and thus excludes the election expenses incurred by the candidates seeking election to the Rajya Sabha, the second chamber of the Indian parliament, and the legislative councils existing in the states, being the upper house of state legislative bodies.[8]

Second, the rules provide the details of the procedures whereby the accounts have to be maintained and the items of expenditure reported. Furthermore, the candidate is required to submit his expense reports within thirty days of the declaration of the election results. The electoral laws also set a ceiling on a candidate's spending in an election. In the 1950s a candidate for election to the House of the People could spend a maximum amount of Rs. 25,000 and for election to the state legislature between Rs. 6000 and Rs. 9000. As the cost of elections kept going up, the Election Commission kept raising the limit. For instance, in 1979 the upper limit for the Lok Sabha election was Rs. 100,000 and for the state legislative assembly Rs. 35,000. These ceilings varied from state to state depending upon the local conditions and cost of living.[9] In 1984 the Election Commission once again raised this ceiling to Rs. 1.25 lakh for the Lok Sabha elections.

Under the present law, however, it is not necessary for the candidate to include in the "account of election expenses any expenditure incurred or authorized ... by a political party" towards his election.[10] The Supreme Court of India in dealing with various election-related petitions has also ruled that "any expenditure ... incurred by a candidate's friends, supporters, well wishers or political party does not fall within the purview" of the election laws.[11] Parties are not bound by the ceilings set by the Election Commission. Obviously this laxity in the rules regarding a party's campaign expenditures and the exemption of campaign spending by political parties from a candidate's required expense report provide a major loophole for the misuse of money in electoral politics.

Regulation of Companies' Campaign Contributions

Until 1956, there were no restrictions in India on companies' contributions to political parties or to the candidates for parliamentary elections. Although candidates for elective offices were dependent on individual contributions to meet their election costs, nevertheless, as the costs increased, both the candidates and the political parties started leaning on the business houses and companies for funds. In January 1956, the Companies Act was amended restricting companies' contributions both to political parties and to individual candidates. The amended Act provided that a public company or its subsidiary shall not, except with the consent of the general body, "contribute to charitable or other funds not directly related to the business of the company or the welfare of its employees, any amount the aggregate of which in any financial year exceeds Rs. 25,000 or five percent of its average net profits during the preceding three years, whichever is greater."[12] The term "other funds" seems to permit the companies to donate money to the political parties, but the Act restricted the amount which companies could contribute towards electoral politics. Despite these restrictions, the realities of electoral politics brought the companies under heavy pressure to donate money to political parties, especially to the ruling Congress party, and more than the limit set by the law.

A fear of the development of close links between big business and politics, however, caused considerable uneasiness both in Parliament and in the influential sectors of Indian society. In 1957, The Bombay High Court Chief Justice, M.C. Chagla, in the case of the Tata Iron and Steel Co. Ltd., observed that

> "we think that it is our duty to draw the attention of Parliament to the great danger inherent in permitting companies to make contributions to funds of political parties. It is a danger which may grow apace and which may ultimately overwhelm and even throttle democracy in the country. Therefore, it is desirable for Parliament to consider under what circumstances and what limitations companies should be permitted to make these contributions."[13]

Justice Chagla suggested that any contributions made by companies to political parties should be made public and preferably through newspapers. The Congress party government, however, made no effort to provide such a provision in the law.

Under these conditions it was not surprising that leaders of the opposition parties inside and outside of Parliament kept pressing the Congress party government either to undertake extensive electoral reforms or to ban companies' campaign contributions. Consequently, in 1969 Indira Gandhi's government passed yet another Companies (Amendment) Act imposing a total ban on companies' donations to parties and candidates or for any political cause. This action of the Congress government, however, did not result just from its desire to reform the political process or to remove or limit the role of money in Indian politics; the action may well have stemmed partly from its desire for self-preservation and partly to improve its image. In the critical elections of 1967, the Congress party had not only lost its dominance at the national level, but in many of the states was reduced to a minority position, resulting in the installation of a coalition, or the united front governments. Thus its precarious position forced it to adopt the 1969 Companies (Amendment) Act lest the companies' donations should end up in the coffers of the opposition parties.[14]

There were, however, many loopholes in the 1969 Companies (Amendment) Act. After winning the 1971 elections, Indira Gandhi was able to collect a very large amount of money for her party by using these loopholes, especially during her Emergency rule between June 1975 and March 1977. Realizing that parties and candidates need funds to contest elections, many groups and influential persons during this period sought the removal of restrictions on companies' contributions of parties and individual candidates provided such contributions were made public. However, the Janata Party, which defeated Indira Gandhi's Congress Party in the March election of 1977, appointed a special committee, headed by Justice Rajinder Sachar, to investigate the issues related to companies' campaign contributions. The Sachar committee, following the Janata party's public posture, ruled against lifting the ban. The committee believed that if the ban were lifted, the large companies and big money would be able to dictate the policies of the parties. In fact in 1979 Chaudhary Charan Singh's caretaker government imposed a blanket ban on direct or indirect donations by businesses and industries to parties or any political cause. It threatened legal action and severe penalties against the companies for any violation of these restrictions.

Despite these restrictions, political parties, especially the ruling party and the candidates for public offices, kept making demands on the businessmen and the companies for funds without much regard for the laws. In 1984 the Rajiv Gandhi government came to power with a promise to introduce extensive electoral reforms in Indian politics; it was his finance minister, V.P. Singh, who tried to break the ties existing between big business and electoral politics. The Companies (Amendment) Act of 1985 is the latest step in regulating the companies' role in campaign finances. The new Act carries a provision allowing private companies to make political contributions not exceeding five percent of their average net profit. The act also "imposed an obligation on every company to disclose in its profit and loss account any amounts contributed by it to any political party or for any political purposes to any person." It raised hopes that now companies' contributions to parties would be made public. In 1986 Rajiv declared that he favored the idea of bringing into the open the accounts of political parties, thus enabling the public to have an idea of the relations existing between the parties and the business world. Until now, however, no such step has been taken.

Laws Dealing with Foreign Contributions

Even though Indian political leaders have frequently hinted about the role of foreign funds in the political process of the country, it was only after the 1967 elections that the issue received serious national attention. In June 1967 many Indian newspapers published a New York Times report summarizing the Central Intelligence Bureau's assertion of the use of foreign money in the general elections of 1967. After frequent debate on the use or abuse of foreign funds in India, both in the Parliament and the national press, in March 1976 the parliament passed the Foreign Contribution (Regulation) Act. The Act imposed three types of restrictions : "[a] a total ban on acceptance of foreign contributions by recipients holding 'sensitive' positions; [b] acceptance, by prior Government permission, by organizations of a 'political' nature, specified in a gazette; and [c] acceptance followed by mere information to Government within a prescribed period."[17] It particularly prohibited the candidates and the parties involved in electoral politics from accepting foreign funds. Political organizations and trade unions could accept foreign funds only with the prior approval of the Government of India. In 1985 the Government of India adopted the Foreign Contributions (Amendment) Act which further tightened the restrictions on the acceptance of such money, and it empowered the authorities to prosecute parties receiving foreign funds in contravention of the provisions of the new law.

Laws dealing with Political Defections

One of the important aspects of Indian politics has been the ease with which the elected members of the Parliament or of the state legislative bodies could defect from their parties and join other groups or parties which would offer them either a position in the cabinet or some other reward. It has been argued that while political parties provide them the tickets, mobilize the voters and spend money on their elections, the parties cannot exercise any control over them if they join other political parties to advance their political careers. Between 1967 and 1983 there were as many as 2,700 cases of defections from one party to another. Fifteen chief ministers changed their parties, causing considerable political instability in the state level politics.[18] In many cases powerful political groups or personalities made efforts to cause defections in order to destabilize a government led by the opposition party. In some cases the legislators were outright bribed to switch parties. Defections are not covered under the electoral laws, but the practice of defection has a very significant impact both on the electoral and political process of the country. In the 1984 election campaign, Rajiv Gandhi promised to introduce an anti-defection law in order to clean up the political process. Both the leaders of the opposition and the ruling parties were committed to stop unprincipled floor-crossings. In March 1985 the 52nd Constitutional Amendment was adopted banning the floor-crossing. It provided that "A member of a House, belonging to any party, shall be disqualified from being a member of the House [a] if he has voluntarily given up his membership of such political party; or [b] if he votes or abstains from voting in such House contrary to any direction issued by the political party to which he belongs ... without obtaining, in either case, the prior permission of such political party ... and such voting or abstention has not been condoned by such political party ... within 15 days from the date of such voting or abstention." The adoption of such a drastic provision was expected to stop the changing of parties by lawmakers prompted by the lure of money or office.

Discrepancies between Laws and Practices

Elections are held for many local, state, and national positions, although it is the elections for the national parliament and state legislative bodies that draw the most attention. In this paper our focus is primarily on the gaps existing between the laws and practices relating to spending on national and state elections.

As noted above, the campaigning period, unlike that of the U.S., is not long. (It is between six and eight weeks.) However, because of the large size of the constituencies and the lack of contact between the voter and the M.P., a candidate needs to campaign extensively to mobilize the voters. "Campaigners who work not for money but out of sheer dedication to the party principles and programs are rare to come by. So perhaps will be the voters themselves in the cash-denuded voting areas."[20]

The candidates need posters, billboards, banners, party symbols, vehicles, loudspeakers, polling agents, booth managers, agents to supervise the counting of votes and hundreds of workers to distribute pamphlets, leaflets, identity slips and other materials. For an assembly seat a candidate may need as many as 150 polling agents and for a parliamentary seat, 316 agents.

We have stated above that the Election Commission has recently fixed a ceiling of Rs. 1.25 lakh on an individual candidate's spending in the Lok Sabha elections. This ceiling is unrealistic and is not followed by the candidates. According to an unofficial estimate, a candidate is likely to spend on paid workers alone as much as Rs. 1,89,480. Transportation and fuel bills may run as high as Rs. 170,000. The candidates also organize public meetings, processions, and rallies and prepare voter lists. According to this estimate the election cost in an average parliamentary constituency is Rs. 584,480.[21] This estimate does not include the money spent on outright purchasing of votes or on the distribution of liquor among the voters before or on the election eve or on the distribution of dhotis and saris or food in the poorer segments of the voting population, all common campaign practices.[22] In 1982 Pranab Mukherji, Indira Gandhi's Finance Minister, stated before Parliament that on an average each parliamentary candidate spends Rs. 5 lakh on his election.[23]

It is common knowledge that the M.P.s. file false election expense reports. A.B. Vajpayee, the Bhartiya Janata Party leader, was candid enough to concede that "most legislators embark on their parliamentary career with a gross lie—the false election returns which they submit."[24] Both the M.P.s and the members of the government are aware of the irregularities practised in the campaign spending and reporting of the election expenditures, yet they have expressed their inability to correct this situation.[25]

Over the years the cost of election has been going up (See Table 1).

TABLE 1
Poll Expenditure for the Lok Sabha Elections

Year	Rs. [in crores]
1952	10.45
1957	6.09
1962	7.32
1967	10.95
1971	14.43
1977	30.00
1980	56.00
1984	300.00 [expected]

[Source : Hindustan Times, January 4, 1985 and Report on the Second General Elections in India 1957, Vol. 1; Report on the Third General Elections in India 1962, Vol. 1; and report on the Fifth General Elections in India 1971-72]

Unofficial estimates put the election costs much higher. Pilloo Mody, a Janata party M.P., for example, estimates that the actual cost of the Lok Sabha election in 1980 was in the neighbourhood of Rs. 300 crores and if one adds the cost of state assembly election it will go up to a staggering Rs. 600 crores. Ramkrishna Hegde, accepting the estimated base figure of Rs. 5.85 lakh per parliamentary constituency per head with an average of three candidates seeking elections, estimates that in each electoral district the cost of election would go up to Rs. 17 lakhs. There are a total of 542 **parliamentary** seats. If the above figure is accepted as the average election expense per seat, the total cost of a parliamentary election would be 92 crores.[27] For the national as well as state elections Hedge believes that the parties and the candidates spend somewhere in the neighborhood of Rs. 400 to 500 crores.[28]

Some of the former associates and closed advisers to Indira Gandhi concede that in the 1971 parliamentary election the range of Congress party spending per seat was between Rs.5 to 10 lakhs. In her own constituency she might have spent as much as Rs. 20 lakhs. In the 1972 state elections, Indira Gandhi insisted on getting a massive electoral victory in Uttar Pradesh and thus spent as much money in U.P. elections as the Congress party had spent on all the parliamentary seats in the 1971 elections.[29] The Congress party candidates are able to raise substantial amounts of money on their own in addition to the funds provided to them by the party.[30] Other political parties, however, are not in such a comfortable financial position except in the states where they are in power. Evidently, the political behaviour of the elites does not conform to the laws which govern the role of money in electoral politics.

Recent reports indicate that an enormous amount of money becomes involved in the direct elections held for Rajya Sabha (the second chamber of India's Parliament) and the Presidential election, where the number of members of the electoral college is small, and where the vote buying is easy."[31]

Sources of Campaign Contributions and Party Finances

There is considerable blurring of lines between campaign contributions made to individual candidates and to the parties. In fact, as we have noted above, since the parties are not accountable for their campaign expenditures, candidates draw heavily on the party funds for their election, even though some candidates may collect funds on their own. In either case the knowledgeable persons list the following as the primary sources of campaign and party finances :

Business Organizations

Indian business organizations can be grouped into many categories. Although the public sector with the largest amount of paid up capital and with more than two million workers dominates the Indian economy, it nevertheless controls only 980 out of some 107,369 factory units. In the second category are privately owned industrial and business organizations with the second largest number of factory units. It is this group of companies which is known as the modern corporate sector of the Indian economy. However, this sector is dominated by 75 business houses, of which the most powerful are the Birlas, Tatas, Singhania, Mafatlal, Kirloskar, Thapar and others. The third group consists of small scale industrial proprietors with 1,275,000 industrial units and employing nine million workers. The fourth sector consists of cottage and village industries producing different types of consumer goods.[33] From among these the privately owned corporate sector and the small scale manufacturer play an important role in the party and political finances.

Before limits were placed on the companies' contributions to political parties, it was the Congress party which received the bulk of the business contributions despite its insistence on democratic socialism and its anti-business public stance. (See Table 2).

TABLE 2
Distribution of Companies' Contributions to Different Political Parties

Years 1966-67

Congress party	Rs.	6,27,528
Swatantra	Rs.	18,820
Jana Sangha	Rs.	2,488
P.S.P.	Rs.	2,030
S.S.P.	Rs.	1,021
INTUC	Rs.	500
Hindu Mahasabha	Rs.	21
Akali Dal	Rs.	10
Total	Rs.	6,46,925

[Source : *Lok Sabha Debates* (New Delhi, Lok Sabha Secretariat, 1967) Fourth Series, Col.3431]

In a later statement in the Lok Sabha Fakhruddin Ali Ahmed, Minister for Industrial Development, gave much higher figures for business contributions to the parties over a longer period (see Table 3).

TABLE 3
Distribution of Companies' Donations to Different Parties for the Period March 1962 to November 1968

Congress party	Rs.	27,307,002
Swatantra party	Rs.	5,593,596
Jana Sangha	Rs.	225,019
P.S.P.	Rs.	105,159
S.S.P.	Rs.	28,236
Communists	Rs.	15,124
Individuals	Rs.	190,888

[Source : *India Backgrounder* Vol. II, No. 6(58), May 9, 1977, p. 656.]

The Congress party received the largest amount of money from such business and industrial houses as the Delhi Cloth Mills (DCM), (Rs. 625, 000), Hindustan Motors (Rs. 550,000), and Tata's Indian Iron and Steel Company (IISCO), (Rs. 5000,000. The figures presented in Table 4 make it evident that it was indeed the Congress party which was favored by all the leading commercial and industrial houses.

TABLE 4
Donations to Political Parties by Leading Commercial and Industrial Houses 1964 to 1967-68

The Birla Groups of Industries

Congress party	Rs.	1,645,000
Jana Sangha	Rs.	21,552
P.S.P.	Rs.	1,500
S.S.P.	Rs.	1,001
Hindu Mahasabha	Rs.	651
Communist party	Rs.	151

The Tata Group of Industries

Congress party	Rs.	540,000
Swatantra party	Rs.	250,000

JK Singhania

Congress party	Rs.	67,500
Swatantra party	Rs.	10,000

Kirloskar

Congress party	Rs.	102,000
Swatantra party	Rs.	375,000
Jana Sangha	Rs.	11,000

Goeneka

Congress party   Rs.   25,000

Sahu Jain

Congress party   Rs.   588,000

[Source : *India Backgrounder*, Vol. II, No.6 (58), May 9 1977, p. 615]

In the post-1969 period, when a blanket ban was imposed on the companies' contributions to political parties, two significant developments took place which brought about some drastic changes in the way the Congress party collected funds from the commercial and industrial houses. First, there was a split in the party which deprived the Indira Gandhi-led Congress party of the support of the party's three biggest fund raisers, S.K. Patil, Atulya Ghosh, and C.B. Gupta, who were the members of the Syndicate, the informal organization of the conservative party bosses, Indira Gandhi had adopted an anti-business populist posture. This alienated the business world, leaving her party short of funds. Even though she had access to one of the trusts set up by Birlas, one of India's leading industrial houses, and she was able to run the day-to-day affairs of her party, she needed a very large amount of money to contest the forthcoming parliamentary elections.

Without making any alterations in the 1969 Companies (Amendment) Act, Indira Gandhi's Congress party devised several new methods to collect funds from companies and businessmen. It was not unusual for Indira Gandhi and her cabinet colleagues to coerce the businessmen and industrialists to contribute funds to the Congress party. In the words of Krishan Bhatia :

The money that Indira's senior Cabinet colleagues collected for the parliamentary elections in 1971 and state election the following year allegedly amounted to tens of millions of rupees and usually changed hands on the basis of a clear quid pro quo. At times ministers deliberately talked publicly about nonexistent government plans to nationalize or regulate a particular industry or trade with the intention of creating nervousness among the people concerned. This naturally encouraged the flow of contributions, especially as the apparent threat ceased once the interests concerned paid up.[34]

Another method used was to seek companies' advertisements to be published in the party's various publications. In 1977 Shanti Bhushan, the Janata party law minister, told the Lok Sabha that Rs. 270,000's worth of advertisements were put in the *Special Republic Day*. The party charged Rs. 10,000 for one full page of advertisement. A similar amount of money was charged for publishing such advertisements in the party's publications in Hindi and various other regional languages.[35] Many companies did not receive copies of the advertisements, however, and in many cases, the money was collected but the advertisements were never printed.[36] Even if this method was not illegal, it went against the spirit of the 1969 Act.

Furthermore, it was disclosed that 882 companies bought advertisement space in the Congress party's various publications and collectively contributed a staggering amount of Rs. 8.04 crores to its coffers.[37] Commenting on the situation at the end of the Emergency in 1977, *The Tribune* observed that

> "such a disclosure was no surprise. Nor does the figure Rs. 8 crore [collection from the 882 companies] give a complete picture of the shady deals between the big firms and erstwhile ruling party at the center to circumvent the law banning companies' donations to political parties. Before the Lok Sabha elections in March it was alleged that the Congress party collected as much as Rs. 30 crores by way of advertisements taken by the companies in a number of so-called souvenirs."[38]

During the Emergency rule of Indira Gandhi [1975-77] many industrial and business houses were active in collecting funds for the ruling party. Kuldip Nayar, a reliable journalist, reported that by circumventing the law, Indira Gandhi extracted as much as Rs. 13 crores during this period for her party.[39] Considering the way L.N. Mishra, one of Indira Gandhi's confidants and a cabinet member, collected funds, the accumulation of such a huge sum of money for the party does not seem surprising. Commenting on the methods used by Mishra, C.S. Pandit observes :

> Often representatives of trade and industry were called by him to Delhi and asked to produce specified amounts. Those who declined were threatened with possible raids by people of the Revenue Intelligence and Enforcement Directorate, which were now operating under the Cabinet Secretariat. In Bombay financial circles stories started circulating of the amounts secured by the Foreign Trade Minister under such threats. Others who came forward willingly with whatever was asked for, received concessions, beyond their imagination, to expand their business and amass further resources.[40]

Other large-scale fund raisers of the Congress party were Umashankar Dixit, Devraj Urs, P.C. Sethi, and Sitaram Kesari who used legal and illegal methods to collect huge amounts of funds from business and commercial houses for the party.[41]

Even the opposition parties, including the Janata party, the Lok Dal, and the Bhartiya Janata party, have been dependent on the business and commercial houses for funds. Both H.M. Bahuguna and Chaudhary Charan Singh were quite successful in raising funds for their parties. Compared to the Congress party, however, the opposition parties, for obvious reasons, have been far less successful in collecting. They have far greater success in approaching the businessmen for contributions in the states where they are in power.

Illegal Donations from Illegal Funds

India has adopted a policy of extensive government control of and regulation of the economy. Various agencies of government are not only engaged in issuing licenses for starting new businesses and industries, but they also regulate the expansion and modernization of industrial plants, labor relations, quality control of industrial products, and the supply of money through nationalized banks and financial institutions. The government also provides funds for agricultural improvement, loans for housing development, undertakes railroad construction, and educational expansion, and sets up primary health care centres and other public service activities. In short, both the national and state governments have a thousand levers of power over the distribution of resources within the society, particularly in relation to business and trade. The ruling parties use these levers of power to establish a kind of exchange relation with business, trade, the other organizations which seek licenses and quotas from the government to undertake economic activities.

Despite the imposition of a legal ban on the companies' contributions for political purposes, the politicians' need for funds on the one hand and the business men's need for access to the center of power on the other have kept the two together. Because of the ban, black money became the primary medium of such contacts.

Black money is defined as the "aggregate of incomes which are taxable but are not reported to authorities."[42] The black economy or the "parallel economy" has very serious implications for the health of the Indian political process. The black economy was in existence even before companies' donations to political parties were banned in 1969, but it was not very extensive, nor was it closely linked with the electoral process until after the ban and the increase in government regulation of the economy in the post-1970 election victories of Indira Gandhi.

Huge amounts of cash money, either in gunny sacks or in plastic bags,are delivered to politicians, particularly to the ministers. S.K. Patil, an erstwhile member of the Syndicate, once declared that he sent Indira Gandhi a 'suitcase full of currency and she did not return even the suitcase."[43] His statement was never contradicted. Cash contributions to the ruling party are always accompanied by some kind of exchange between the donors and the minister, to the profit of the former.[44] Commenting on the situation Prem Shankar Jha, one of India's noted journalist, wrote that "the government came more and more to resemble a bargain basement, where a rise in sugar price, an increase in export subsidies, and an import license for scarce material, would be exchanged for cash donations to the party."[45] Such contributions, however, do not go to parties alone ; they are given to the candidates seeking elections and sitting members of Parliament as well as the state legislators.

The electoral practice of not observing the financial ceiling on political campaigns has given big money a dominant role in Indian politics. Chief Election Commissioner K. Trevedi asserted that :

> this malady [of big money], I am afraid during the last decades has assumed an alarming proportion. The huge expenditures incurred by the candidates and the political parties have no relationship to the ceiling prescribed under the law. The candidates and their political parties look to big money-bags for their funds to contest elections, thereby adopting a formula which establishes the chances of winning in direct proportion to the money spent. That this in course of time triggers a chain reaction leading to corruption at various decision-making levels does not seem to bother them.[46]

The pernicious nexus existing between the tax evaders, smugglers, mobsters, black-marketeers, and the politicians have become dominant within the Indian political process.[47]

And the black money is perhaps the most important source of electoral finances.

What is the extent of the black money in Indian politics? There are various estimates. According to a report published by the National Institute of Public Finance and Policy:

> Based on some rough norms Pendse [1983] estimates that Rs. 170 crores of "black money" was spent in the 1980 Lok Sabha elections. Allowing for the leakages enroute he suggests that something like Rs. 400 crores have had to be generated to assure the Rs. 170 crores becomes available for actual election expenditures. And this is for Lok Sabha election alone. When we take into account the election to state assemblies, and to various local bodies, as well as the inter-election requirements for political campaigning and manipulations, it is quite clear that the demand for political funds could easily average several hundred crores per year.[48]

It further adds that

> such funds are in the nature of transfers, but the greater the demand for such transfers, the greater is the inducement for generation of black income. Political contributions are raised from a wide range of sources of which industry and trade are believed to the principal ones. "Black" income made through tax evasion of legal sources of income along with income from all manner of illegal sources provides the "base" for the political "contributions."

> Political domination over the apparatus of licenses and permits and over public expenditures ensures the means by which this base can be enhanced at will and individual enterprises induced to contribute.[49]

Some sources, however, believe that the report of the National Institute of Public Finance and Policy is too conservative in its estimate of the amount of black money in politics. Piloo Mody, a Janata Party M.P., believes that as much as Rs. 5,000 crores of black money was in circulation in Indian politics. His estimates are based on the cost of elections, the day-to-day running of political parties, rallies and public meetings, as well as the personal enrichment of politicians.[50]

Despite the recent lifting of the ban on companies' contributions to political parties, both the businessmen and politicians have been reluctant to talk about the political money. An official of the FCCI (Federation of Indian Chamber of Commerce) in various interviews asserted that since no company will be willing to talk about its contributions to a political party, it would be almost impossible to get reliable figures.

But a recent estimate suggests that companies' direct contributions to parties and individual politicians may not account for more than 20 percent of the political money.[51] It is the individual businessman and the industrialist who contribute directly to either a minister or the party leaders, the lawmakers or the candidate for public office. The new class of entrepreneurs, running small manufacturing units, are eager to seek favors from the lawmakers and party leaders, and they are becoming the major direct contributors to individual politicians.

Fund raising by such politicians as A.R. Antulay, the former chief minister of Maharashtra, established unique and somewhat questionable practices. In fact, there are not only questionable methods used to collect funds, but there is also now a blurring of the lines between personal and political finances. Antulay set up several trusts, some named after Indira Gandhi and others in the name of her son, Sanjay Gandhi, which were managed personally by the former chief minister. He collected a huge amount of money, running into crores of rupees, by pressuring the contractors, wine merchants, builders, co-operative sugar mill owners, industrialists, and others. Many of these contributions were received by the Chief Minister personally. There was little known about the auditing of the accounts or the ways the money was being spent.[52] Similar practices were followed by Devraj Urs and many other state level Congress party leaders.[53]

Even the Janata party ministers and high party officials showed scant regard for the laws dealing with electoral and party finances. Many of them did not hesitate to collect funds for the party or for private trusts using illegal or questionable methods. Since party discipline was virtually nonexistent, ministers were independent power centers and could use money to benefit their supporters and clients both within and outside of the Parliament.[54]

Kickbacks from Business Deals

The government of India not only regulates the nation's economy and runs the public sector industries but also enters into numerous business contracts with local and foreign business and industrial concerns. Astute observers of political money in India have privately recognized the existence of the system of kickbacks between the ministers, businessmen, government contractors, and the financing of the ruling party. After the 1977 defeat of the Congress party and subsequent desertion of Indira Gandhi by the party's stalwarts, many of its financial sources dried up, although Indira Gandhi kept receiving financial support from, in addition to the Birlas, two new business tycoons : Swaraj Paul, based in London with his Caparo empire, and Dhirubhai Ambani, based in Bombay with his Reliance Kingdom.[55]

Despite the availability of such business support for Indira Gandhi's Congress party, her son Sanjay Gandhi found the Indian businessmen and industrialists an unreliable source of financial support. Instead he found kickbacks, through business deals with foreign companies, a much more reliable and rewarding channel for raising funds. Therefore, the techniques of collecting money for party and political purposes underwent a drastic change after Indira Gandhi's return to power in 1980. *The Hindustan Times* noted that between 1980-1985, industrialists were puzzled by the drop in the demand for political contributions."[56] The ruling party now concentrates on "kickbacks from huge government purchases, for defense and major public sector projects.[57] India also invests around Rs. 800 crores a year on projects related to power generation and fertilizer, and almost half of this investment is made in foreign exchange. According to one observer, "on a mark-up of 10 percent, which is not considered high in this country, you have a net pay-off of Rs. 400 crores a year, which is shared, on a suitable basis, between several parties involved."[58]

The government also contracts suppliers and builders to set up oil refineries and build gas lines, so the public sector companies get involved in projects worth crores of rupees. In most of these business deals the ministers and officials of the ruling party are likely to take cuts. It is, however, in the area of defence purchase that the relationship between kickbacks and party finances has been most frequently observed. The purchase of a German submarine was one of the first such cases reported; it is believed that a commission of Rs. 30 crores was paid on this deal. *The Hindustan Times,* a respectable and pro-Congress party newspaper, recently declared, "the Congress party has been repeatedly accused in the press of loading 'front-end commission' on defence contracts to raise funds for the election and to meet other party expenses."[59] The multi-million dollar deal with Germany for the submarine confirmed the charge. In another important defense contract with the Bofors company of Sweden for the supply of artillery for the Indian army, it is alleged that Rs. 80 crores was paid in commission, and the common assumption is that the money went into the coffers of the ruling party headed by Rajiv Gandhi. Reliable sources both within and outside of the Congress party estimate that the party needs around Rs. 150 crores every five years to contest national elections.[60] When in 1987 Vishvanath Pratap Singh, then holding important portfolios in Rajiv Gandhi's cabinet, instituted inquiries into kickbacks in the defence deals the question was asked, "Doesn't Vishvanath Pratap know where the money to fight elections comes from ?"[61] Subsequently, V.P. Singh was not only fired from the cabinet but was also expelled from the Congress party. These two deals are only the tip of the iceberg. It is widely believed that earlier large kickbacks were paid on the Sea Harriers, the Mirages, the Jaguars, and other defence contracts.[62]

Foreign Funds

Both inside the outside of Parliament allegations are made about the role of foreign money in Indian politics. The flow of this money has been rising every year : in 1978 around Rs. 170 crore came from abroad,[63] in 1985 it was Rs. 230 crores, and in 1986 it became a staggering Rs. 434 crores.[64] Even though a major portion of this money is used for cultural and social purposes, much of it ends up in the coffers of many secular organizations such as the trade unions and the political parties.

A large part of this money comes from the countries of Western Europe and the U.S., and frequently a substantial portion of this money ends up for the electoral use of political parties. Senator Daniel Moynihan, who served as U.S. Ambassador to India during the Nixon presidency, stated that the U.S. Embassy frequently gave money to the Congress party, especially in its fight with the Marxist parties in West Bengal. "Communists in turn," says Mohan Guruswamy, "receive money from businesses whose sole market is the Soviet Union and its allies. The Communist turned Capitalist is a bizarre yet common sight that adorns our landscape ... Over-invoicing is the usual Soviet way of transferring funds into India. Some of this money does find its way to other parties also. Both the Congress and Janata seem to have been recipients from this conduit."[65]

Multinational corporations have also contributed both to parties and to individuals. In the words to Guruswamy,

It is well known that the company executives, even MNC executives, hand over packets of currency notes to party bosses. Eyewitness accounts abound. It might be coincidental that the companies received later prized industrial licences, for instance, to set up synthetic fibre plants, etc. The point is money flows to political parties from all manners of people, it is extremely unlikely that any top politician will pass a polygraph test denying this."[66]

"Foreign patronage to political parties also comes in the form of advertisements in souvenirs and newspapers, large printing orders in their presses, and commission to select monopoly companies through which indigenous items were exported under trade agreement.[67]

Despite the passage of laws imposing stringent penalties for the violation of regulations dealing with foreign donations and despite frequent violations of these provisions reported in the press, it is widely known that not even a single case has ever been registered under these laws.[68]

Conclusions : Implications for Polity and Society

Democracies are delicate systems and they are difficult to maintain. It is often asserted that the stable democracies are products of an environment which inspires trust and confidence among its citizens. Although elective officials are not moral leaders, their public conduct and behavior are nevertheless expected to conform to certain basic ethical standards. Their conduct in public should look right and proper in the eyes of those who elect them.

In India, Mahatma Gandhi and his associates were able to set certain high standards of public conduct. Although Gandhi's moralistic approach to politics may be inapplicable to the competitive nature of a democratic polity, nevertheless the persons who followed him and held offices in the post-independence period were committed to certain ethical norms of behavior. These norms restrained them from exploiting their public positions for personal gains. They were willing to put the corporate interests of the state and society above their personal, psychological, and material needs. Their commitment to these rules of behavior ensured the validity of the electoral process, inspiring trust and confidence in the citizenry.

Furthermore, as Max Weber has said, the authority of modern political leaders is based on legal-rational norms. It is the law which ensures their legitimacy in the eyes of the people. Laws also, as we quoted Locke earlier, ensure the liberty which is the foundation of a democratic society.

Discrepancies between the observance of electoral laws and the political behavior of the elites, as seen above, seriously undermine the validity both of the electoral process and the moral basis of the political authority. It must be conceded that money alone has not helped the parties or the individuals to win the elections, as is evident in the defeat of Indira Gandhi in the 1977 elections. However, the flouting of electoral laws by politicians and political parties seriously undermines the authority of the laws themselves. First of all, it seriously weakens the ordinary citizens' voluntary compliance with the existing system of law. As is well-known in India, economic offenders such as the tax evaders, smugglers, and others get "off the hook" because of their links with the powerful politicians. In addition, the obvious links between the black money and politics give the ordinary citizens reason to question the legitimacy of the democratic authority. Consequently, many citizens have come to believe that the chances of their achieving justice within the system, or a fair hearing from the administration, or redress of their grievances through peaceful means are becoming slimmer every day.

It is no overstatement that the existing linkages between big money and electoral politics have led to widespread corruption. It is openly asserted that, "corruption is rampant in every sector of our society ... A large number of politicians and ministers are corrupt. Corruption is universal in the lower ranks of public services, it has affected the middle ranks as well and is now afflicting the apex of our administrative structure—the All-India Services."[69]

There is a widespread belief that the earlier high level of public behavior and the normally accepted individual code of conduct have taken a rapid downward plunge. One may not entirely agree with B.K. Nehru when he declared that "we have degenerated in one single generation, from being an honest society into a dishonest one.[70] On the other hand, though, it is hard to disagree with James Manor who stresses that even though normlessness has not overtaken the entire Indian society, anomie is pervasive among the professional and semi-professional politicians.[71] Furthermore, if in less mobilized periods of Indian history, various segments of Indian society were able to maintain their autonomy and isolate themselves from politics, such a situation is today becoming rare. The role of electoral mobilization and its implications for the society are perceptively summarized by R.S. Khare :

> Popular democratic politics has intensified the quest for power and profit in old [i.e. caste] as well as new [i.e. adult franchise] terms. As the traditional centers and positions of power have become empty and as the democratic institutional centers have only imitated the actual power, the chase for the *satisfying* position, power, and authority is evident throughout India. Diverse groups and individuals are intensely power hungry. But whatever transitory power and position one corners takes much effort and strategy and usually means little because in such a scheme as one gets more one coverts more, and the more one seeks the stable power the more elusive it becomes. Hence the twin feelings of insufficiency and dissatisfaction never leave the new Indian within whom social duty, competition, and rationality churn but only halfway in an ethos of uncertainty and ambivalence.[72]

Since Indian politicians seem to have adopted C.B. Macpherson's attitude towards democracy as being a kind of market mechanism where the voters are perceived as merely consumers with varied demands and the politicians as the entrepreneurs out to buy their votes,[73] their conduct has rendered politics devoid of ethical premises. The use and abuse of political money has further confounded the already chaotic situation existing in India in both a moral and a social sense.

Within this marketplace model of Indian democracy Indian political parties play a critical role. If, as in the U.S., politics in India has become a big industry, political parties are the major partners in this industry. However, Indian political parties differ from American political parties in organization, authority patterns, and delivery of goods and services.

Until 1967 the Congress party functioned as a collection of regional political machines "which taken together formed the largest and the most formidable agency for the distribution of spoils and the extraction of electoral support that the world has ever seen or is ever likely to see.[74] Money, gifts, jobs, contracts, and other political favors were distributed on a decentralized basis. The party held its elections regularly and the party bosses mobilized and delivered the votes to the party's national leadership but they maintained their regional and local autonomy. With the advent of Indira Gandhi as the boss of both the government and the Congress party, the power was centralized; this mighty machine became oligarchic and a tool of personal authority. With the rise of her son Sanjay within the party and the new methods of raising funds, the machine degenerated into an instrument of enormous corruption within the society without having any democratic accountability. It promoted the recruitment of criminals and persons with questionable background into Indian politics. With control over enormous amounts of money, a small number of Congress party leaders not only exercised almost total control over the political future of the party members and corrupted the electoral process but they even tried to subvert legally elected state governments controlled by the opposition parties by bribing the legislators. This position further deteriorated in 1988 when the party is being led by Rajiv Gandhi.[75]

The other minor parties (perhaps with the exception of the Marxists and the Bhartiya Janata Party), also are oligarchic in their organizational structure with little or no accountability to their rank and file. Political notables, representing kinship or caste-based organizations, form the factional networks on which the parties are based. Factional leaders distribute political patronage and funds among their kinship groups and clients. Because of the existence of personal and parochial loyalties, party leaders find it hard to ignore the needs of their economic dependents. Since the parties are non-democratic and oligarchic they are unlikely to inspire confidence in the operation of the electoral process. In the absence of interparty democracy, as the recent events indicate, the laws like the Anti-Defection Constitutional Amendment are likely to stifle debate on issues raised by the dissidents within the party and strengthen the hand of the entrenched party leadership. It is not surprising that the Chief Election Commissioner of India was forced to admit that "unless the role of political parties, so far as it concerns elections, was properly regulated, any attempt directed toward the furtherance of the purity of elections would be frustrated."[76] He further recommended that in order to achieve this goal Parliament should pass a law regulating the internal party functioning to maintain inter-party democracy.[77] However, no such action has yet been taken.

Maintenance of the purity of the electoral process is not only vital for the operation of Indian democracy; it is crucial to the very survival of the nation state in India.

NOTES

1. On the theoretical basis of democracy see S.M. Lipset, "Some Social Requisites of Democracy : Economic Development and Political Legitimacy," *American Political Science Review*, 53 (March, 1959), pp. 69-105; Phil Cutright, "National Political

Development : Measurement and Analysis," in Charles F. Canudde and Dean E. Neubauer (eds.), *Empirical Democratic Theory* (Chicago, Markham Publishing Co. 1969), pp. 193-209; Samuel Huntington, "Will More Countries Become Democratic ?" *Political Science Quarterly*, 99.2 (Summer, 1984), pp. 203-215; Charles Lindblom, *Politics and Markets : The World's Political and Economic Systems*, (New York, Basic Books, 1977) ; and Barrington Moore, Jr., *Social Origins of Dictatorship and Democracy* (Boston, Beacon, 1966), Chapter 7.

2. S.M. Lipset, *Political Man : The Social Basis of Politics* (Baltimore, MD., Johns Hopkins University Press, 1981), p. 27.

3. Quoted in Paul Wilkinson, *Terrorism and The Liberal State* (New York, John Wiley and Sons, 1977), p. 5.

4. V.A. Pai Pandiker and Ramshray Roy, "Financing," *Seminar*, September, 1979, p. 4.

5. Herbert E. Alexander, *Financing Politics : Money, Elections and Political Reforms* (Washington, *Congressional Quarterly Press*, 1984), p.3.

6. Quoted in A.J. Heidenheimer (ed.), *Comparative Political Financing of Party Organizations and Election Campaign*, (Lexington, Mass., D.C. Health and Co., 1970), p.3.

7. *A Handbook for Candidates : For the Election to the House of the People* (New Delhi, Election Commission of India, 1979), p. 74.

8. M.M. Dube and K.L. Jain, *Elections : Laws and Procedure* (Indore, MP India, Vedpal Law House, 1984), p. 64.

9. *A Handbook for Candidates*, p.75.

10. *Ibid.*

11. Dube and Jain, *op.cit.*, p. 69 and B. Shiva Rao, "Election Practices and Machinery—Need for Reforms," in S.C. Kashyup (ed.), *Elections and Electoral Reforms in India* (New Delhi, The Institute of Constitutional and Parliamentary Studies, 1971), p. 24.

12. *Indian Express*, March 8, 1977.

13. *Ibid*.

14. *Ibid*.

15. *Statesman*, September 6, 1978.

16. V.K. Agrawal, "Political Donations : A Danger to Democracy," *The Economic Times*, July 28, 1988, pp. 5-7.

17. *India Backgrounder*, May 24, 1976, p. 69.

18. *India Today*, February 15, 1985, p. 28.

19. *Hindu : International Edition*, March 2, 1985. Also Hindu : International Edition, February 9, 1985.

20. *Hindu*, February 4, 1978.

21. Ramkrishna Hegde, *Electoral Reforms : Lack of Political Will* (Banghlore, Karnatak Janata Party, n.d.), p. 101.

22. *Parliamentary Proceedings : Rajya Sabha Debates*, vol. 130. N. 11, Col. 358-59.

23. *Statesman*, October 6, 1982.

24. *Statesman*, February 3, 1978.

25. *Lok Sabha Debates*, Fourth series, Vol. 15, Col. 2509-11 and *Lok Sabha Debates*, Fourth series, Vol. 17, Col. 1779.

26. *Statesman*, October 6, 1982.

27. Hegde, *op.cit.*, p.101.

28. *Ibid*.

29. Interview 19, February 27, 1987 and Interview #15, April 10, 1987.

30. Prem Shankar Jha, "Cutting One's Own Throat," *Hindustan Times*, April 17, 1987.

31. Inder Malhotra, "Political Commentary : Big Money and Politics," *Times of India*, March 17, 1988 and *India Abroad*, (New York) March 11, 1988, p. 9. On this point also see Janardan Thakur, *All the Janata Men* (New Delhi, Vikas Publishing House, 1978), p. 106.

32. Stanley Kochanek, "Briefcase Politics in India : The Congress Party and the Business Elite," *Asian Survey*, December 1987, p. 1280.

33. *Ibid.*, p. 1279.

34. Quoted in *Ibid*. p. 1291.

35. *The Lok Sabha Debates*, Vol. 15, No. 55, Col. 389-90.

36. *Tribune*, September 8, 1977.

37. *Hindustan Times*, September 8, 1977.

38. *Tribune*, September 8, 1977.

39. *Indian Express*, November 23, 1977.

40. C.S. Pandit, *End of an Era* (New Delhi, Allied Publishers, 1977), p. 70. Also see *Times of India*, September 3, 1977.

41. Janardan Thakur, *Indira Gandhi and Her Power Game* (Vikas Publishing House, 1979), Chapter 7.

42. National Institute of Public Finance and Policy, *The Black Economy in India* (New Delhi, National Institute of Public Finance and Policy, 1985), p. 296.

43. Inder Malhotra, *op. cit.*

44. *Ibid.* Also see Kochanek, *op. cit.*

45. Prem Shankar Jha, *India : Political Economy of Stagnation* (New Delhi, Oxford University Press, 1980), p. 273.

46. Quoted in National Institute Public Policy and Finance, *op. cit.* p. 294-295.

47. *Business India*, July 3—August 12, 1984, p. 74.

48. National Institute of Public Policy and Finance, *op. cit.*, p. 296.

49. *Ibid.*

50. *Statesman*, October 6, 1982.

51. Kochanek, *op. cit.*, p. 1287.

52. Hannan Ezekiel, "The Donation Issue : The Facts and the Law," *Economic times*, September 7, 1981.

53. Janardan Thakur, *Indira Gandhi and the Power Game*, Chapter 4.

54. G.K. Reddy, "The Nation : Fund Raising Extravaganza," *Hindu*, September 6, 1981 and *National Herald*, September 3, 1981.

55. Nikhil Chakravartdy, "The Colour of Money, "*Times of India*, April 19, 1987.

56. *Hindustan Times*, April 20, 1987.

57. Chakravarty, *op. cit.*

58. Jay Dubhashi, "Kickbacks Through Defense Deals," *Tribune*, April 13, 1987.

59. *Hindustan Times*, April 13, 1987.

60. Prem Shankar Jha, "Cutting One's Own Throat," *Hindustan Times*, April 17, 1987 and Dubashi, *op. cit.*

61. Chakravartdy, *op. cit. Hindustan Times*, April 20, 1987 and Girilal Jain, "Challenge Rajiv Cannot Ignore,. " *Times of India*, April 13, 1987.

62. *Hidustan Times*, April 20, 1987.

63. *Parliamentary Proceedings, Rajya Sabha Debates*, Vol. 130 No. 11, Col. 358-59.

64. *Times of India*, July 24, 1986 and *Statesman Weekly*, October 24, 1987.

65. Mohan Guruswamy, "Black Money and Political Parties," *Indian Express*, January 31, 1985.

66. *Ibid*.

67. *India Backgrounder*, Vol. 1, No. 8 (May 19, 1976), p. 70.

68. *Patriot*, January 24, 1985.

69. National Institute of Public Finance and Policy, *Op. cit.* p. 297.

70. Quoted in *Ibid*.

71. James Manor, "Anomie in Indian Politics : Origins and Potential Wider Impact," *Economic and Political Weekly* (Annual Number, 1983), pp. 732-33.

72. R. S. Khare, *Culture and Democracy : Anthropological Reflections on Modern India*, (Lanham, University Press of America, 1985), p. 54.

73. C.B. Macpherson, *The Life and Time of Liberal Democracy* (New York, Oxford University Press, 1977), pp. 79-81.

74. James Manor, "The Electoral Process amid Awakening and Decay : Reflections on the Indian General Elections of 1980," in Peter Lyon and James Manor [eds], *Transfer and Transformation : Political Institutions in the New Commonwealth* [Leicester, Leicester University Press, 1983], p. 88.

75. *India Today*, August 31, 1988 p. 5.

76. Quoted in L.P. Singh, *Electoral Reform* (New Delhi, Uppal Publisher, 1986) p. 79.

77. *Ibid*.

4

GREGORY C. KOZLOWSKI

SHAH BANU'S CASE, BRITAIN'S LEGAL LEGACY AND MUSLIM POLITICS IN MODERN INDIA

Bent with the burdens of age and indigence, a toothless and frail lady, swathed in a *burqah*, knocks at the courthouse door in search of justice. Arrayed against her, blocking her path to judicial redress, is a strange phalanx composed of slick, young politicians and bearded, turbaned *mullahs*.[1] While the former count the votes of communal constituents, the latter hold aloft the Holy *Quran* and wave the banner of *shariah* in an effort to rally the support of the mass of their undereducated, potentially violent, coreligionists. Shah Banu's effort to force her ex-husband to pay alimony, and the subsequent parliamentary maneuvers which brought forth legislation making it impossible for other Muslim women to follow Shah Banu's example, have inspired many emotional images of this type.

Explanations for the acrimony displayed by almost all participants in debates over *Mohammed Ahmed Khan vs. Shah Banu Begum*,[2] decided by India's Supreme Court in July of 1985, and the *Muslim Women's (Protection of Rights on Divorce) Bill*[3] which passed the Lok Sabha on 6 May, 1986, are easy to find. Journalists, social scientists, activists, politicians, and religious scholars have taken every opportunity to present their opinions in popular and scholarly forums. Whether they abhor the Supreme Court's decision and applaud the Women's Bill, or *vice-versa,* almost all commentators seem to carry on their arguments in a time warp. Either they refer to "Islam" as if that faith were wholly defined in the Prophet's lifetime and the two or three centuries which followed his death, or, at the opposite temporal extreme, they assume that all of the events explaining the ill-will Shah Banu's case stirred only occurred after 1947.[4] Clearly, the historical middle ground needs to be described; particularly the role which British legal institutions played in creating the context in which the issues raised by the Shah Banu case have been argued out.

A Family Dispute

While questions of Muslim women's rights, or the lack thereof, came to dominate public discussion after the Madhya Pradesh High Court and the Supreme Court handed down decisions in Shah Banu's favor, the origins of the political controversy lay in a private dispute.[5] In the early 1930s, Shah Banu had married her first cousin Mohammad Ahmed Khan. Cross-cousin marriages among some Muslims in South Asia were common enough. Indeed, Mohammad Ahmed later contracted a second marriage with yet another first cousin, Halima Begum.

Marriage between close relatives was often part of a social strategy designed to protect the status of fairly affluent families.[6] It seemed to answer a fear that if women married "strangers," they would claim their inheritance rights and call for a partitioning of an extended family's estate. Such moralization could lead to a decline in social and economic standing. As the beginnings of the Shah Banu dispute demonstrated, cross-cousin marriage was not entirely successful in forestalling inter-family wrangling. The very closeness of the parties involved, both in terms of kinship and residence, often made such conflicts sharper. Something of this sort happened within the extended family to which both Shah Banu and Mohammad Ahmed Khan belonged.

That family enjoyed some prosperity and prominence. It provided Mohammad Ahmed with a good education and he became a highly regarded advocate with an income sufficient to support two wives and twelve children, five by Shah Banu and seven by Halima Begum. All lived in a *"mahal"* or *"haveli:"* a "traditional" dwelling consisting of a rambling set of rooms arranged around a central courtyard.[7] The *haveli* provided the initial battlefield where Shah Banu, Mohammad Ahmed, and other members of the family squared off. They began quarreling over the disposition of a piece of property in which the entire family had an interest. The squabble may have begun in the previous generation and continued to agitate the family group well into a third generation.

When arguments in an extended family occur, members can employ several tactics widely-known and sanctioned in the culture. In an old-style mahal, with its several rooms, roof, and access to a common courtyard, individuals can engage in an elaborate game of "now you see me, now you don't." People can avoid each other by ducking out of a room, scampering into a roof or they can pounce suddenly to confront one another in the courtyard. More drastic measures can include setting up a separate kitchen and even walling off one set of rooms from the rest of the house. Finally, one party can admit to complete exasperation by leaving the *haveli*. Since the *haveli* had belonged to Mohammad Ahmad's parents, because he had his law offices there and his income supported the household, Shah Banu had little choice but departure; she claiming to be driven out and her husband saying she left of her own accord.

When she left her husband's house in 1975, Shah Banu had three grown sons who were employed in high-status, well-paying jobs who could have supported her. In addition, she still had claim to some of the family's property. She was hardly a pauper. After a brief stay in her "home" village, she began living with her youngest son who had some rooms adjacent to his father's *haveli*. Her sons and daughters were upset at their mother's leaving the mahal. They feared, apparently, that they would be at a disadvantage to their half-siblings when it came time to divide up their father's sizeable estate. A half-brother who was a partner in Mohammad Ahmed Khan's law business did seem to be a special favorite who might be able to take advantage of that position to disinherit Shah Banu as well as her children. These encouraged their mother to initiate a suit for control of the disputed property and, perhaps to further vex their father, maintenance as a wrongfully ejected spouse. Law suits often become an end in themselves, a way of causing *taklif* (grief) to the human object of one's anger.[8] We can never know whether Shah Banu or her children expected to win or merely wished to strike a blow. For his part, Mohammad Ahmed tried to head off an extended legal battle by divorcing Shah Banu. The ploy did not work and his ex-wife's case began a slow, but steady, progress through the courts.

When a law suit comes under the purview of a court, the institutional framework transforms it. The original sources of grievance, the highly personal passions which gave rise to the dispute in the first place, can be forgotten. In their place, a "point of law" appears. Recalling that a plea for maintenance had been only one aspect of Shah Banu's original plaint, the court's focus on this demand to the exclusion of the old arguments over family property abstracted one issue from a complex of interpersonal relationships.

The Indore First Class Magistrate's court solved the question of maintenance by referring to section 125 of the Code of Criminal Procedure, an act adopted by the Government of Independent India almost verbatim from the British original promulgated in 1874. Its intent was to prevent female vagrancy by forcing husbands to support legally married spouses whom they had forced out of the marital domicile. Indian courts had invoked this act in other cases,[9] but it was Shah Banu's case which attracted nationwide attention and led to many more women lodging similar plaints. Mohammad Ahmed Khan even represented some of these women. Shah Banu's case came to the fore partly because both she and her husband displayed a knack for handling the press. Shah Banu's age, illiteracy, and seeming helplessness made her a good story, while her husband's wealth and assurance that he stood for Muslim law made him a perfect foil.

In late 1985, the dispute prompted a new level of interest when the Congress government chose sides by allowing the introduction of a parliamentary act which exempted Muslims from the force of section 125 of the Code of Criminal Procedure. The bill's supporters argued that the application of this article to Muslims violated the social status their personal law enjoyed. By this time, almost everyone seemed to have forgotten the human dimensions of the conflict and the temporal context in which they occurred. "Muslim law," the status of women, communal rights, and the relationship of Muslims to the Government of India occupied peoples' minds. The discussion of the issues became dominated by a discourse whose historical provenance became less clear as more parties entered into the disagreement. These assertions and counterclaims need to be placed in a clearer historical context.

Past and Present

Many of those taking part in the debate prompted by the courts' decisions and the Women's Divorce Bill of 1986 had recourse to an appeal to the founding of Islam. For them, the matter had to be seen in the light of this ancient and unchanging faith. The supposed essential immutability of Islam did not, however, solve the problem. It appeared to serve the purposes of those holding two divergent views. It supported those who believed that the courts created a new law for Muslims, something which a revealed religion could not tolerate, but it also provided ammunition to those who opposed the Women's Bill because it imposed an innovation.

In a similar fashion, the proposition that in Islam, law and faith are one, sustained almost any side in the argument. The notion that in the time of the Prophet, Islamic law enhanced the rights of women was a weapon for those *defencing* the status quo as well as for those who saw that as a spur to Muslims to accept a greater extension of those rights as the logical consequence of Prophetic example *(Sunnah)*. Those who appealed to the Holy *Quran* and incidents from the Prophetic era to support either view did not convince anyone in the opposing ranks.

The period since 1947 constituted the second temporal frame in which much of the discussion of Shah Banu's case and its aftermath took place. Everything from the violence which accompanied Partition, through the Bangladesh war, to the struggle over the Babari Masjid has been summoned up as part of an explanation of the extremes of emotion prompted by Shah Banu's case. The terms modernization and progress as well as their antonyms have a prominent place in arguments which focus on the past forty years. Once again, both those who criticize and those who support the legal verdict or the Women's Bill have been able to deduce opposite conclusions by referring to the same events and the same terminology. For some of them, Muslims represent a backward group whose conservative religion prevents their adaptation to the new order created by the modern Indian state.[10] They argue that a similar religious obscurantism keeps Muslims out of modern schools and tied to occupations which consign them to poverty. This makes them easy marks for the preaching of their *mullahs* who are themselves ignorant of and averse to everything connected with progress.[11] From this perspective, Muslims' backwardness will never let them accept the positive change implied in the Shah Banu ruling. But that same familiar litany can be converted into an *apologia* for their special psychology. How can Muslims commit themselves to change when they are a minority, uncertain of their status in a country where the majority never abates its criticisms?[12]

A close analysis of both scholarly and popular commentary reveals that with few exceptions the historical perspective on these issues is curiously abstract. While references to particular events and persons abound, the general historical context remains vague. Either the Prophetic age, with only an occasional *salaam* in the direction of the Mughals, or the happenings of the period since Independence are called up to illuminate the whys and wherefores of the Shah Banu case and its repercussions.[13] Few people even mention, much less seriously consider, the great span of years during which the British ruled India and the ways they shaped the institutional framework in which the controversy occurs.

When India gained its freedom in 1947, the laws promulgated during the raj, together with the system of courts which administered them, remained substantially the same. The political identity of the country's inhabitants did not alter dramatically. While the Constitution of 1950 envisions a secular state, India's citizenry, as the polemics surrounding Shah Banu illustrate, continues to be defined by their association with one or another religious tradition, each of which supposedly has its own religious law.[14] Though constituencies are no longer reserved for those adhering to a given faith, members of parliament still consider themselves the de facto representatives of religious communities. This close connection between religion, religious law, and communal political identity survives as one of the most enduring legacies of British imperial rule. Contemporary Indians are indeed "Midnight's Children," but they are the grandchildren of the raj as well.

Several of the raj's legal and political bequests have direct influence on the questions raised by all parties to the public side of the Shah Banu dispute. The first concerns the character of Shariah and its relationship to a Muslim Personal Law. The second involves the way in which the British created a law of private property and the impact of the courts' enforcement of those laws on the rights of women to control wealth. A third has to do with the ways that litigation and politics became inextricably linked when religious leaders found that a centralized, bureaucratized state could be an effective ally in any effort to extend their influence over Muslims.

Colonial Courts and the Creation of Islamic Law

Most participants in the Shah Banu controversy accept the notion that what Muslims call "*shariah*"is law, that when Muslim princes ruled India it was the "law of the land," and that Muslim Personal Law is *shariah*. The wide acceptance of those propositions probably has more to do with the effectiveness of the legal and judicial system the British created than it does with the actual practice of Muslim states.[15] In pre-colonial states, the *shariah* lacked the narrowing of acceptable rules and judicial authority which served to define law in the history of Western Europe from the eighteenth century to the present. Not only were the rules of *shariah* diffuse, but no single set of state-sponsored institutions enforced those guidelines.

In the period before the advent of British rule, Muslim scholars in India had acknowledged the authority of dozens of works on *shariah*.[16] These texts were not carbon copies of each other. They contained a wide range of views. Even within the same "school" *(mazhab)*, individuals disagreed on both major and minor matters. Abu Hanifah, the eponym of the Hanifi school to which most Muslims in India presumably belong, frequently held opinions from which his star pupils, Abu Yusuf and Imam Mohammad, dissented. Such internal divergence has continued to the present day. Though Deobandis, Barelvis, Ahl-e Hadisis and Firangi Mahalis are all Hanifis, they disagree on matters of principle and retain some personal animosity. With reference to Shah Banu , her local *mullah*, a Barelvi, was very upset when a group of Deobandis persuaded Shah Banu to repudiate the Supreme Court's verdict in her favor. He approved of the repudiation, but regretted that Deobandis obtained it.[17]

The education of the *ulama* placed a great deal of emphasis on developing forensic skills.[18] Almost any *alim* felt he possessed the right to contradict even the most highly regarded authorities. Collections of the writings of those scholars as well as compilations of their formal opinions (*fatawa*) never attempted to rectify divergent views. Such works simply listed the conflicting assertions making no effort to reconcile them. No single "code" of *shariah* existed prior to the arrival of the British.[19] Since the objective in *shariah* application was to find a religiously correct conrse of action in a highly specific set of circumstances, such a code would never have to be created. A *fatwa* does not seek to establish or apply a firm, fixed rule applicable in every particular instance. Every set of circumstances is unique and calls for a fresh course of reasoned inquiry into the sources of revelation, followed by a scholar's own appraisal of those sources and the events which prompted a request for his advice.

Texts on *shariah* did not provide equal scrutiny to every facet of life. They commonly gave the most attention to ritual and spiritual matters. The proper etiquette of the *Hajj* or the nature of pollution and its remedies took up the bulk of treatises on the application of shariah.[20] More mundane matters got less attention. While certain types of transaction involving property, contracts for example, did receive a fairly extensive treatment, other vital matters, land tenure for instance, had only brief expositions, if brought up at all. Muslims often guided their behaviour in these matters by the customs which prevailed in their region or they sought the advice of sufis or *ulama* whose religious authority did not depend on the states' commands.[21] At the time of the British conquest, no single Islamic code dictated the acquisition, distribution and transmission of wealth.

As the British began to assume control of the administration of justice in the subcontinent, they provided the impetus for the codification of *shariah*.[22] William Jones contemplated the creation of a single book of "Muhammadan law," but the died before the task began. Jones and other British lawyers found their inspiration in the efforts of Coke and Blackstone to provide England with a common set of rules applicable throughout the British Isles. Jones and the other scholars were also acquainted with similar efforts on Europe's continent to devise sets of law which would have force in an entire nation. The desire for legal regularity, therefor, seemed inspired by trends within the British legal tradition.

Translations of books on shariah played a minor role in the British administration of justice. Apart from short treatises, 150 years of British effort produced only two translations of Islamic texts: the *Hedaya*, a *qazi's* handbook put together by al-Marghinani in the twelfth century A.D, translated by Charles Hamilton and published in 1791, and Neil Baillie's *Digest of Muhammadan Law*, a compendium of brief excerpts from the *Fatawa-i Alamgiri* published in 1865.[23] Textbooks on "Mohammadan Law," ranging from W. MacNaghtan's *Principles of Mohammedan Law* of 1825 through the works of Amir Ali (1892), Abdur Rahim (1911), and F.B.Tyabji (1913) had considerable influence because they were written along the lines of textbooks on European law and were familiar to the judges of the Anglo-Indian courts who were either Britons or Indian trained in British sponsored law schools.[24]

The practice of the British courts in India was the single greatest influence on the present form of Muslim Personal Law. The organization and authority of those courts were quite different from those which had prevailed in Mughal times. In the Mughal empire authority to settle disputes resided in the overlapping jurisdictions of several types of individuals, not all of whom had government sanction. Though much attention falls on the office of *qazi*, the duties and status of these officials were detailed in theory, but unclear in practice. Many *qazis* inherited their posts, sometimes from individuals appointed by the dynasties preceding the Mughal. They may well have been primarily religious figures whose most important function was leading the Friday prayers and mentioning the ruler's name before delivering the Friday sermon.[25] Moreover, as elsewhere in the Islamic world, religious scholars who accepted governmental appointments elicited a contemptuous opinion from their fellows.[26] Pious Muslims sometimes avoided *qazis*, preferring to take the guidance of sufi *pirs* of independent *ulama*. Also, issues which should have been subject to the *shariah's* prescription, and hence the province of *qazis*, came under the state's regulations *(qanun)* administered by Mughal officers who were not members of the learned class. *Kotwals*, for example, punished crime and settled any disputes which threatened the peace. Matters involving land revenue, and this included questions of inheritance and the transfer of grants such as *madad-i maash*, the former being definitely *shariah's* preserve, went before the agents of the treasury *(diwan)*.[27]

Under the authority of the raj, overlapping and competing jurisdictions disappeared. Especially after the court reforms of 1863, lines of appeal and authority, from the courts of *munsifs* and assistant district magistrates through High Courts to the Privy Council in London, were set in the context of a single, hierarchically organized, bureaucratized, and governmentally sanctioned system. This was something even the Mughals had not contemplated, much less created. The work of these courts had far more influence on the shape of Islamic law as it exists in modern India.

Judges in these courts were usually Englishmen. Indians slowly made their way into the bench, but even in the 1930s and 40s they were outnumbered by their British colleagues. Limiting our discussion to Muslim judges, those who sat on Indian courts in the nineteenth and twentieth centuries were trained in the same fashion as British lawyers in Indian universities' law schools established by the British who also set their syllabi; or they were called to the bar in England itself. Of the noted Muslim judges of the Anglo-Indian courts Badr ud-din Tyabji, his son Faiz Badr ud-din, Sayyid Mahmud, Amir Ali and Abdur Rahim, all received their training in that fashion. None of them came from families which maintained a tradition of learning in *shariah* and many of them belonged to *Shiah* sects.[28] Were any of these judges, both Muslim and non-Muslim, qualified by the standards of *shariah* to establish rules for the faithful? The answer must be "no". Yet, they were the individuals who decided which portions of the *shariah* applied in India. They ignored most of it as unenforceable.

When they did find some element which appeared justifiable, they invariably encountered the divergent opinions of Muslim scholars mentioned above. Faced with a lack of unanimity in their sources, judges turned to British legal principles such as equity. One of these notions, precedent, became a major influence in determining the character of Muslim law.

If one reviews the judgment of Justice Chandrachud in Shah Banu's case, one finds some token verses of the Holy *Quran* cited, a quote, somewhat incongruously, from *Manu*, a brief quote from the nineteenth century British Orientalist Edward Lane, but the crucial sources informing the opinion are court cases, most of which date to the raj. Justice Chandrachud is careful to give special mention to two cases on which Muslim justices sat. Thus, *stare decis*, precedent, established the major guidelines used by the Chief Justice in writing his verdict in Shah Banu's case. These he took to establish the character of Islamic law. The history of English law demonstrates the potentially deadening effect of the over-application of precedent. Is not the same consequence evident in Muslim Personal law? If this set of rules appears staic, incapable of adapting to the circumstances of modern India, perhaps the fault lies with Anglo-Indian jurists, not with the essential unity of faith and law in Islam.

Those Muslims who defend Muslim Personal Law as *shariah* seem to be ignoring many unpleasant realities. Only bits and pieces of this body of law were connected with views expressed by pre-colonial Islamic thinkers. Precedents, legislative acts, and textbooks of Muhammadan law have had far more influence on the precepts of Muslim Personal law.[30] A few of the *ulama* have criticized the practice of permitting non-Muslims to rule on Islamic law,[31] but on the whole, even they are not calling for a complete overhaul of the Indian legal system. Muslim Personal Law seems to survive from habit or inertia rather than by its close connection to the Islamic tradition.

Most immediately relevant to the issues raised by the Shah Banu decision are the Muslim Personal Law's rules concerning women's rights to property. Once again, the most important period in the formation of current attitudes toward legal guarantees for women was that of the raj. Legal action since independence have done little, before 1986, to expand or restrict the rights admitted by the Anglo-Indian courts.

Colonial Courts and Women's Rights to Property

The image of Muslim women suffers from some of the same penchant for caricature which characterizes descriptions of almost anything preceded by the adjective "Muslim". The stock portrait to Muslim women as poor, silent, and abused creatures does not convey anything of the variety, and ambiguity, which marks the place of females in almost all societies, including Muslim ones.[32] As noted above, the discussion of Shah Banu's case prompted a spate of rather abstract references to the inferior place which women have supposedly always had in the Muslim world. For some, their lot excites rage or pity, but neither or those is effective as a descriptive or analytic category. At the same time, painting an idyllic portrait of women's life does not appear to be a rational way of combating ignorance and vilification.[33] On balance, whether or not women enjoy property rights and the social prominence which usually accompanies them, depends on the vagaries of time and place.

In the Mughal period, women in the highest ranks of society were able to control considerable wealth. The women of the imperial harem issued decrees in their own names and under their own seals. They invested in and directed trading ventures. They distributed their wealth in the form of gifts to servants or favorite religious figures as they pleased.[34] Slightly lower down on the socio-economic scale, the wives and daughters of those who held *madad-i maash*, *wazifah*, or other types of imperial grants were able to retain control of at least a portion of the incomes when the original incumbent died.[35] No prohibition on women controlling property or exercising the rights of ownership existed. Documents of the period assume, without comment, that women could maintain an independent income.

Even so, the property rights of women were limited by such variables as the amount of wealth a given family controlled and the number of individuals who had to be supported. When resources were limited and demands upon them great, some women were denied the rights which a strict interpretation of *shariah* would have granted them. In straitened circumstances, males probably did pressure women to renounce legitimate claims to an inheritance.[36] Some Muslim groups; the Khojahs or Punjabi Jats for instance, routinely excluded women from opportunities to obtain control of property.[37] Particular economic and class conditions as well as caste traditions, rather than a basic principle of the Islamic faith, forced these decisions. Indeed they differed little from practices in Europe and North America.[38]

A major change in the social context in which rights to wealth were either attained or lost occurred when the British began to enforce law which turned land into private property. In the Mughal period, most individuals seemed more interested in the income which land generated than in the land itself.[39] The earlier focus on cash and the things which cash procured made it easier to divide estates so that women could receive a portion of their inheritance. Were the forcible division of land among heirs recognized by the Holy *Quran* and *Shariah* carried out, however, estates would soon be cut up into tidbits. When land became the measure of wealth and status, a family which once had these things faced the eventual loss of them through excessive fragmentation.

Anglo-Indian courts tended to enforce a textbook version of the *shariah's* rule of inheritance. [40] On the surface this would have been an enhancement of women's rights to a share of a parent's or husband's estate, since in pre-British times Muslims did not always strictly adhere to those rules.[41] In a similar fashion, those courts demanded the full payment of a bridal gift *(mehr)*, even when that meant that a woman gained lifetime control of her husband's property.[42] Such appearances were in a number of ways deceiving. What the courts gave with one hand, they often took away with the other. For example, in 1894, the Privy Council ruled that an endowment *(waqf)* must be founded for a "charitable or religious purpose.[43] Prior to the Privy Council's ruling, endowments provided Muslims with a way of mollifying the rigors of the *shariah's* inheritance regulations which the Anglo-Indian courts so carefully observed. According to those rules, when a male died leaving no sons, but only daughters, the daughters' share in an estate did not markedly increase. That which would have been a son's portion went to male first cousins. By contrast, the establishment of a *waqf* gave its founder the ability to select those who would manage the endowment and receive its income. In that way, a man could pass on an intact estate to his daughters.[44] By eliminating this way of settling an estate, the British courts closed one avenue by which Muslim women asserted their right to landed property. Not the least of the ironies in the Shah Banu controversy is that the Muslim Women's Bill requires local *waqf* boards to support indigent divorcees by way of charity.[45] Institutions which once allowed women to enjoy the income of an undivided estate, to control that estate as custodians and pass it on to heirs of their choosing, are now required to give them subsistence.

So far as the rights of women to property were concerned, the courts of the raj were a mixed blessing. Though they sustained some rights, while enhancing others, they eliminated some others which gave Muslim women independent status. In a larger sense, they made it more difficult for women to exercise independent control of property by subjecting land to the varying pressures of "the market." While savants argue over whether or not a Muslim landlords suffered more than others from the imposition of the notion of private property in land,[46] Muslims themselves believed that their estates were in greater danger. This sense of impending catastrophe continued to frighten them until well after independence. Zamindari abolition laws, even when they were evaded, have usually harmed the Muslim gentry class.[47] In an environment in which the basis of social prestige seems to be shrinking., women are likely to suffer the loss first. Once again, however, this deprivation stems from economic necessity and not from a conscious Islamic bias against women.

Litigation and Communal Politics

The bureaucratic structure of the British empire made it impossible to separate law and politics. Not only were the courts politically sanctioned, but they seemed to operate with many of the same ideas about the nature of Indian society that British officials had. For them, as for judges, India appeared as a patchwork of separate religious ethnic and racial groups, each of which had its own law based on its faith. Perhaps because judges were often completely ignorant of Indian languages and Indian social realities,[48] courts were reluctant to recognize subdivisions within such abstractions as "Hindu" and "Muslim." For example, they did not recognize a distinction between "Shiah" and "Sunni" until the 1840s and the status of groups like the Khojahs remained uncertain throughout the raj.[49] An awareness of the subtle and shifting character of such social identities was rare. The courts and the politicians shared a preference for growing social generalizations, a tendency all too evident in the discussion of the Shah Banu affair.

Had the approach used in the courts been restricted to that venue, politics in contemporary India would be very different, but the terminology of the courts received a much wider circulation. As the British slowly and reluctantly admitted Indians into the government, the legal perception of India entered the language of politics. Lawyers made a habit of entering political life. The Anglo-Indian courts became in effect, the nursery school of Indian nationalist politics. Though the conditions of Indian participation were strictly circumscribed with the franchise going to a favored few, once the principle of representative government was introduced, would be politicians had to have some body to represent. The system favored those who could give the impression that they spoke for a united constituency. Then, as now, claims to the unfailing support of one or another community carried greater weight with the administration.

Since this proved an effective way of dealing with government, the rapid acceptance of the style by would-be leaders is only logical. A somewhat more complicated problem arises when considering the response of Muslim religious scholars. In the aftermath of the revolt of 1857, most of the *ulama* adopted political quietism as their stance toward the imperial government. The scholars of the seminary at Deoband, for example, tried to isolate themselves from the influence of the raj.[50]

In the later years of the nineteenth century, however, the *ulama* began to shift their position. Rather than remaining aloof from the British, they began to take advantage of the government's predisposition to heed the views of any who asserted that their constituency was based on religious interest. Beginning with the agitation that lead to the passage of the Mussalman Wakf Validating Act of 1913, through the Cawnpore Mosque incident and the Partition of Bengal and its revocation, religious scholars from different traditions dropped their indifference to the raj and became lobbyists.[51] What brought about the change in tactics? The *ulama* evidently realized that a centralized state presented them with an opportunity to influence their coreligionists more than ever before. The state's authority commanded more attention than the purely private efforts of religious scholars.

When the nationalist movement demonstrated its power in the years between 1919 and 1924, a number of religious scholars attached themselves to it. Though the independent state the nationalist leaders sought did not emerge for another twenty-five years, this experience forged personal bonds between a number of religious scholars and political leaders. While some have been puzzled by the preference which many so-called "orthodox" Muslim scholars showed for India over Pakistan, years of active cooperation accounted in some measure for the loyalty. Pakistan was for many of the ulama an unknown quantity, but India's leaders were friends and potential benefactors.[52] The close association of the Congress and Janta parties with scholars of the Jamait ul-ulama-i Hind and other Muslim groups is simply the latest expression of an alliance which dates back to the end of the last century.

In the years before Indian independence, the *ulama* learned that protestations of communal solidarity resulted in government action. Their experience since 1947 has only reinforced that impression. Do the *mullahs* really control the minds of India's more than seventy million Muslims? Probably not, but they do control access to the politicians and so they possess power in government's eyes. While today's journalists worry about "fundamentalism, " the British fretted over "Wahabism." In both cases, the dire predictions of *jihad* have not materialized because Muslims in the subcontinent have always been a minority, but a minority whose largely self-appointed leadership have turned a deficit into an asset through the skillful manipulation of religious abstractions.

Perhaps there is some symbolic connection between Shah Banu's case and the relationship of Muslims to the society in which they live. Like personal grievances, social and political complaints often percolate for years on end. When they finally erupt, explanations have difficulty locating the time when problems began. The tendency is to seek a reason in the distant past: "We never got along," or in the immediate past, "Last week you........" The period between the beginning and last week seems insignificant. In the the controversy over Shah Banu's suit, the long middle period of British rule has been largely forgotten, but the fundamental social, economic, and political misunderstandings originated there. India, as other emerging nations, began its independence with the resolve to reject the colonial part and build anew. That has not proved an easy task. Disremembering the ways in which imperialism set the stage for independent life does not help. A sober assessment of the foundations of contemporary Indian life, rather than constant mutual recrimination, might help point to a new path for all parties concerned. These might well meditate on the words of an Indian colleague of mine who once said, only half in jest,

"British rule in India began on August 14, 1947."

NOTES

1. In order to simplify printing, no diacriticals including ayn and hamza, will be included in the following essay.

2. *All India reporter*, vol. 72, 945ff; a text of the judgment is reprinted in *The Shah Bano Controversy*, ed., A.A. Engineer, (Bombay: Orient Longman, 1987), 23-34.

3. Texts of the bill can be found in *Asian Recorder*, XXXII/24 (June 11-17, 1986) 18927-29; also *Shah Bano Controversy*, 85-88.

4. Nawaz B. Mody, "The press in India: The Shah Bano Judgment and Its Aftermath," *Asian Survey*, XXVII/8(August, 1987) 935-53.

5. Most of the following information on the family dispute is based on Saeed Naqvi, "The Shah Bano Case: The Real Truth," In *Shah Bano Controversy*, 66-70.

6. Cross-cousin marriage has been extensively described by scholars of the Middle East; see Dale F. Eickelman, The Middle East: *An Anthropologica Approach*, (Engleweed Cliffs, N.J. : Prentice Hall, 1981), 123 ff; however, the strategies involved in these marriages in the Indian context do not appear to have been systematically investigated.

7. David Leyveld, *Aligarh's First Generation*, (Princeton: Princeton University Press, 1978), 35-54.

8. G.C. Kozlowski, *Muslim Endowments and Society in British India*, (Cambridge: Cambridge University Press, 1985), 79-95;

also, O. Mendelsohn, "The Pathology of the Indian Legal System," *Modern Asdian Studies*, 15/4 (1981), 823-863.

9. *Ahmedalli Mohammad Hanif Makandar vs. Rabiya, Bombay Law Reporter*, 1977, 238 ff.

10. Imtiaj Ahmed points out that "modernization" for many Indian social scientists has become just another excuse for savaging Muslims, "Introduction,"*Modernization and Social Change Among Muslims in India,* (New Delhi: Manohar, 1983), xvii-xlix.

11. "A Community in Turmoil," *India Today* (January 11, 1986),90-104.

12. "Anger and Hurt,"*Ibid.,* (March 15,1986), 40-43.

13. K.R.Malkani, "Prisoners of their Past, " *Far Eastern Economic Review*, (March 20, 1986),35.

14. One of the best discussions of what "secularism" means in the modern Indian context remains V.P. Luthra, *The Concept of the Secular State and India,* (Calcutta: Oxford University Press, 1964); also, G.C. Kozlowski, "Indian Secularity and the Islamic Law: A Liberal Muslim's Response, " *Islamic Quarterly*, XVIII/3-4 (July-December, 1974),33-47.

15. The following summarizes arguments that I have made more exclusively elsewhere, see, G.C..Kozlowski, "When the 'Way' Becomes the 'Law": Modern State and the Transformation of Halakha and *Shariah*," in *Studies in Islamic and Judaic Traditions*, II, eds., W. Brinner and S.D. Ricks , (Decatur, Ga.: Scholar's Press, forthcoming) and my, "Muslim Women and the Control of Property in North India," *The Indian Economic and Social History Review*, 24/2 (1987), 163-181.

16. J.H. Harrington, "Remarks Upon the Authorities of Mosulman Law,"*Asiatik Researches, Asiatic Society of Bengal*, X(1811), 475-512.

17. For a report of the Indore *mullah's* disappointment, Saeed Naqvi, "The Real Truth; " for a scholarly account of the divergence of these groups, see, B.D. Metcalf, *Islamic Revival in British India,* (Berkely: University of California Press, 1982).

18. G. Makdisi, *The Rise of Colleges,* (Edinburgh: Edinburgh University Press, 1981), 106-120 and M. Fischer, *Iran: From Religious Dispute to Revolution,* (Cambridge, Mass.: Harvard University Press, 1980),12-60.

19. Despite its title the *Fatawa-i Hind* is not a collection of scholars' *Fatawa*, but an anthology of other textbooks. It preserved all of the differences of opinion and was not intended to serve as a "code" for all Indian Muslims; see, J.Schacht, "On the title of the *Fatawa al-Alamgiriyya,"* in *Iran and Islam,* ed. , C. Bosworth, (Edinburgh: Edinburgh University Press, 1971), 475-78.

20. For example, *Fatawa-i Deoband*, (Deoband: Dar al-ulum, 1968).

21. K.M. Ashraf, *Life and Conditions of the People of Hindustan,* (New Delhi: Manoharlal, 1970), 50-51; 101-112.

22. While the students of the *dharmashastra* have long admitted that the British, in effect, created "Hindu Law," students of *shariah* have not drawn the same conclusion from a similar process, see, J.D.M. Derrett, *Religion, Law and the State in India,* (New York: Free Press, 1968); for a very subtle, though not entirely convincing attempt to modify this view, see, C.J. Fuller, "Hinduism and Spiritual Authority in Modern Indian Law, " *Comparative Studies in Society and History* 30/2 (1988),225-248.

23. G.C. Kozlowski, *Muslim Endowments,* 123-127.

24. *Indian Judge,* (Madras; G.A. Natesan, 1932?); Ibid, 130-131.

25. "Life of Guru Nanak,"in *Shri Guru Adi Granth*, trans., E.Trumpp (London: Tuebner, 1877), 20-30.

26. M.G.S. Hodson, *The Venture of Islam*, (Chicago: University of Chicago Press, 1974), I, 238; 318; 351.

27. B. Cohn, "The Initial British Impact on India," *Journal of Asian Studies*, XIX/4 (1951),418-431.

28. *Indian Judges* (op. cit.).

29. Kozlowski, *Muslim Endowments*, 97 ff.

30. A.A.A. Fyzee, "The Muhammadan Law in India," *Comparative Studies in Society and History*, 5 (1983), 401-415.

31. S. Mitra, " The First Rumblings," *Sunday* (March 9,1986), 14.

32. D. Waines, "Through a Veil Darkly: The Study of Women in Muslim Societies," *Comparative Studies in Society and History*, 24 (1982), 642-59.

33. Charis Waddy, *Women in Muslim History*, (New York: Longman, 1980).

34. *Edicts of the Mughal Harem* , trans., Tirmizi, (Delhi: Idarah-i Adabiyat-i Delhi, 1979) and E.B. Findly, "The Capture of Maryam-uz-Zamani's Ship: Mughal Women and European Traders," *Journal of the American Oriental Society*, 108/2 (1988), 227-238.

35. Z. Malik,"Documents of *Madad-i Maash* during the Reign of Mohammad Shah, 1719-1748," *Indo-Iranica*, XXVI/2 (1973), 97-123; S. Rashid, "*Madad-i Maash* Grants under the Mughals" *Journal of the Pakistan Historical Society*, 9 (1961), 90-108.

36. C. Vreede-de Stuers, *Parda*, (Assen, Netherlands: Van Gorcum, 1968), 13-15.

37. C. Dobbin, *Urban Leadership in Western India*,(Oxford: Oxford University Press, 1972), 113-21; J. Hollister, *The Shia of India*, reprint edition, (New Delhi: Manoharlal, 1979), 378-412 and D. Ibbetson, *Punjab Castes*, reprint edition, (Delhi: B.R. Publishing, 1974), 97-163.

38. Kozlowski, "Muslim Women," 165.

39. W. Neale, *Economic Change in Rural India*, (New Haven: Yale University Press, 1962), 5-7; 20-37; also, appropriate papers in *Land Control and Social Structure in Indian History*, ed., R. Frykenburg, (Madison: University of Wisconsin Press, 1969).

40. *Cassamally Jairajbhai vs. Sir Currimbhoy Ibrahim*, Indian Law Report, Bombay Series, XXXVI, 241ff.

41. Note by Sir Sayyid Ahmed Khan in *Home-Judicial Proceedings B-Files* national Archives of India, October, 1879, 44-45.

42. *Hamina Bibi vs. Zubaida Bibi*, Indian Law Reports, Allahabad Series, XXXIII, 182 ff.

43. *Abul Fata Mohammed Ishak vs. Russamoy Dhur Chowdhry*, Indian law Reports, Indian Appeals, XXIII, 76 ff.

44. *Abdul Rajak vs. Bai Junbabai*, Bombay Law Reporter, XIV, 295 ff.

45. Asian Recorder 14929.

46. W.W. Hunter, *The Indian Musalmans*, reprint edition, (Lahore: Premier Book House, 1974),139.

47. T. Metcalf, "Landlords Without Land, "*Pacific Affairs*, XL/1-2 (1968),5-18.

48. G. Rankin, *Background to Indian law,* (Cambridge: Cambridge University Press, 1946), vii.

49. Cassamally's case (note 40), 260.

50. B. Metcalf, *Islamic Revival.*

51. Kozlowski, *Muslim Endowments,* 156 ff.

52. The noted "orthodox" thinker, A.A. Mawdudi, did not support the demand for Pakistan and moved there only because of threats on his life. The organization he founded, Jamait-i Islami has maintained close relations with leading politicians. see C.J. Adams, "The Ideology of Mawlana Maududi, " in *South Asian Politics and Religion,* ed. D.E. Smith (Princeton: Princeton University Press, 1966),371-97.

5

CHHATRAPATI SINGH

LAW, POVERTY AND WELFARISM

The Basis of Anti-Poverty Programmes

The war against poverty in India is simultaneously a war against casteism, especially that afflicting the Scheduled Castes and Tribes, who happen to be the poorest among the poor. Any critique of poverty in India must, therefore, address itself, first of all, to the conditions of these castes and tribes. Proclaiming that something new can be said about the methods by which their conditions can be improved, forty years after Independence and almost a century after the British, Dr. B.R. Ambedkar, and Gandhi, may sound presumptuous. Questioning the universally accepted strategy of affirmative state action of reverse discrimination may sound even more foolhardy. The fact, nonetheless, remains that even after half a century of state programmes, the Scheduled Castes and Tribes remain poor, atrocities against Harijans are wide-spread and the amelioration schemes, by and large, remain ineffective. Mass killing of Harijans in Bihar, violence caused by anti-reservation agitations in Gujarat and Assam, are other indicators of the shortcomings of affirmative action. Unless, at this stage, we earnestly seek the structural alternatives historically open to the Indian state for poverty alleviation and frontally address the assumptions of the existing anti-poverty programmes, it is unlikely that any major change can occur for many years to come. The usual way of looking at the matter is to assume that, evidently, the methods demanded by Dr. Ambedkar and the Constitution are correct, affirmative state action is the right, and perhaps the only strategy. The problem, it is argued, lies in the incompetent or half-hearted *implementation* of affirmative state action programmes, as well as in the fact that for various reasons the scheduled caste and tribe members have not been able to derive as much benefit as they should from such programmes.[1] In the last three decades, numerous doctrinal and empirical studies have been done, based on these assumptions, to show how the legislative measures for affirmative state action have been ineffectively implemented, or how the backward classes have benefited little from government schemes, or how the judiciary or the legislature have intervened in an attempt to improve the situation. The most detailed account of the affirmative action scenario culminates in Mark Galanter's *Competing Equalities*.[2]

In light of this monumental failure to improve the lot of Scheduled Castes and Tribes over this century, one must venture to question the fundamental constitutional and political assumptions once again, however improper or uncommon it may seem at the moment. Is it really the case that the condition of the scheduled castes and tribes has not improved due to the failure to properly implemented affirmative state action? May it not be the case that such failures of implementation are inherent, from the very beginning, in the nature of the programmes and the law? The claim that various laws are good but that they have not achieved their goals because they have not been properly implemented, is the usual conclusion of various legal research in India. Such research hardly ever stops to consider whether these laws could be implemented in the first place. The inability to implement a particular law, for various reasons, is one thing, but the legislation of laws that can be implemented raises a different sort of question about the very purpose of legislative processes and the nature of the state. An alternative ideological perspective is generated if one assumes, for the moment, that the legal framework for affirmative state action for the ameliorative of the Scheduled Castes and Tribes is beyond implementation from the start. It is possible, given the evolution of the monopolitic/capitalistic state in India, that all such affirmative action, laws, and programmes are in fact not ameliorative, but ways of further oppressing, containing, limiting, restraining or side-tracking the interests of the poor and backward classes! Preposterous as this possibility may seem, it cannot be brushed aside as an unwarranted conclusion, especially when it still needs to be shown that India is a socialist democracy within which the state can really alleviate poverty. Thinking of the nature of the Indian state it seems more natural and consistent to believe that in a capitalistic state, capitalist modes of control will evolve which will not favour the poor. This is not to suggest that all affirmative action in India is in fact exploitative, but, first, only to point to the fact that there is an alternative way of looking at the phenomenon of affirmative action, which needs to be explored and taken seriously. The problem, hitherto, has been that it is so ubiquitously assumed that affirmative action, of the type prevalent, is a good thing, that one never thinks of questioning its basis or of seeking alternatives; all research is confined to the details of the existing system. This type of analysis also ignores the obvious; how can a socialistic measure (of seeking social economic justice) succeed within a capitalistic market economy?

Now the assertion that the so-called ameliorative laws may actually be social legitimation of non-ameliorative strategies, may seem to go contrary to the general belief that measures which were, after all, championed by people such as Dr. Ambedkar who were truly interested in the improvement of the underprivileged castes and tribes, cannot be wrong. Dr. Ambedkar's sincerity of purpose is evidently beyond doubt. His knowledge, however, as to what will constitute the appropriate strategy for the amelioration of the under-privileged people, was a product of his times and of political contingencies. It was an expression of a liberal ideology which had its roots in a certain understanding of political democracy and the dignity of man in a civil society. It did not emerge from an economic theory of exploitation or state formation. Perhaps, if it had, he might have fought for altogether different ends. To argue, therefore, that the political and social demands made for the improvement of the under-privileged classes by Dr. Ambedkar and other members of the Constituent Assembly, have not been of a type which can achieve the desired ends, is not to show disrespect for them in anyway, or to cast any aspersions on their sincerity but only to suggest that the philosophy of action advocated by them should be open to question, as much as any man's knowledge is.[3] The fact that forty years after Independence the goals they desired have not been achieved, clearly shows that either the demands they made on the political system were inaccurate and insufficient, or that the types of demand they made were of a kind which could be subverted by the political economy to serve the ends of a capitalistic market, in other words economy in which the underprivileged or exploited classes do not rebel against the system because they are kept at bay by socially legitimized illusion of state action for a melioration. In either case, one has to face up to the fact that there has been something fundamentally incomplete or wrong with the strategy demanded and adopted by statesmen who have desired the salvation of the underprivileged classes.

The aim of this essay is not merely to criticise affirmative state action, but first to demonstrate the claims made above, by showing how affirmative action of the type practised presently achieves non-ameliorative ends, and the role that law plays in this result then to go on to show how a totally different type of affirmative state action and law are necessary if amelioration is desired. The link between what is the case and what is desired is our understanding of the root causes of poverty and underprivileged status. The work, therefore, will necessitate looking closely at not the reasons for the economic conditions of the Scheduled Castes and Tribes but also at the theories of poverty which have structured the current poverty alleviation, and what is ideologically presupposed in them.

There are some *prima facie* anomalies which can be observed even before we begin detailed analysis. To start with, from the economic point of view there is little justification, for jumping together the tribes with the Scheduled Castes. The community resources management system, means of livelihood, property rights, possession, culture, habitat skills and educational needs of the tribals are all very different from those of the Scheduled Castes. To assume that the strategy for upliftment of the tribals will be the same as that of the Scheduled Castes is to exhibit a gross ignorance of the economic conditions of Indian people. The economics of the tribals are, by and large, land based (forest lands): they can claim occupancy rights on such lands, and even under the existing forest laws they have usufruct rights to the land resources. The price for their labour has largely been governed by the state-made rules under the forest laws. The scheduled castes, on the other hand, are by and large landless, doing menial or agriculture labour, earning their livelihood through their skills, and getting prices for their labour which depend upon the existing market forces and exploitative power of those who employ them. Clearly, different types of economic strategies are required for the liberation of the scheduled castes and tribes. Yet the Indian law and the Constitution speaks of Scheduled Castes and Tribes in one breath. As is generally known, this scheme became part of the Indian Constitution when the British drafted the Government of India Act in 1935. It is also known that the colonial rulers had a *political* and *not* an *economic* reason for lumping the Scheduled Castes and Tribes together, that of identifying and creating a separate political faction of people who were assumed to be outside the Hindu fold. This is not to say that atrocities were not being perpetuated by upper caste Hindus on lower castes, and, in fact, worse atrocities were being perpetuated by the British on the Tribals during the same period (such as by abolishing all traditional land rights of the tribals, acquiring forest land and resources for the crown, and classifying some tribal groups as criminal tribes). Yet when it came to the political front, the castes and tribes were grouped together, for reasons which political history has repeatedly pointed out: the "divide and conquer policy, that is, of creating antagonistic political factions where they did not exist before. Having understood the various colonial practices of communal divisions, the first taste before the Constituent Assembly should have been that of undoing the basis of such divisions and finding alternative for amelioration, and surely not adopting *en bloc* the colonial practices.

Adoption of the 1935 Government of India Act with respect to percentile treatment of some people by the state created a series of anomalies for post-Independence Indian Constitutionalism. These concern equality before law and the state, right to property, right to education and public services, uniform civil code, right to association and political representation of the people. It will be best to discuss these in the context of the detailed analysis of the amelioration approaches, the reason for adopting them, and the ensuing consequences. Here it may suffice to mention that this work attempts a philosophical and jurisprudential critique of the affirmative state action which expresses itself in terms of affirmative laws and anti-poverty programmes. It seeks to expose its ideological and historical roots, so as to show the true character of such laws and programmes. The structural alternatives for state formation, in which poverty can really be removed, necessitates exposing the basic presuppositions of the existing anti-poverty programmes and outlining the new principles on which the laws and the programme need to be based. The aim of this paper is limited to this basic task.

Approaches and Amelioration

Since the beginning of this century untouchability and excesses of caste hierarchy presented a problem whose solution was inextricably involved in all approaches to nationalism in India. The question remained how such problems were to be overcome. The possible solutions may be roughly classified into three types. The Evangelical approach, which stressed a form of paternalism in which moral, spiritual, and economic help is to be given to the untouchables for their upliftment. The Reformist, leading to a caste-less society, and perception of untouchability as something external to Hinduism; such purified Hinduism would accept the Harijans and tribals as equals within the Hindu fold. At the other extreme, the Secular approach focused on the denial of civil rights and economic opportunities and stressed a separate political identity for the lower castes and tribes, so that this separate group could be given preferential treatment by the state. Subsequent legislation, programmes and other affirmative state actions have obviously been influenced by all three ideologies in different measure. The assumption, the advocacy of specific action, and the consequences of each of these approaches can, nonetheless, be analysed separately.

The Evangelical and Reformist Approach

The logical consequence of the Evangelicalism of the Christian administrations and missionaries is state *paternalism*, especially when such administrators become functionaries of the state. Paternalism is the belief that the state needs to protect and help either a part or the whole of the people it governs, as the father helps his children. Paternalism tends to view the governed people as state subjects who are in special need of the sovereign's help. The ideology opposed to paternalism would be one of comradeship and non-interference, one in which the state views the people as citizens and not merely subjects and comrades or equal partners. Then the role of the state becomes different. First it does not exploit the people it is concerned with and second, it attempts to do way with all those external exploitative measures or practices wich retard the growth of the people. By removing these obstacles it provides the necessary opportunities to citizens for their own development.

Both the Evangelical and Reformist movements are primarily concerned with removing the social injustice of untouchability in India. To comprehend one aspect of the differences in their strategies, one has to pay attention to the notion of social injustice as understood by the two approaches. Although the preamble of the Indian Constitution mentions social justice separately from economic justice, the difference has never been made explicit in theory or practice in the Indian context. It is interesting to see how then nations of social and economic justice have played interchangeable roles in the developmental process. To begin with, the difference between social and economic justice can be sustained only if the concepts can be defined in different terms. If social justice is a matter of social status and social status a matter of economic opportunities, then the difference between the ideas of social and economic justice is lost, because economic justice is itself definable in terms of economic opportunities. This is not of course, the way the idea of social and economic justice was entirely distinguished. From about the time of Raja Ram Mohan Roy, social injustice was perceived to be constituted not by economic disparities but because there was a hierarchical stratification of social status in which the members of the society did not have a choice about their individual dignity within the social scheme. If social injustice, as distinguished from economic injustice, is so constituted then what was required was to repeal or abolish the sources which gave validity to the old social structure, on the one hand, and transform social practices and attitudes internally, on the other. This indeed was the enterprise of the Reformists, both in the social and the legal sphere. In the social sphere the Brahmo Samaj, Arya Samaj, Rama Krishna Mission. Aurobindo Society and other similar movements are evidence of such attempts. In the legal sphere the legislation of the *Hindu Code* through a series of Parliament Acts in 1955-56, which abandons *varna* distinctions, the Untouchability (Offences) Act, 1955, and also the earlier acceptance of a uniform Indian Penal Code, the Criminal Procedure Code and the Civil Procedure Code account for the major Reformist movements unlike the laws, did not make any caste distinctions in procedure or penalties these. It is evident, therefore, that both during the British period and after Independence the Reformist movement had a significant impact on law reform. The question then remains: why did the jurists and politicians not apply the same Reformist ideology to Constitutional drafting? In the spirit of the Hindu Code and the Penal Codes all varna distinction should have been abolished in the Constitution, yet it adopted a three varna system: the Scheduled Castes, the Scheduled Tribes, and ordinary citizens. The answer is two-fold; first, the Reformist movements have never had an economic programme for the upliftment of the underprivileged, and the second, (which is a corollary of the first) legally and politically social deprivation has not been perceived merely as a matter of social injustice. It has in fact been synonymous with economic injustice, especially from the point of view of the Evangelical and Secular ideologies which have had equally significant impact on constitution-making.

The Evangelical enterprise has unfolded itself in two ways. First it has resulted in mass conversion of Scheduled castes and tribes into Christianity and Buddhism. Such conversions have not carried with themselves an economic programme of upliftment, hence the consequences of this aspect of Evangelicalism is comparatively limited. Second, as mentioned, the main aspect of this ideology has been paternalism, which in legal terms has implied reservations of economic opportunities (seats and offices) for the underprivileged. The fact that the jurists both before and after Independence did not proceed to rectify social status by merely legislating new equalitarian laws but instead adopted a form of paternalism can be interpreted to show that they clearly saw that within a new individualistic, capitalistic or industrial economic order, where possession of wealth is itself a value of a person's worth and excellence, the social status could not be improved by simply declaring everyone as equal. In ancient India the social status was independent of the economic status; a Brahmin could be poor but still respected. In modern India this is not so. Hence in ancient India social inequities could be corrected without interfering with the economic system, as was done through Buddhism or Jainism. In modern India, since social status is directly dependent on the economic status, social justice cannot be obtained without affecting economic justice at the same time. If this perception can be attributed to the jurists and politicians, it, of course, justifies economic aid and legal paternalism, but it has a serious logical consequence, namely, that this type of paternalism is to be extended to all those whose social status is low in modern India, due to their economic status. It does not, ipso facto, provide the argument that the paternalism is to be extended only to untouchables or scheduled castes and tribes. One has to then ask what are the external or extra grounds for delimiting paternalism to certain classes, and moreover, of defining the beneficiaries of economic justice in social terms and not in economic terms?

To understand the motivation, as well as the assumptions and consequences of the motivations, one has to take a deeper look at the roots of paternalism itself, i.e. the historical circumstances within which this type of paternalism took shape.[4]

A society can be reformed internally, without the use of sanctions or force. Buddha, Mahavir, Nanak, Kabir, Chaitanya, Khusro, Gandhi, were all reformists who successfully transformed society in various ways, without imposing authoritative laws from above. But the British government of India could not introduce legal reform to benefit the poor because internal reform requires understanding the culture, reasons, and beliefs which structure the society; it also requires ability to communicate with the people, in their own language. Reform through a legal system presuppose an unselfish motive of genuine compassion and caring for the people. This was, evidently, not the colonial orientation. Not knowing the society internally it was impossible for the British to bring about extensive internal reforms which would benefit the low caste poor.

Reform through law, however, did not begin with paternalistic assumptions. The first conscious movements to introduce English legal principles into India arose out an attempt by the British Parliament to control the excess of the servants of the East India Company. Lord North's Regulating Act, 1773 instituted the Calcutta Supreme Court, the chief purpose of which was, in Edmund Burke's words, "to form a strong and solid security for the natives against the wrongs and oppressions of the British subjects in Bengal".[5] This attitude, however, totally changed with Cornwallis, the Governor-General from 1786 to 1793. He had the choice between consolidating British rule on the basis of the Mughal system in keeping with the company's tradition, or of adopting an entirely new foreign foundation. The Sialcot Committee on the Affairs of the East India Company, in fact, suggested both alternatives. Cornwallis, however, chose the latter.[6] He sought to reduce the functions of the government to the task of ensuring the security of persons and property through law. This was a frank attempt to apply the Whig philosophy of government. He thought the rule of law could be achieved by permanently limiting the state revenue demands on land, for like all Whigs, he was convinced that landed property was the agency which affected the reconciliation of freedom and order. There would flow from a landed property, according to Cornwallis, a natural ordering of society into ranks and class, "nowhere more necessary than in this country for reserving order in civil society".[7] Cornwallis' Whigian perspective did not concern itself with the landed property of the tribals at this time, nor did it stop to consider how order in society could be preserved when the majority of lower caste people were landless and poorly prepared to have property rights. What it did realize was the legitimization of the property rights of the Zamindars, who are already landed.

In the post-Wiggian period, the utilitarians and the liberals had a powerful influence on the people in control of Indian affairs. The liberal current began to assert itself in India at the same time as it did in the English political life, albeit in a radically different way. James Mill's *History of British India* resulted in this employment in the East India House and after 1819 of his son John Stuart Mill, thus firmly establishing the utilitarian influence in Indian affairs.[8] These influences consist of, among other tings, the idea of proportional representation and defining the dignity of man in terms of his civil and political rights. It is interesting to note that when it came to the actual application of his theory, John Stuart Mill thought it could be applied to only certain types of people and societies, amongst which of course were not the Indians. What could he applied to the Indians, as Fitzjames Stephen argued after his return from India, was the Benthamite and Austinian types of authoritarianism.[9] Stephen's experience resulted in significant negation of modern liberal ideologies and is historically valuable in-so-far as it was the actual ideology applied in India.

Stephens' authoritarianism had a close connection with Evangelicalism. Two founding members of the Evangelical Clapham sect—Charles Grant and John Shore (later Lord Teignomouth)—were company servants who had been Cornwallis' advisers concerning the Bengal Permanent Settlement. The aggressive Christianity of the Clapham sect became a force in public life mainly through the cause of the Indian mission. Because of the close tie with India enjoyed by the Grants, the Thorntons and the Stephens, the Clapham and its offshoots were able to send forth generations of civil servants stamped with evangelical assurance, earnestness of purpose, and religious convictions. So many Claphams naturally left a deep impression on the Indian administration, so much so that evangelicalism instead of being a religious mission, became a prevalent administrative culture. James Fitzjames Stephens was one such administrator with ingrained evangelical persuasiveness.

The precedence for evangelism to express itself as authoritarian paternalism was laid by T.B. Macaulay, who although theoretically opposed to the benthamite idea that law was meant to reform society, turned out to be the most reformist in practical terms. The existence of different indigenous legal systems in India, such as Mitakshara and the Dayabhag, before the Charter Act, inspired a hope for a great chain of codes for the Indian empire. Bentham had long recognized the opportunity which India presented, but it was left to Macaulay to make the reality of a uniform penal code a matter of practical politics. In his speech on the Charter Bill on 10th July 1833 Macaulay echoed the sentiments which Bentham had expressed half a century earlier, and which James Mill had written in his *History of British India*.[10]

After the 1840s, with the departure of Holt Mackenzie and Bentick and with Metcalfe's lessening influence, a reformed Whiggism again took hold of the government, in which besides Macaulay, Alexander Ross was the main representative. Ross opposed the *laisez faire* alternative to the attempt to unite the utilitarian programme with the authoritarian paternalism which had developed in the Sir Thomas Munro tradition. He took the *laisez faire* doctrine and transformed it, as did his contemporaries in England, into a criterion for radical reform. With Ross, the law became the sole instrument of social change. He, in fact, advocated a rapid and complete transformation of the complex inter-subjective personal relationships between Indians, replacing it with something similar to the economic and social structure of England.

It was against this background that J. Fitsjames Stephen took up his work. Legal paternalism, or the imperialism that expressed itself through law, took its clear and final shape with Stephen. He held the office of law member for only two and a half years, yet his influence has been most significant in affecting the development of the Indian legal system. Like Bentham's *Anarchical Fallacies*, Stephen attacked the abstract doctrine of liberty and the rights of man. From his theory emerged practical arguments against the denigration of power and force by which John Bright and the Manchester liberals condemned the very existence of the British rule in India. He used these against the notion that Britain had a duty to educate India towards self-government, and against the policy of self-effacement and surrender to abstract moral ideas of liberty. Besides having a powerful influence as a law member, which brought about, amongst other things, the Evidence Act of 1872, Stephen had a lasting effect on the mind of Lord Curzon, the Governor General from 1989 to 105. Stephen drew his solution to the Indian problems mainly from the philosophy of Thomas Hobbes. He conceived law in authoritarian terms as the command of the sovereign: the state operated by force and threat and it was the whole nature of law to make the operation regular and deliberate.[11]

This historical account of the English involvement with special reform, is by no means exhaustive, nor does it mention any voices which spoke against the legal philosophy practised by the establishment. It does, nonetheless, capture the important ideological forces which controlled, created and led not only to the Government of India Act, 1935, with its clear paternalistic, evangelical and authoritative scheduling of the castes and tribes, but also to the Independent Indian Constitution, which openly adopted such schedules from the 1935 Act. Most members of the Constitutional Assembly were lawyers who carried with them the legal culture and world view left behind by Stephens and Macaulay. Generations of civil servants, lawyers, and politicians have believed and continue to believe that the poor are in need of help, that they have to be 'salvaged' through ameliorative measures, instead of asking why are these people poor in the first place, who made them poor, and how shall we stop such people from making them poor? We have seen in modern India that providing social justice is seen to be directly dependent upon providing economic justice. The question then needs to be asked who has continued to do economic injustice to the Scheduled Castes and Tribes, and how shall we stop this through law? Helping others is a virtue only when one does not continue to be responsible for the misery of the other, else it is a hypocracy. For making altruism a state policy and claiming it to be virtuous, it would have to be shown how the policies carried on by the state have not been responsible for the misery of the lower castes and tribes. It would have to be shown, for example, how the British, while taking away all the resources of the tribes through various Forest Acts, did not impoverish the tribals.

The subsequent part of this work will analyze the impoverishment programme of the lower castes and tribes, both by the British and the independent government. Here, before preceding to the analysis of the secular approach, it will be important to briefly review the alleged advantages of the ameliorative programmes and preferential treatment.

Some of the major (alleged) advantages and disadvantages are neatly tabulated by Marc Galanter in his *Competing Equalities*. These can be classified into economic, political , psychological, and social.[12] The advantages and disadvantages he mentions, of course, emerge from the status quo, that is accepting the legal framework as it is, including the ideologies and motivations that underline it. From a different ideological perspective, as will be shown, one may come with a different list of disadvantages of the given scheme of things. Amongst economic advantages Galanter mentions two; redistribution of resources and incubation, that is a greater protection period for the acquisition of resources and skills. He states, "Preferences provide a direct flow of valuable resources to the beneficiaries in larger measures than they would otherwise enjoy" and "By broadening opportunities,preferences stimulate the acquisition of skills and resources needed to compete successfully in open competition".[13] Now, as far as the flow of resources is concerned forty years of the so-called preferential treatment has still kept the Scheduled Castes and Tribes poor, so evidently there has been only a marginal flow of resources. The argument, therefore, is false, it cannot be a justification for preferential treatment. The crux of the argument lies in the assertion that "preferences provide .... resources .... in larger measures than they would otherwise enjoy". How do we know this? Has the state tried any other method to allocate resources Have we made a study of alternative methods of providing resources as a result of which we know which of them achieves this in larger measure? Does the state know who is depriving the poor of the resources and has it made any attempt to check this? Galanter, evidently, echoes the usual propaganda and mentions an 'advantage' of the preferential treatment, in a simplistic way, without researching the more basic aspect of what the statement pre-supposes or implies. As for 'broadening the opportunities for the acquisition of skills', one must ask what skills? Is the state broadening the opportunities for the skills which the scheduled castes and tribes already have? Does it economically respect their skill? On the contrary, through "preferential treatment" the state neglects the skills possessed by the lower castes and tribes. It tells them: "if you want help from the state change your skill; become doctors, engineers, clerks, etc.for which we are reserving special seats for you, we only respect the skill of the bourgeois. If you want to remain confined to your menial proletariat or tribal skills, you can go to hell for all we care". This is the paternalistic evangelical spirit speaking through the state. It amounts to saying," Look here you scheduled caste and tribe people, we have and we shall continue to respect and pay well for only the work done by the upper caste people: if you people want to be respected and get a larger measure of resources, quit doing what you have been doing and begin doing the work hitherto done by Brahmins, Vaishyas, Kshatriyas, and other higher castes, that is become higher castes, only then can you fit into our scheme of things." This is the opposite of what Gandhi taught. He wanted us to learn respect for all kinds of labour, especially manual labour. The tragedy is that the scheduled caste and tribes people, having been brainwashed for so many centuries to believe that the upper caste work is more respectful, begin to fight for and demand the so-called upper caste work, instead of fighting to make their own skill and labour socially better respected and economically more resourceful.

We shall return to the question of resources and labour in the subsequent section on poverty. Here it is important to discuss the other alleged advantages.

The other major advantage of preferential treatment, mentioned by Galanter is political. "Preferences", he states, "provide for participation in decision making by those who effectively represent the interest of the beneficiaries, interest that would otherwise be under-represented or neglected".[14] The major question here is: Do the political representatives really reflect the interest of the scheduled castes and tribes or do they reflect party and their personal political interest? Any number of analyses have shown that it is doubtful if our election system is now capable of generating true representation of people's interest.[15] There is the larger question of whether anyone who wishes to(and manages to) represent the political or social interest of some people, knows economically what is in the best interest of the people and for their welfare. The basic argument for political preference, however, is not merely representation of interests, but from the secular perspective, the generation of a separate political identity, so that one assumes, the bargaining power of this separate group will increase. The fact, once again, is that we do not observe any significant economic betterment of the scheduled castes and tribes merely because they have had political representation over the last forty years. The politicization of the castes and tribes has generated its own peculiar problem within Indian democracy. Before drawing any conclusion as to the merits and demerits of separate political representation it will be necessary to understand the background from within which the secular movement arose, the ideologies that motivated it, and what influence it has had on the legal system. It is only with this understanding that one may be able to seek feasible alternatives which are possible within our democratic set-up.

The Secular Approach

Secularism is the idea that different communities must co-exist peacefully, respecting each other's identity and helping each other towards development. With reference to the scheduled castes and tribes the basic issue at stake, from the very beginning, has not been of peaceful coexistence, but whether, to start with, they are or need to be, a different community. Gandhi's and the Reformist approach had been to assert that the scheduled castes and tribes form a part of the Hindu community,. untouchability is an injustice perpetuated within Hinduism, it was Hinduism, therefore, that needed to be purified and reformed. The counter-assertion that the untouchables should be enumerated as a class separate from Hindus became definitive when the Census Commissioner (for 1911) accepted the suggestion, followed by prompt endorsement by the Muslim League.[16] The League's apprehension about a continued Hindu majority must have been in the light of the then current estimate that the untouchables (then known as Depressed Classes) numbered 50-60 million, about a fifth of the total population.[17] State recognition and identification of different people suffering from similar disabilities provided the grounds for a new sense of 'Community' of untouchables. Untouchability, was thus propelled into a prominent place on the Indian political stage. The idea of the state reserving special communal quotas for public offices and opportunities, did not, however, emerge from the issues of untouchability. It was already preceded by movements of the middle class Hindus against the Brahmin pre-eminence in Madras and Bombay. The Justice Party (South Indian Liberal Federation) was founded in 1916; the organization of non-Brahmins in Bombay began in 1917. The Princely State of Mysore instituted a system in which all communities other than the Brahmins were designated backward classes"; from 1918 places were reserved for them in colleges and state services. The non-Brahmin's demands for a greater political representation were promptly recognized by the British through the Government of India Act, 1919. At first the non-Brahmin or "Backward Classes" movement undertook to represent the interest of the lowest strata as well as the upper but as they proposed, their voices increasingly reacted their personal interests.[18] The 1919 Act provided a few nominated seats for the Depressed Classes. These were followed by legislative resolutions and administrative orders- which were honored largely in the breach. The idea, however, that welfare consists of political representation and reserving public and educational opportunities, was by now well-rooted. The state had strategically divested the notion of welfare from any connection with basic resources needs and community management of available resources. For the middle caste non-Brahmins such an interpretation of welfarism did not necessarily affect their livelihood, their 'backwardness' did not necessarily reflect their economic status.

For the Depressed Classes, however, the situation was otherwise. The assumption, therefore, that the preferential treatment shown to the non-Brahmins, constitutes welfarism when extended to the untouchables through the 1919 Act, is fallacious. The requirements for the two classes were different. The need for such an extension, as noted, was more political than economic.

The political aftermath of the welfareist assumptions is well documented. Both Gandhi's and Dr. Ambedkar's struggles, though often at variance with each other, remained confined to the limits and notions of welfarism as generated by the 1919 Act. All the battles for welfarism were, inadvertently, fought within the confines of ideologies and fields of praxis that the British had promoted and propagated. Consequently, before the Simon Commission in 1928, Dr. Ambedkar demanded a similar treatment for the untouchables as the non-Brahmins had demanded in 1916, and, as before, the Commission promptly accepted it. In the first Round Table Conference, which Gandhi refused to attend, Dr. Ambedkar went on to demand separate electorates for the untouchables. Gandhi was unable to change the British opinion, in the Second Round Table Conference, that he alone represented the interest of all Indians and especially the untouchables. Consequently, the British drove the axe of division of the Indian people further by announcing the Communal Award in August, 1932 which gave separate political identity not only to Muslims, Christians, and Sikhs but also to the untouchables. Gandhi's subsequent fast into death to revoke separate electorate for the untouchables resulted in the Poona Pact of September, 1932, which set the stage for the subsequent pattern of representation for the untouchables. The Poona Pact, unfortunately, did not make any substantive change in the Communal Award. It did, however, re-establish the Congress claim to equally represent the interests of the untouchables.[19] When Independence came in 1947 Dr. Ambedkar became one of the principle architects of the constitution with the result that it incorporated much of the secular programme he had championed. The evangelical, reformist and secular ideologies, all had significant impact in reconstituting Indian law, and so did the notions of welfarism, as evolved through the 1919 and the 1935 Government of India Act.

A major consequence of constitutionally legitimatizing the Communal Award, including the creation of a new political community of untouchables, has been the antagonistic polarisation of the classes, mainly due to the politicization of such classes. To assure that the recognition of separate political identity necessarily betters economic prospects of a particular group is obviously falacious. The Muslims in India, for example, have not become economically better off merely because the Communal Award gave them a new identity, there is little ground to believe why the situation should be any different in the case of the untouchables. Where some people have became economically better off, there are various other reasons than that of political identity.

This is not to say that a few people have not benefited from preferential treatment; the point is that under a different economic programme (not merely a political one) aimed at all underprivileged people (and not merely at those who can come up to receive it), it is possible that a majority of the people could have benefited. We shall see subsequently what such economic alternative can be. Here it is important to understand the logic of communal politicization. Falsely tying up economic betterment with political or religious identity is historically not a new thing. This has been the usual strategy whenever political forces have wanted to create a new social and economic space for themselves. There are sufficient counter examples to show that the alleged economic advantages do not emerge from political or religious identity, or conversely ,that economic deprivation is not necessarily tied up with alleged political or religious identity. The vast majority of Muslims in Pakistan, for example, did not become economically better off than Indian Muslims; the Jews in the United States are not economically poor because they do not have a political identity, nor are the Indians. Hinduism, Which many orientalists tied up with poverty, has not prevented many Hindus in North of America, Europe, or even India now, from becoming rich.

Antagonistic political polarization has been the main consequence of positive discrimination. It is important to understand the reasons for this. On the classical Madisonian view of representation the parliamentarians represent the will and the interest of only their individual groups. While, in accordance with the utilitarian view, such as that of J.S.Mill, they are supposed to represent the 'people' and hence have the mandate of the nation as a whole. Whereas the People's Representation Act, 1952, attempts, to elect the representatives of the 'people' in India on a utilitarian basis, the constitutional laws, providing separate electorates for minority groups and scheduled castes and tribes, provide the basis for factionalism in interest and hence the necessity of representation of interest groups, in a Madisonian way. Herein lies the reason for the politicization of the preferred groups. Whereas the election laws provide for universal franchise, without taking into account caste, creed, status or sex (including Articles 325, 326 of the Indian Constitution), the laws demarcating grounds for affirmative state action define precisely those characteristics through Presidential orders. Article 330 of the Constitution reserving seats for people who have been identified on the basis of caste and creed, defeats the intent of universal suffrage and the neutrality of the election laws. There are similar contradictions between Articles 15 and 16 which prohibit individuals from discriminating on the basis of religion and cast and Articles 29 and 30 which allow groups to invoke precisely these criteria. The alleged need for tolerance towards such legal contradictions has been the belief that it is the price for alienation of the underprivileged, but this, as we have seen is not happening, nor is there ground to believe that this is the only way amelioration can be achieved. By and large, if it does achieve the economic amelioration of someone, it is of those who have political ambitions. To comprehend this it is important to remember that politics has its own logic.

As opposed to the legal institution, the political institution exists because of the divisions amongst people's interest, identity and future prospects. If there be no such divisions, there will be no conflicts between communities, and if there be no conflicts, no political agents will be required to represent those interests. It is, therefore, essential to the very existence of the political institution that it must constantly seek to create division amongst people, if there be none and if it wishes to continue to exist. The stronger the factions become the more necessary it is to have political agents to negotiate amongst them. This is not to say that all factions and differences amongst people are created by the politicians; there are some genuine situations in the history of societies when political agents are required as representatives to negotiate amongst the factions. However, if a Madisonian type of factionalism is going to be generalized through Constitutional and election laws for all times, then so must be the historical conditions for the existence of representatives of such factions. These are some of the deeper problems in the theory of democracy which cannot be discussed here.[20] However, the consequence of an electoral strategy which promotes or rests on factionalism, can be comprehended without going into any deeper analysis of democracy. It is not surprising, therefore, that the major preoccupation of politicians is creating new vote banks, promoting communal disharmony between Hindus and Muslims, or Hindus and Sikhs, or as of late, between Hindus and Harijans. The goal of secularism promised by the Preamble to the Constitution becomes unattainable because of its the acceptance of the Government of India Act, 1935 in the later part of the Constitution. This 'secular' path cannot lead to the amelioration of the vast majority of the scheduled castes and tribes.

Theories of Poverty

Seeking the answer to the amelioration of the backward classes needs,means first of all, understanding what the basic causes of this backwardness are. Unless the basic causes are identified and dealt with, merely treating the effects of poverty is like trying to treat the ill effect of cancer without being able to get at the root cause. The victim, unfortunately, perishes no matter how potent the ameliorative measures may be. Fortunately, poverty, unlike cancer, is not genetic or natural, it is a condition brought about by human failings. Its cure, therefore, lies in counter-acting such failures. As well and again unlike cancer the type of actions that will bring about poverty, is very well known: those that will take away more from a person than will be returned to him. There is only one way a well or a lake can dry up : if more water is withdrawn from it than is supplied to it by underground or over-ground. Similarly, there is only one way natural forest can be turned into a desert: if more vegetation is felled than the earth can regenerate within the same time period. Exactly the same principle applies to man: a person can become poor only if more is taken away from him than was previously available to him through his own labour or from nature. If poverty has increased in absolute terms than there can be only one basic reason for this: That there has been a continuous exploitation of wealth, both natural and from human labour, of some people.

The major task of social sciences and economics then becomes one of understanding and exposing this process of *impoverishment*; of explaining how and what type of human effort brings about the poverty of others, how it makes them underprivileged, and consequently of seeking and suggesting alternative methods to stop this process.[21] Blinded, as the social sciences are, with the knowledge system of those who seek to exploit both natural and human resources, they are unable to take much interest in these economic and social processes of impoverishment. Instead they limit their interest to describing who the 'poor' are, what the 'poverty-line' is. Numerous variables and parameters are invoked to arrive at the criteria and the debates in this knowledge system multiply into volumes.[22] The social scientists, similarly, spend an enormous amount of their effort in finding out or determining the criteria for lower 'castes'. Undoubtedly, it is important to know who the underprivileged and the poor are, but it is more important to know the processes by which they got there so that we can reverse them. There is very little, however, that economics and social science have provided that will enlighten us by way of theories of impoverishment. Their major time is spent on working out 'theories of development, but whose development? Evidently the development of those who use this knowledge system.

In India's 'garibi-hatao' or anti-poverty programmes, what one may ask , is the underlying theory of poverty? A critical review of the Five-Year Plans reveals that this issue has never been dealt with. Such plans do not ask why such people are poor or who is impoverishing them. The plans begin with the fact of poverty, as though this just naturally occurs like earthquakes so the state then has to provide relief money to sustain the people: The "fact" on the contrary, may stem from the state's own impoverishment programmes. In the absence of a clear understanding of what is causing poverty, the allocation of funds by the center or by the states can at best be arbitrary, in other words, funding is the perspective of poverty elevation, not from that of the government's priorities and felt needs. When, for example, we are told that in the seventh Five-Year Plan the total allocation of funds for poverty alleviation for the scheduled castes and tribes (during 1986-87) was Rs.637.98 crores, how are we to evaluate whether this amount was fair, just, or constitutional? Is there any criteria of entitlement, deserved or merited spelled out? Obviously not since this is impossible without a proper theory of poverty.

Processes of Impoverishments

With reference to Scheduled Castes and Tribes then we have first of all to understand the basic cause for their poverty, that is the methods by which they became impoverished. In what follows I shall identify and outline some of the primary causes and methods of impoverishment. Alternatives for amelioration will then emerge from these outlines. Evidently, each of these identified causes and methods will stand in need of elaboration and further justifications, the alternatives suggested will also require detailed exploration. I shall however, not undertake such an enterprise at this stage. Since this essay is mainly a critique of the affirmative action programme, and perhaps a first radical critique of the Indian situation, it will suffice to lay bare the basic principles on which alternative ameliorative programme can be developed, and which arise from an alternative ideological perspective.

In its most elementary form, a theory of poverty must take into account the following factors:

(a) Generally, the input and output of wealth: Is what the people are getting equivalent, in economic terms, to what they are giving?
(b) Availability, acquisition, and utilization of basic need resources, specially, housing resources, food, fodder resources, water resources, fuel resources.
(c) The utilization of and returns for labour resources;
(d) Community resource management systems;
(e) Forum for conflict resolution.

Each of these factors is a topic for a separate thesis. In general terms however, let us turn now to see how they apply to the actual conditions of the Scheduled Castes and Tribes.

Taking the tribes first, it is well-known that through a series of laws the British took away whatever occupancy and land rights the tribals had in their ancestral forests.[23] The so-called record of rights under the Forest Act are in fact records of some usufruct 'rights' which the forest settlement officers granted them as a privilege. Such rights do not entail getting any compensation for the usufructs in case the government decides to fell all of the trees in area. In deforested area the right are vacuous, not amounting to any further entitlements. Thus even in constitutionally "scheduled areas" where the settlement rights of the tribals are protected, the government has the right to fell trees, make the land barren, and divest the tribals of the enjoyment of any usufruct rights. The British had a consistent policy of exploiting the forests for internal and

European markets.[24] The Indian government has continued with the 1927 Forest Act and reduced the forest coverage to barely 10%.

The enormous amount of wealth that has been taken out of the Indian forests over the last 150 years can be calculated by adding up the total annual revenue for those years, for each of the Indian states, as shown in the Annual Records of the Forest Departments. Taking a very low average estimate of Rupees 40 crores income annually the total revenue yielded for the state and central exchequer amount to about one and half lakh crore rupees.[25] This, figuratively, would have been the value of the wealth at the disposal of the tribals to utilize for their basic needs, if the Indian government had not exploited the forests ruthlessly. The wealth exploited was earlier transferred to Europe; and now it goes to the Indian urban class; it does not go back to the tribals. What goes back is a small fraction of the allocated funds, which in its totality—taking all of the seven five-year plans together—is microscopic as compared to the extent of the wealth which the tribals have been deprived of over the years.[26] This, then, is the general outline of impoverishment, where the input is infinitesimal as compared to the output.

Turning to the basic needs, and beginning with shelter; more than 3000 large and small dams have been built so far in India, most of them in dense forest areas. These dams have submerged not only thousand upon thousand of hectares of rich tropical forests but as well the homesteads of the tribals. There is very little evidence of the ousted ones being properly rehabilitated anywhere. These projects have turned lakhs of tribals into landless labourers.[27]

The impoverishment is not limited to ousting the tribals from their homestead lands. Even where the tribal and the rural poor live on their own land, the cost of housing has been phenomenally increased for them. The tribals and the rural poor built their houses with bamboo timber and mud available naturally in the non-cash economy; this was a wealth at their disposal. Through various legislations, especially the Forest Acts, the governments have usurped the ownership of most of such housing resources, largely because these same resources are required for the paper and pulp industries which produce commodities for the urban class. Tribals and the rural poor—most of whom are Scheduled Castes and Tribes—now buy bamboo in rural areas at a price of Rs.18-20 per bamboo, whereas the same is sold to the industries at subsidized rates, as low as Rs.1/- per ton. Usurpation of the housing resources wealth is thus another way of impoverishing the rural and tribal people. The various forest laws have also been instrumental in taking away the fuel resources from the tribals and the backward classes. [28]

Regulation of food resources involves one in a complex narration. Here there is a systematic neglect of indigenous food resources and habits as well as also of local irrigation and agricultural practices. State-supported scientific research has sought the propagation of monocultures, of wheat or varieties of rice. It has not sought to improve the yields of what the people have been traditionally eating in those regions, and about which there have been systems of traditional knowledge, both in nutritional and agricultural practices. The common property base for food resources in the non-cash economy has been gradually eroded or privatized in favour of a controlled market, as a consequence of which the prices of essential commodities in the village are often more than those in the urban areas. The usurpation of common lands, such as village forests, *goachar*, *shamlats*, *parambokes*, etc, for purposes of industry, public services, and domicile has also resulted in a phenomenal increase in fodder prices for cattle in the villages.[29] The technology for irrigation has been of a type which has benefited the agricultural practices of only the rich landlords or those with large consolidated holdings; it leaves out all marginal farmers and landless labourers.[30] In short, the whole food policy and agricultural planning in India has assured further impoverishment of the landless labourers, marginal farmers, and tribals most of whom belong to the scheduled category.

Turning to the scheduled castes, most of whom are landless agricultural labourers or semi-skilled craftsmen, it becomes important to consider the labour laws. Agriculture labour is officially governed by the Minimum Wages Act, which in rural areas is often followed in the breach, that is, the daily wages are even lower than what the Act prescribes. The point is not about the non-implementation of the Act, but its very rationale. Why one must ask, is the state trying to ensure that the labourers get the minimum wage? The basic argument is that the state wants to make sure that such people get at least the minimum wage for the subsistence level, given the general exploitative nature of the labour market. This argument looks very sound, on the face of it, and has consequently continued to fool people for generations. An inquiring mind must ask: what is the basis of the assumption that a state must strive to get at least the "minimum" for the labourers; why not at most the maximum? Which welfare theory or which economic policy of this country assigns to the state the role of seeking only the minimum? Should not a state which is genuinely interested in the welfare of the people attempt to get for the underprivileged people the maximum it can within the economic and labour market structure? One must emphasize, it is not a matter of semantic quibble here between the terms "minimum" and "maximum" it is a matter of two totally different perspectives on welfare theory. Consider the fact that when the trade unions bargain for the wages, they seek the maximum from the employers. Similarly, private enterprise tries to pay the maximum to their senior employees. Maximum here means the highest competitive wages within the market system, which on the one hand will allow the employers to retain the employees, and on the other, guarantee the enterprise's economic continuity. The government's pay commission, too, works on the basis that it determines the fair or the best salary payable within the concerned economic infrastructure; so does the University Grants' Commission vis-a-vis its employees. Why then, when it comes to the poor, must the state make a volte-face, and seek the enforcement of minimum wages.

To understand the double standard involved in the enforcement of wages and determination of salaries, one must look at the deeper presuppositions of the Minimums Wages Act and the rules made thereunder. The wages under this Act are determined by finding out the subsistence requirements of the poorest (in terms of housing, food, clothing, and other needs) and then translating them into fiscal terms by using the price index.[31] Fixing the wages in this manner amounts to the following statement by the state: "Look, we need your labour; we have found out what is required by you to keep your soul and body together; through our laws we will bother ourselves only to make sure that you continue in this state". The Minimum Wages Act, thus, becomes a powerful instrument in the hands of the upper classes to maintain the status quo of subsistence, since this is all they are required to pay, and a social legitimization by the state of the exploitation of labour. The labour of the vast majority of scheduled castes and tribes comes under the purview of the Minimum Wages Act. The double standard of wages and salaries, one for the private and public sectors and another for the agricultural and unorganized labour sector, ensures impoverishment of the latter and gradual enrichment of the former.

The exploitation of tribal labour is even more striking. It is, by and large, not even governed by the Minimum Wages Act; it is governed by labour rules under the Forest Acts, wherein the wages are even lower than under the Minimum Wages Act. Most of the forests in India, ironically, have been felled by using tribal labour by the Forest Departments or contractors, with ridiculously low wages governed by the Forest Act.

The impoverishment of community resources management systems and local mechanisms for conflict resolution is correlated with the loss of power over locally available natural resources and exploitation of labour. As the resources and fruits of labour have been usurped gradually, the necessity to retain the traditional management systems has become redundant. Community resources, such as wells, tanks, grazing lands, village forests, minor forest produce, wild life, including fish, birds, etc, have all been traditionally managed in the villages by indigenous management systems which are governed by customary laws and practices. These systems have been grossly impoverished by enactments of the Panchayat Acts, in which the traditional systems find no representation and the panchayat themselves lack all economic powers. A "development" administration at block levels has been superimposed on these panchayats which has little to do with local systems of management or traditional resource use.

All this is only an outline of the massive impoverishment programme that the governments have been undertaking. Considering their size and impact all anti-poverty, garibi-hatao and poverty alleviation schemes pale into insignificance when a wholistic loss-benefit analysis is done, that is when who is locating control, possession and utilization of resources and who is gaining it is considered. The analysis here has limited itself to the basic needs and labour resources. When the larger context of natural resources utilization, such as of ores, electricity and land, is taken, a more dismal picture will appear. The poverty that the state is trying to get rid of is one that it itself, perpetuates, at a much faster rate and to an amazingly greater extent, than the rates at which any anti-poverty programme can work.In the light of this, any evangelical, secular, philanthropic, or altruistic affirmative state action for scheduled castes and tribes is a sheer mockery or hypocrisy.

Let us turn now to take stock of the basic principles that cannot do justice in any poverty alleviation programme and those that can. To begin with, a radical reorientation is required in perspective and planning for poverty removal schemes. This emerges from our understanding that poverty is not a state; it is not a condition of misfortune which naturally belongs to the human condition; it is an end result of a process of impoverishment, the root cause of which lies in the acquisition, distribution, and utilization of natural resources, including labour resources.

Our current ameliorative programmes and planning are based on an assumption that poverty is a natural social condition—perhaps an act of God—which has to be tolerated, and that it is the task of a benevolent state to somehow bring the people up from below the poverty line. In such an assumption both the real causes of poverty and the real nature of the state get hidden. The evangelical benevolent welfarism of the state turns out to be a farce because the state itself has and continues to perpetuate poverty. The actual amount of wealth distributed to the people through the schemes, such as the Integrated Rural Development Programme, the National Rural Employment Programme, the Tribal Welfare Programme etc, is miniscule as compared to the natural wealth they are being deprived of. The secular philanthropy of reserving seats in the legislature does indeed bring about economic benefits to the politicians, but it leaves the vast majority untouched.[32] Reservation of seats in educational and employment opportunities has again benefited few,[33] but from the perspective of equity and justice the question is not how many it has benefited but is it a right state policy in principle? Such reservation, as we have seen, amounts to showing disrespect for certain types of human labour and skills. Such a state policy is not only contrary to human dignity but an antithesis of the Gandhian philosophy.

So much for the critique of the existing ameliorative programmes and the ideologies that motivate them. Let us turn to see what type of programmes can possibly be conducive to poverty occasion and what types of principles must amelioration be based on. What can be indicated here is the framework and the basic directions; the details will need to be explored once the general perspective is comprehended.

Conservation and generation of assets at the local rural level need prime attention, especially those concerning basic needs. Evidently, conservation and generation require two different strategies, and both of them require their own respective organizational and managerial infrastructures.

The basic principles which direct the state to remove impoverishment are already embodied in the Constitution; one does not have to go very far to seek them.

These provisions of the Constitution (as provided in Article 39) pertain to natural resources—the material resources of the community, such as common water tanks, rivers, lakes, village forests, gochar land, embankments, and coastal areas. In its full connotation they also include ores, minerals, hydrocarbons, coal the sun-light and the air. In short all common property resources which are naturally at man's disposal for use and which are to be utilized to serve the common good. The material resources that these common property resources yield provide the means of livelihood for the vast majority of scheduled castes and tribes.

Now, the basic question is, are our natural resource laws in accordance with the constitutional directives? Most of these laws are products of the colonial period and no fundamental revision has been made in any of these laws so far. It is therefore unlikely to expect that they would be consistent with the Constitution. The Forest Laws, which deprive the rural and tribal people of fuel, fodder, food and housing resources, are of 1927 vintage. They give the government unlimited power to oust the people from any forest, by mere notification.[34] The forest laws together with the Land Acquisition Act of 1894, not only deprive the people of land resources, they have scant respect for rehabilitation and compensation to ousted ones.[35] The water laws, similarly, take away all power from the people to decide on agricultural and domestic water needs. There is a large corpus of natural resources laws in India and common to them all is not only their colonial exploitative nature but also the fact that they are at gross variance with the post-Independence Indian Constitution. Article 13 of the Constitution says that all pre-Independence laws, before the commencement of the Constitution, which are inconsistent with the fundamental rights, shall be void. The natural task for the Indian law-makers would be to find out how many and which aspects of the pre-Independence law violate fundamental rights, especially those which concern the immediate life and livelihood of the people, and then to declare them void. No such task has been undertaken so far. Even where it can be demonstratably shown that some natural resources laws (such as the Indian Forest Act, 1927) are in violation of fundamental rights, neither the courts nor the judiciary has bothered to amend them so far.[36]

If cessation of impoverishment is to be achieved, the immediate task before the Indian legislature and government is to amend the natural resources laws so that they are in keeping with the Constitution, especially Articles 39 (a), (b) and (c). The forest laws for example, will have to be amended so that the forests are used for the common good, that is, for benefits which include the poor rural and tribal people. Housing, fuel, and fodder needs of such people must take priority in the forest laws. So far the forest produce has been used mainly for the good of the urban and the rich people.

Social forestry needs to aim at recreation of permanent village forests so that assets are build up at the local village levels.[37] Common lands and village forest lands which have been taken away from the villages through various forest and land laws need to be re-allocated to the villages, as permanent pastures or forests for local use only. This will require some major amendments to the Land Reform and Land Development laws. Such laws have not concerned themselves with development of pastures or forests for rural purposes. In the name of "reform" and "development" they have cared only for acquisition and utilization which end up in favouring the rich.

There is a need to a new, and appropriate land use policy. This must concern itself not only with agriculture but with forestry needs, pasture land needs, and housing settlement needs at the rural levels.[37]

What is true of other basic needs is also true for water. The state has propagated a technology for water harvesting and utilization which has grossly neglected the creation of water assets at the rural levels. Even the traditionally available assets, such as common tanks, ponds and wells, have been reclaimed for agricultural purposes. The poverty alleviation programme requires first, a protection and conservation of the still existing water resources at the rural levels, for rural needs, and second a massive investment in the re-creation of water assets, common tanks, wells, etc. so that the rural people are not entirely dependent for their water needs on external sources.

Regeneration of natural assets and their protection against inequitable exploitation by outsiders, requires some basic infrastructural changes. This necessitates major amendments in the Panchayat Acts. Under the existing Acts although common lands, forests and water tanks, ponds, etc. are vested in the panchayats, they are deprived of all legal power to keep them for village use if they want to. The Land Acquisition Act overrides the panchayat's whenever they wish. Also , the panchayats have been granted negligible funds to be able to maintain the common rural assets.

In their poverty alleviation programmes the Ministries of Rural Development, Environment and Forest; Agriculture; Social welfare; and others, work through new village level organizations such as Village Development Committees; Village Forest Committees; Mahila Samitis, Yuvak Mandal Dals; etc. Such associations are adhoc creations and have no legal capacity to bargain. Besides being in conflict with the existing panchayats, the creation of such organizations is a farce. It is a replication of organization without understanding the reason for the failure of the earlier organization, namely the panchayats.[39] The state, through its laws, has first of all totally incapacitated the elected association of the rural people. It then goes out to create new associations, with even lesser capacities, and then hopes there will be rural development. What is required is not creation of new rural development organizations, but an understanding of why the existing one does not work, and then amending and facilitating in all ways so that it works. For the creation, protection, and utilization of assets at the rural level, by the rural people, for poverty alleviation, it is necessary first to vest land, for common use, for forests, grazing and tanks, in the panchayats, where such rights do not already exist. Most villages now do not have such forests, gochars, or tanks. On the other hand great areas of lands now with the Forest and Revenue Departments are precisely those which were usurped by them from the villages. These and the surplus land acquired by them need to be redistributed to the villages, as common lands vested in the panchayats. The panchayat Acts would have to be amended to endorse the non-alienability of such lands (and water resources) and the non-transferability of their use. The income from such assets and additional revenues from the state and the centre will also necessitate appropriate change in the Acts. The point here is not about the various necessary changes in the panchayat Acts—these can be worked out but about the fact that such an Act should, in the first instance, ensure creation, protection, and utilization of the natural resources for the rural people and under their own control.[40]

In-so-far as the basic principle concerning labour resource is concerned, this too is laid down in the Constitution: Act.38(2):

'The State shall, in particular, strive to minimize the inequalities in income, and endeavour to eliminate inequalities in status, facilities and opportunities, not only amongst individuals but also amongst groups of peoples residing in different areas or engaged in different vocations.'

This clearly includes the tribals who reside in particular areas and the scheduled castes who are engaged in different vocations. As we have seen, through the Forest Laws and the Minimum Wages Act, the State has endeavoured to achieve precisely the opposite of what the Constitution demands. If poverty alleviation is desired, these unconstitutional provisions need to be immediately amended so that the skilled or semi-skilled labour of the scheduled caste (including agricultural labour) and tribal labour (including that involved in the collection and sale of minor forest produce) will receive the maximum, and not the minimum, wage. In fact article 43 of the Constitution directs the state to legislate labour laws which will yield living wages and not those which will maintain the people at a mere subsistence level. Interestingly, Article 37 clearly states that all directive principles are fundamental in the governance of the country. Neither the Planning Commission, nor the Finance Ministry and not even the Prime Minister's Cabinets have ever found it necessary to consult the Constitution while drawing up any plan to govern the country. Unless those who govern abide by the Constitution, it is difficult to see how the situation of the poor can be bettered.

The framework of thought and facts presented here do not in themselves provide detailed action plans for poverty alleviation, but they provide the necessary background and understanding from which specific actions can emerge. The crux of the argument has been to show that poverty is a consequence of how the wealth of a nation is utilized, and by whom. Alternative strategies for poverty alleviation must address themselves directly to the utilization of this wealth, especially when it concerns basic needs, resources, and the dignity of human labour. The work has also presented a critique of the existing ameliorative programmes, exposing their ideological and historical roots and showing their true character within the capitalistic economy.

NOTES

1. Galanter, Marc., "Compensatory Discrimination in Political Representation: A Preliminary Assessment of India's Thirty Year Experience with Reserved Seats in Legislatures." *Economic and Political Weekly* XIV 437-54 (1979).

2. Galanter, Marc., *Competing Equalities*, Oxford; New Delhi 1984.

3. Ambedkar's basic political and legal ideologies are clearly outlined in his *State and Minorities: What Are Their Rights and How to Secure Them in the Constitution of Free India*. Thacker & Co. Bombay 1948. Also his 1916 monograph: *Caste*

in India: *Their Mechanism, Genesis and Development,* is revealing.

4. For a more detailed account of legal paternalism see: Chhatrapati Singh, 'Ideological Root of Legal Paternalism' in *Indian Journal of the Indian Law Institute,* Vol.24:1, 1982.

5. Burke, Edmund, *Works* Vol. VI at 384 (1852); Ninth Report of the Select Committee on the Indian Affairs (1783).

6. Fifth Report of the Select Committee on Affairs of the East India Company, 18 Ordered by the House of Commons to be printed on 28th July 1812.

7. Charles Ross (Ed.), I, *Correspondence of Marquis Cornwallis,* Vol. I at 554. "Dispatch to Court of Directors." 2nd August, 1789.

8. For an extended discussion of the influence of the utilitarian in India see Eric Stokes, *The English Utilitarians and India* (1959).

9. See J. Fitzjames Stephen's *Liberty, Equality, Fraternity* (1875); see also Hunter: *Life Of Mayo,* Vol.II (1875). Stephen's view is summerised in the letter to The Times of 4th January, 1820.

10. Mill, James, *History of British India,* Vol. V at 479 (2nd Ed.) 1820.

11. Hunter: *Life of Mayo,* Vol.II, at 165-166 (1875).

12. Galanter, Marc., *Competing Equalities,* pp.81-82.

13. Ibid. p. 81, 106.

14. Ibid. p. 82, 107.

15. For example, S.V.Pande, "The politicization of the Special Constitutional Provisions and the Perpetuation of Casteism." XVI *Indian Political Science Review* (1980).

16. In 1909 when the Minto-Morley reforms were promulgated, separate electorates were provided for the Muslims. For discussions see: Zelliott, Eleasnor, "Dr. Ambedkar and the

Mahar Movement. " Ph. D. Dissertation, University of Pennsylvania in *Indian Review,* September 1910: and in *Contemporary Review* 1913 (103: 376-85).

17. The Government of (British) India, on the one hand, professed to refrain from any official classification of people (until 1936) on the ground that it would be unfair to stigmatize people (See: The Indian Statutory Commission, 1930: V, 1341), and on the other hand, promulgated various government bodies to make official estimates of the numbers. The Franchise (South Borough) Committee which was established to advise on the franchise (separate electorates) under the 1919 reforms, found 42.2 millions of the Depressed Classes in India. Since there were one-third as many more in the princely States, a figure of 50-60 million was acceptable. The 1921 census and the Reforms Enquiry (Muddiam) Committee of 1924 arrived at comparable figures. The grounds for political divisions and stigmatization of people were thus being worked out from the very beginning, despite the proposed official policy to the contrary.

18. On the isolation of the untouchables from non-Brahmin movements see: Irschick, Eugene F. *Politics and Social Conflicts in South India: The non-BrahminMovement And Tamil Separatism. 1916-1929.* Berkeley: University of California Press.

19. Ambedkar, B.R. 'What Congress and Gandhi have done to the Untouchables' 2nd edn. the Bombay; Thacker & Co.1946. See also Lelah Dusbkir, "The Policy of Indian National Congress Towards the Depressed Classes: A Historical Study. "University of Pennsylvania.1957.

20. For a more detailed analysis of the issues see: Chhatrapati Singh,' The Idea of Political Representation' *Philosophias.* 1 (1981), University of Ottawa.

21. For a more detailed critique of the social science see Upendra Baxi's 'Introduction' to Baxi (Ed.) *Law and Poverty* Tripathi. Bombay.1988.

22. For example, V.M. Dandekar and N.Rath "Poverty in India" VI *Economic and Political Weekly* 31 (1974); also, P.Bardhan, "On the incidence of Poverty in Rural India in th Sixties. "VIII

Economic and Political Weekly 245 (1973); D.S.Tyagi, "How Valid are the Estimates of Trends in Rural Poverty?" XVII *Economic and Political Weekly* A 54-62 (1982).

23. Singh, Chhatrapati, *Common Property and Common Poverty* Oxford. Delhi 1985. See also; Baden-Powell: *Manual of Jurisprudence for the Forest Officers*, Calcutta 1882.

24. Guha, Ramchandra, "Forestry in Pre-British India." *Economic and Political Weekly*. Vol XViii No. 44-45, 1983.

25. This is a very rough estimate calculated merely to make the point. The actual value of each tree, taking into account the soil it conserves, the biomass produced, water retention, shade, etc., would be far greater than the cost of mere timber. The forest department do not take into account the actual economic and social value of trees, merely the current market value of timber. For a discussion on the actual socio-economic cost of submergence of tree in one case—the Tehri dam, see: Vajay Paranjpye: *Evaluating the Tehri Dam* INTACH, New Delhi 1988. See also, Chhatrapati Singh & P.K. Chaudhary: *Dam and the Law* Indian Law Institute, New Delhi. 1987.

26. Even according to the Planning Commission's own evaluations of the poverty alleviation programmes, scheduled castes and scheduled tribes have remained relatively unaffected by the implementation of the programmes. As of 1983-84 the per capita consumption expenditure per month of the scheduled castes and tribes was respectively Rs.67.08 and Rs.61.44, as compared with Rs. 70.94 for all below the poverty line. See: C.H. Hanumanth Rao, "Changes in Rural Poverty in India" in XXIV *Mainstream* 9 (Jan.11, 1986). Other official reports too bring out a similar story about the poorest of the poor. See; Evaluation Report on Integrated Rural Development Programme (Government of India, Planning Commission, Programme Evaluation Organization,1985) National Bank for Agriculture and Rural Development's 'Study of Implementation of Integrated Rural Development programme" (Mimeo, not dated); Reserve Bank of India's Report of the Committee to review Arrangement for Institutional Credit for Agriculture and Rural Development (1981). Even independent research and studies bring out a

similar non-efficacy of the anti-poverty programmes, especially with reference to the scheduled castes and tribes. See, for example Sandeep Bagchee, "Poverty Alleviation Programmes in the Seventh Plan" in *Economic and Political Weekly* XXII, 139 (1987) ; Mukul Sanwal, "Garibi Hatao: Improving Implementation," in *Economic and Political Weekly*, XX 2176 (1985)' V.M. Rao, "Changing Village Structure: Impact of Rural Development Programme" *Economic and Political Weekly* XXII, A-2 (1987).

27. The details of those ousted because of dams are recorded in various reports of the Irrigation Commission and the Central Water Commission, Studies of their rehabilitation problems, however, are very few. See , for example, Vidyut Joshi, Submerging Villages: Problems and Prospects, Ajanta Books ..Delhi, 1988.

28. For more details concerning the forest situation in India and the Government's policy for the sale of timber, especially bamboo, see: *The State of India's Environment: A Citizen's Report* (1984-85) Centre for Science and Environment, New Delhi. pp.50-98. The price and labour involved in cooking (fuel price) in rural area is now many times more than in urban areas, because the cost and amount of gas or electricity required for cooking is urban areas is far less than the cost of timber or kerosene in rural areas. For details see A Citizen's Report (ibid) pp.146-161.

29. See *India's Environment : A Citizen's Report* (1986) pp. 3-14. Also: Brara. H., Shifting Sands. Institute of Development Studies, Jaipur. 1986 Jodha. N.S. 'Farming Systems in Dry-Tropical Region of India." ICRISAT. Hyderabad 1986.

30. *The Citizen's Report* (1982), pp. 15, 29; 1986: pp. 27-42.

31. Chopra, D.C., '*The Minimum Wages Act, 1948*' Eastern Law House, Calcutta. 1981. pp. 90-134.

32. Galanter, Marc., *Competing Equalities*, pp.44-45.

33. *Ibid*.pp.55-64.

34. For an analysis of the unconstitutional aspects of the forest laws see Chhatrapati Singh, *Common Property and Common Poverty*, Oxford University Press. New Delhi 1986.

35. The *Citizen's Report* (1985), pp.103-110. See also: Proceedings of the "Workshop on Rehabilitation" Indian Social Institute, New Delhi-1988.

36. For a more detailed discussion see: J.Bandhopadhyay, Chhatrapati Singh, N.Jayal. (ed.): *India' Environment: Crises and Response*, Natraj Pub. Dehradun 1986.pp247-275.

37. For details see the Social Forestry project appraisal reports done by Chhatrapati Singh for the Government of Tamilnadu and SIDA (1985); Govts. of Rajasthan, Gujarat, Himachal Pradesh and Uttar Pradesh, and the World Bank (1988): Govt. of Orissa and DANIDA, (1987); Govt. of Bihar and SIDA (1985). Govt of India (National Wasteland Development Board, Ministry of Environment and Forests, 6 Volume Reports), 1986.

38. The abstracts of the 6 Volume Reports has some discussion on this issue: Chhatrapati Singh 'Forestry and the Law' in *Journal of the Indian Law Institute*, Vol.29"1,1987.

39. For some relevant discussions see: Vijay Kumar, *Panchayati Raj*, Ph.D. dissertation, University of Kurukshetra, 1988.

40. Singh, Chhatrapati, *Panchayats, Forestry and the Law*. Report submitted to the Ministry of Environment and Forests, National Wasteland Development Board. 1986.

6

ARADHANA PARMAR

WOMEN AND THE LAW

In the last few years there have been significant changes in the laws affecting women, as well as in the role of women in the Indian society. These changes are not accidental but the result of certain discernible trends such as an increase in literacy and education among the masses, an increasing acceptance of the principle of equality of sexes, increased awareness in society of the injustice done to women in the past, and an increasingly progressive judicial approach to the various issues of women. These trends called for a change in the traditional role of women and their participation on equal terms with men in political, social, economic, and cultural life. Consequently, new thinking on the questions of women has started at all levels of society, including the areas of law-making and enforcement of law.

The effort in this study is to analyze the relationship between law and women from the ancient to the modern times. The status of women has varied greatly through the ages owing to political and cultural reasons, and the difference between the freedom and importance of women in ancient times and their subservience in the modern age is striking. A survey of ancient literature shows that the journey of women has been downhill. The concern for the rights of women which voiced itself continually was largely smothered by the duplicity and hypocrisy of society toward women. In theory, society placed women on a high pedestal but in practice it made them the receptacle of its frustrations, fears, and perversions. The Indian society has demonstrated a schizophrenic personality insofar as its attitude to women is concerned, and this split is evident in its social and sexual morality as well as in its laws. One of the best ways to understand the spirit of a civilization and appreciate its excellence and limitations is to study the history of the status of women in it. In the infant stages of social evolution, no other social group experienced such absolute dependence upon men as did the women, and the degree to which this dependence has been voluntarily reduced serves as a rough test of the justice and fair play developed in a community.

The different periods which saw marked fluctuations in the status of women are broadly three : 1) the Vedic age (up to 500 B.C.) ; 2) the post-Vedic age (500 B.C. to the advent of Muslims in India) ; and 3) the Muslim, the British, and the post-independence period. The first two periods constitute the ancient past of India ; the third, the modern age.

The Ancient Period

Information regarding the position of women in the earliest periods of Indian history presented in this section relates to the elite sections of society, viz., the high castes and the upper strata. Very little material is available on the conditions of the life of women from the non-elite groups. In the patriarchal school system of the Vedic age, the cultured parents were as anxious to have a daughter as they were to beget sons. A rational social set-up ensured numerous opportunities for girls and prevented them from being a burden on their parents. They could be initiated in Vedic studies and were entitled to offer sacrifices to gods, a function for which a son was not absolutely necessary. In the Vedic age, the marriage of the daughter was not a difficult problem and was often solved by the daughter herself. A liberal atmosphere added to the status of women and therefore the birth of a girl in the family was by no means unwelcome.

Marriage was a sacramental affair and many religious and social ceremonies were incomplete without the presence of the wife on the occasion. The marriage of girls took place at the age of 16 to 17, and the educated brides had an effective voice in the selection of their life partners. In royal and rich families there were instances of polygamy though monogamy was the rule. The wife was not a shadow of her husband and had an independent self. If her husband died, she did not have to ascend her husband's funeral pyre,[1] as she had to in later periods. The *sati* custom, as it developed later, was unknown. On the contrary, she was allowed to remarry either in a regular fashion or under the custom of *Niyoga*.[2]

The main disability that women suffered from in the Vedic age was that they did not enjoy proprietary rights : they could not hold or inherit any property. Nevertheless, the overall position of women in the Vedic time was fairly satisfactory and respectable.

In the post-Vedic age, the position of women in India deteriorated considerably. By 500 B.C., the Aryans were well-established in India and had taken to a life of ease and luxury. In the Vedic age, the father was anxious to have strong and numerous sons, more for secular than religious reasons. In the post-Vedic age, the son had become a religious rather than a secular necessity.[3] The marriageable age of boys and girls began to be lowered. One of the major adverse consequences of lowering the marriageable age of girls was that the *Upanayana*[4] and education of girls were discouraged. The very young and inexperienced brides ceased to have any effective voice in the settlement of their marriages. Quite often the parents were in a hurry to give away their daughters in marriage before they attained puberty, and the matches were often ill-suited. Under these circumstances, the ill-equipped and immature wife could not but be subservient to her husband and this started the tale of unbridled domination of female by the male in Indian society.

During this period, the marriages of Aryan men with non-Aryan women became common. The introduction of the non-Aryan wife into the Aryan household was mainly responsible for the general deterioration in the status of women. The non-Aryan wife with her ignorance of the Sanskrit language and Hindu religion obviously could not enjoy the same religious privileges as the Aryan consort. It appears that the orthodox priests were shocked at the gross mistakes made by the non-Aryan wife who was otherwise the favourite of her husband and was associated with religious ceremonies. To save the situation, the custodians of religion declared that the non-Aryan wife was unfit for association with her husband in such ceremonies.[5] But a mighty king who was infatuated with his non-Aryan beloved, would ignore the wishes of priests who were dependent upon him for their subsistence and would insist upon having his own favourite of her race and caste. To achieve their objective, the priests eventually declared the whole class of women to be ineligible for Vedic studies and religious duties. This new arrangement would not hurt any one section of women for it denied rights to all women indiscriminately.[6]

By this period, the age of city or small states was over and the Hindu Kingdom had become fairly extensive. The splendour of royal courts had increased and kings had begun to keep much biggar "harems" than those dreamt of in earlier times. Such example was followed by their numerous feudatories and rich subjects. The growing harems of kings made them jealous and some of them sought to keep their wives in seclusion. This seclusion of women, however, was confined only to a very small section of the royal families and a majority of kings did not care to adopt it. But the new developments had very unfavourable consequences for the status of women of all classes, including the widows. They strengthened the hands of those who were opposed to *Niyoga* and widow remarriage. No doubt, *Niyoga* deserved to be stamped out, but widow remarriage was desirable.

Further erosion of the rights of women in all areas, except that of proprietary rights, continued. Significantly, the right of the widow to inherit her husband's property came to be recognized all over the country by 1200 A.D. On the other hand, the deterioration in the condition of women was reflected in the fact that *Upanayana* of women went completely out of vogue; women came to be regarded as the equals of Sudras. The marriageable age of girls, with the exception of Kshatriya's, was lowered to 10 or 8; widow marriage was prohibited. Only among the Kshatriyas, girls continued to be married at the age of 14 or 15, for the Kshatriya father always dreaded the possibility of his son-in-law dying in the frequent warfare before his daughter had come of age. In fact, many Kshatriya ladies were called upon to assume the reins of government as regents; therefore training in administrative duties and military exercises had to be given to them. This also necessitated the postponement of their marriage to a somewhat advanced age.

In contrast, the non-Kshatriya girls, who were married at the age of 10 or 11, received no worthwhile education. In the beginning, only a widow from a respectable high caste family could not remarry whatever her age might have been at the time of her husband's death, but in due course remarriage was adopted even by those lower castes which were anxious to "Sanskritize" and gain respectability. The prejudice against widow remarriage was so deep-rooted that the legislation passed in the matter much later by the British rulers in 1856 A.D. allowing widows to remarry had no appreciable effect on the situation for more than half a century.

A greater calamity that befall the widow during this period was the *Sati* introduction system. It was started among the warrior castes but it gradually spread throughout the society. The action of *Sati* came to be regarded as a great religious sacrifice which deserved to be imitated. Despite vehement opposition by some, the custom continued. The custom of *Sati* came to be surrounded by a halo. Even the Brahmans adopted the custom, as they did not like to be excelled by the Kshatriyas in the pursuit of ascetic practices. Widows now had dismal prospects : they could not only not remarry but also had to ascend the funeral pyres of their husband.

Modern Period

Muslim : The Muslim rulers, as a rule, did not like the *Sati* Custom. Humayun (ruler from 1530 to 1555 A.D.) unsuccessfully tried to ban it in the case of widows who had passed the child-bearing age. In the later part of his reign, Akbar (ruler 1556-1605 A.D.) also opposed the custom. He appointed inspectors to see that no force was used to compel widows to practise *Sati* against their will. As a consequence, *Satis* became a rare phenomenon in the surrounding areas of Agra, practically the whole of north India. However, the custom remained firmly entrenched in the ruling Rajput families of north India. The average Rajput princess preferred to be a *Sati* and would not allow her husband to be cremated alone.

As regards the Sikhs, Amardas, the third Sikh Guru, condemned the *Sati* custom, and it was not followed by them for a long time. But when Sikhs developed into a fighting community, they did not like to lag behind the Rajputs in following the time-honoured traditions, including the practice of *Sati*. Consequently, the *Sati* custom became common in the Sikh aristocracy in spite of its prohibition by the Gurus.[7]

Another system supported and strengthened by the Muslims was the *Purdah* system (veil). The *Purdah* system was confined to a small section of the Hindu society up to the beginning of the 11th century A.D. With the advent of Muslim rule, it started spreading to different communities. There were several reasons for the adoption of the custom. The times were unsettled and there was a general feeling of insecurity. The Hindu life and honour did not count much for the conquerors. The *Purdah* offered an additional protection from the unscrupulous soldiery to the beautiful women while out on a journey. It became quite common among the rich Hindu families of north India in the

Women and The Law

15th and 16th centuries. In Rajputana, the custom became universal among the ruling families and was regarded as an essential insignia of respectability and high breeding. Women of the peasant and working classes could not of course afford to remain in seclusion, for they had to move out for their daily work.

British : By 1850 the condition of women further deteriorated. Literacy among the Hindu women had reached its lowest.[8] Feeble attempts were made by the British Government in India to improve this situation by providing educational opportunities to women. However progress remained very slow, primarily because the girls were married at the ages of nine or ten and could attend school only for three or four years.

The radical changes in the political climate of the country did have a tremendous impact on the *Sati* system. Lord William Bentick launched a personal crusade against the system and in December 1829, declared the custom illegal in British India. His subordinate English officers were opposed to his reform and considered it an act of interference in the personal religious affairs of the Hindus. The 1829 regulation to the Privy Council was met with resentment by the orthodox Hindus. The appeal to declare the regulation illegal was, however, supported only by 800 signatures. The enlightened Hindu opinion welcomed the new regulation, and a memorandum was presented to the Governor General for his humane step. Raja Ram Mohan Roy went to England and pleaded with the members of the Privy Council not to annul the new regulation. Impressed by his advocacy, the authorities in England rejected the pro-*Sati* memorandum in 1832. Though the custom of *Sati* was prohibited in British India, it continued to prevail in different parts of the country, especially in Rajputana where it was most strongly entrenched.

During the subsequent years, some Hindu widows who intensely believed that it was their religious duty to accompany their dead husbands tried to ascend the funeral pyres, but they were usually prevented from achieving their object by the public and the police. The practice of *Sati* is not totally dead in India today but its occurrence is almost negligible.

The *Purdah* system was dealt a serious blow during the Indian nationalist movement when women joined it by the thousands. Education was another factor which brought Indian women out of their secluded environment.

Post-Independence India

Women's participation in the nationalist movement made them equal partners in the nation-building tasks which lay ahead in an independent India. They received rights that had been won in the West only after a long struggle. The urban women, in particular, made rapid headway in almost every walk of life. The founding fathers remembered the contribution of women to the nationalist movement and were aware of the potential of women. They made necessary provision in the Constitution to guarantee equal rights and equal opportunities to women. After independence, the states and the Centre took measures for the betterment of women. The most significant step was the reform of Hindu Law, recognising women's right to property, divorce, guardianship, etc., on a nearly equal footing with men. After 41 years of independence, a favourable change in the status of urban women is clearly visible, but there is not much evidence of such a change in the rural areas.

The Constitution of free India, adopted on January 26, 1950, guarantees certain fundamental rights to all Indians irrespective of their religion, gender, and race (Article 14). The Constitution ensures social, economic, and political justice; liberty of thought, expression, belief, faith, and worship; equality of status and opportunity; and dignity of the individual. It also lays down certain goals which the state should realise over a period of time. Besides, certain classes of persons who by themselves are not able to get the full benefit of the socio-economic change, have been given special protection.

While all the provisions of the Constitution are applicable in equal measure to men and women, parts III and IV are of special significance to women.

Protective legislation for women is enshrined in these sections. The phrase "equality before law" has been further elaborated in Article 15 (1) which lay down that the state "shall not discriminate against any citizen" on the ground of sex or on any other ground. However, the provision of non-discrimination on this account does not prevent the state from making special provisions for women and children as has been laid down in Article 15 (3). Thus, while discrimination against women is prohibited, there is no pressure to discriminate in their favour with a view to providing them with special facilities or to solving their special problems.

Another important provision which is an extension of the principle of equality before law, is equality in the matter of employment or appointment under the state. Article 16 (1) states : "There shall be equality of opportunity for all citizens in matters of employment or appointment to any office under the state." And Article 16 (2) provides : "No citizen shall, on grounds of religion, race, caste, sex, descent, place of birth, residence, or any of them be ineligible or discriminated against in respect of any employment or office under the state." In the light of these provisions, a woman has the same rights in the matter of employment under the state as a man.

Part IV of the Constitution has some special provisions for the welfare of women and for the improvement in their social and economic status. The Directive Principles of State Policy proclaim that "the citizens, men and women equally, have the right to an adequate means of livelihood" (Article 39 (9)).

Some other provisions in the Constitution concerning women provide "that there is equal pay for equal work for both men and women;" "that the health and strength of workers, men and women, and the tender age of children are not abused and that citizens are not forced by economic necessity to enter evocations unsuited to their age or strength"; and "that childhood and youth are protected against exploitation and against moral and material abandonment." Besides, Article 42 provides that the "state shall make provisions for securing just and humane conditions of work and maternity relief." The 1961 Maternity Benefit Act provide women employees, in different types of employment, maternity relief in the form of leave of up to 90 days with full wages.

The Constitution assigns supremacy to law as an instrument of directed social change. It demands of the legislature, judiciary, and executive continuous vigilance and responsiveness to the relationship between law and social transformation in contemporary India. However, despite these provisions in the Constitution, there were no serious efforts on the part of the various state governments and the Central Government to treat women as a separate category and to assess their progress. The community development programmes of the late 1950s and 1960s did not make a separate mention of the programmes for women.

It was during the early '70s and during the Fifth Five-Year Plan period (1975-80) that the Government of India felt that while the lot of urban women had substantially changed after independence, there was virtually no change in the status of rural women. The government, therefore, felt the need to examine the question of status of women in the country with a view to formulating effective policies. Accordingly, a Committee appointed by the Government of India in 1974 on the Status of Women in India, under the Chairmanship of Veena Mazumdar submitted its report in 1975, observing that the condition of women in India had worsened since independence. In almost all significant sectors the representation of women was lower than the percentage of their population. The main indicators of women's worsening condition were education, employment, and health. The Committee noted the following trends :

1. An excessive mortality rate among women and small children;

2. A decline in the male-female ratio, for there was a lesser number of women per thousand men in the successive decades from 1901 to 1971;
3. A disparity between women's and men's access to health care and medical service;
4. An increasing gap between the two sexes in terms of literacy, education, and training for employment;
5. A decline in women's employment since the 1950s;
6. An increasing rate of outmigration from village to village among women in comparison with men.

The Committee also noted that the process of development had marginalised the poorest women who lived from hand to mouth.

The above observations of the Committee on the Status of Women in India, though startling at the time, have been corroborated by subsequent analyses and research. It is now conclusively established that the process of modernization and development has not decreased the social and economic handicaps of women; on the contrary, they have been aggravated. Many of their traditional occupations such as processing of foodgrains, cottage industry, spinning and weaving, production of vegetable oil, and baking have been wrested from them by machines.

The backsliding of women despite modernization and technological advancement has identifiable reasons. In most parts of India, women's roles remained rigidly fixed in men's minds even after independence. Especially the upper caste women in rural areas found it difficult to avail themselves of whatever opportunities were made available to them due to prejudice and resistance at home, in society, and in the administration. Women's movements and organisations, too, which had been strong and active in the pre-independence days, became passive and made peace with the formal equality granted by the Constitution. In addition, the five-year plans for development from 1951 onwards did not treat women as a separate category, and the allocation of funds for the development of human resources was reduced in the successive plants.

It was the sixth Five-Year Plan (1980-81) document which for the first time carried a separate chapter on women and viewed them not merely as beneficiaries of social welfare measure but as an active component of the human resources, which would benefit and be benefited by the development effort. It is encouraging that the seventh Five-Year Plan has increased the financial allocation for women by three times in comparison with the sixth Five-Year Plan. This indicates the government's increasing concern for women.

In the post-independence period, the government has made numerous efforts and passed social legislation to improve the general condition and status of women. But the painful fact is that not many women are able to make use of this legislation. India seems to have given its women an opportunity to use their capability and judgment without losing their feminity. But there is no real breakthrough in the lot of the Indian women, and the available opportunities are not grasped by women at all levels of society.

As noted earlier, mere enactment of laws cannot help the oppressed whether they are women or any other social group, nor can such enactment by itself set the pace for economic and social development. What is necessary is that the oppressed should understand the law and show readiness to use it in their favour. In India, law has not been able to become a mover of society because the intended beneficiaries do not fully appreciate its significance.

Despite social and legal efforts, the condition of Indian women is at best paradoxical. On the one hand they participate, as women in advanced societies do, in the decision-making process at the highest level in virtually every field; on the other, many of them are still subjected to the degrading *Purdah* system and are victims of evil social customs and religious rites. The reasons for this paradox and the low status of women are both institutional and attitudinal. While institutional changes have been attempted by the state agencies, the change in attitudes is hard to bring about. It is mainly because of the absence of attitudinal change that the reforms to improve the status of women have not had the desired impact on a majority of Indians.

Traditional, religious, and cultural beliefs and practices still largely determine women's participation in the social and economic life in India. Despite regional and class differences, male domination continues to be the hallmark of male-female relationship. Prejudice against women is expressed in the practices of all religions in the country.

Hinduism, the religion of the majority of India, greatly conditions social behaviour. Patriarchy is the way of life and male domination in the family undermines the equality of roles of the husband and the wife, the mother and the father, and the son and the daughter. The result is that the most important economic, social, and personal events in a woman's life are determined by man, allowing her very little say, for example, in marriage, sale or acquisition of property, her life outdoors and her occupational pursuits. The treatment of widowed relatives, single women and unmarried daughters, is a matter for men's decisions. The overprotection of females, which is an inevitable feature of the patriarchal family, restricts women's independence and freedom of movement. Interestingly, our Constitution also does not see the negative aspects of patriarchy and, like the Indian society, views it as perfectly natural. "The Constitution does not see patriarchy as problematic, it perceives it as natural, the Indian Constitution coolly contemplates a male-dominated Indian society."[9]

A bias against women in India is reflected in the allocation and rating of occupations of the two sexes. A higher prestige is assigned to the tasks predominantly associated with the male : ploughing against post-harvest operations; masonry against female assistance in the construction industry (by rezas) : operating of the potter's wheel against preparation of the clay for it, etc. The bias prevails despite the fact that the former kinds of jobs by no means involve a greater skill. Since society has ordained that the women must not touch the plough or handle the potters' wheel, women have no chance to prove their skill in these crafts. The self-esteem of women is kept deliberately low, for they are to be groomed to play the subordinate roles of wives and mothers, and are prevented from taking an interest in serious matters and participating equally in decision-making. Thus, in a patriarchal family, the woman is reduced to economic dependence. Her work within the family is not recognised as work, and she is looked upon as a burden. When she gets married and goes away from her father's house to her in-laws, the latter are compensated for taking the girl in terms of dowry. This is why the dowry system has become the sine qua non of Hindu weddings, especially in the northern states, with the possible exception of the hill states. It includes gifts ranging from cars and jewelry to household utensils, depending on the status of the father. For a father, his daughter's marriage is both an occasion to show his wealth and an opportunity to ensure that his daughter spends the rest of her life in safety and comfort. The non-egalitarian nature of Indian society is reflected in the dowry system, to which the modern youth is unashamedly a party.

The final destiny of the girl if her marriage and, therefore, her education is of secondary importance and is often neglected. The girl is so thoroughly indoctrinated that she starts thinking on similar lines in respect of her own daughters. Thus, the devaluation of a girl continues from generation to generation. A daughter is a drain on the family's resources and so her birth is not welcome. It is perhaps due to the deliberate neglect or indifference of parents of girls that the mortality rate of female infants is higher than that of male infants, especially in the northwestern states where the bias against female infants is reflected even in the demand for pregnancy tests to determine the sex of a child. It is quite revealing that such a demand seems to be greater in states where the practice of dowry is more rampant. The intention is to have an abortion in case the child conceived is a girl.

The unfair treatment meted out to the woman runs counter to the spirit of the Constitution which prohibits dowry and accords equal status to women. Notwithstanding the Dowry Prohibition Act, 1961, hundreds of brides have committed suicide or have been burnt to death by their in-laws out of greed for more dowry. These happenings have made the eradication of dowry a major issue for social reformers and has perhaps received more attention than any other issue in the last ten years or so. Ironically, the dowry system, instead of getting weaker, has flourished and spread to all levels of Indian society. In 1975 the Report of the Veena Mazumdar Committee on the Status of Women in India pointed out that the Dowry Prohibition Act was completely ineffective.

The worst consequence of the inferior status of women and prejudice against them is the burning of brides. If newspaper reports are any indication, in this decade indeed, it has become an epidemic. "Brushing aside sheaves of legislation, it has spread like a plague across the country. Harassment and burning of brides seems to have become a ghoulish symbol of national unity for the pattern of burning brides is painfully common."[10] The burning of brides led to a public controversy and certain changes were made in the Criminal Procedure Code, the Indian Penal Code, and the Evidence Act in 1983. These amendments to the criminal laws can be useful to women since they extend the definition of cruelty to include mental and psychological harassment of a wife, and also extend the definition of abetment to suicide. But despite such laws, women are looked upon by some sectors of society as commodities to be bought, sold, used, and burnt. A Joint Committee of Parliament appointed to examine the ineffectiveness of the Dowry Prohibition Act remarked : "Despite the existence of central enactment as also the amending enactments passed by the various state governments and the steps taken both by the central and the state governments, neither of them has been able to curb the social evil of dowry. The central enactment brought into force with the ostensible purpose of curbing the evil, if not eradicating it, has singularly failed to achieve its objective. In spite of the rapid growth of the practice of dowry, there are practically no cases reported under the Act. The evil sought to be done away by the Act has, on the other hand, increased by leaps and bounds and has now assumed grotesque and alarming proportions."

People's prejudices are too deeply rooted to be removed by law overnight. Strangely enough, even the rape laws of the country are not able to give sufficient protection to the victim; instead, the law invariably treats the woman-victim as the accused. In *(Tukaram vs. State of Maharashtra,* 1979, Supreme Court), a young tribal girl, Mathura, of about 16, was raped by policemen while her relatives stood outside the police station waiting helplessly. The sessions court declared the policemen innocent and Mathura "a shocking liar." The Bombay High Court reversed the judgment and sentenced the accused, Tukaram and Ganapat. On appeal, the Indian Supreme Court reversed the decision of the High Court and acquitted the rapists on the ground that the victim, Mathura, was of immoral character and hence must have consented to sexual intercourse.

The Supreme Court judgment in the above case aroused anger and indignation. Four law teachers wrote an open letter to the Chief Justice of India requesting him to have the case reheard by the full bench of the Court. The letter raised several important questions and quoted the decision in the *Nandini Satpathy* case (1978) in which the Supreme Court had condemned the practice of calling women to police stations in gross violation of section 160 (1) of the Criminal Procedure Code. The authors of the letter went to the extent of saying that nothing short of protection of human rights and constitutionalism was at stake.

Following the media coverage and public protests against the Supreme Court judgment in the Mathura case, the Union Government requested the Law Commission to make a special study of the law pertaining to rape. This study led to the amendment to the rape laws contained in the Indian Penal Code, the Criminal Procedure Code, and the Indian Evidence

Act, and introduced several reforms concerning the punishment for rape and the procedure and the rules of evidence. But the amendments left a number of loopholes. One such loophole is that the victim is vulnerable to attacks on her character in the court, and this can deter any victim from going to court.

Another important legislation affecting women is the Family Courts Act, 1984. This act provides for "the establishment of family court with a view to promoting conciliation in, and secure speedy settlement of, disputes relating to marriage and family affairs." There are many provisions in the Act modifying the law of procedure and evidence in relation to family court.

Sad to say, the passage of the Family Courts Act, 1984 has by no means improved the lot of women. Objectively judged family disputes arise as a result of inequalities within the family. Adjustment, as settlement or conciliation means that women have to adjust to this inequality. As well, one basic fact is not taken into consideration by this new family court act. The idea behind the family courts is that family disputes are a private matter and should be heard in privacy as is done within the family itself. So women are taught to bear with beatings, humiliations, and molestation but not to speak out because the honour of the family would be put in jeopardy.

While dealing with the family disputes most of the judges display the same attitude toward women as society on the whole does. Ironically, even in those cases here there is evidence, the courts choose not to believe the woman. Sometimes, even her dying declaration is not believed. In *States vs. Udham Singh and others* (1984), a young woman called Shanni Kaur, mother of a one-year-old boy, died of burns in a Delhi hospital. Before dying she gave her statement three times, once to the police and twice to the doctors, stating that her husband had poured kerosene on her and burnt her. All the three dying declarations were disbelieved by the Court on one ground or another. This bias against women was even more evident in *Sarad Birdhichand Sardar vs. State of*

Maharashtra (1984). Sarad, a chemical engineer, was found guilty of murdering his twenty-year-old wife, Manjushree, by suffocating her and by administering potassium cyanide to her. He was found guilty by both the sessions court and the Bombay High Court. But he was acquitted by the Supreme Court. The Honourable Judge said, "Manju (from the evidence on the record) appears to be not only a highly sensitive woman who expected the whole-hearted love and affection from her husband but having been thoroughly disappointed out of sheer disgust, frustration and depression she may have chosen to end her life. At least this possibility is clearly gleaned from her letters and mental attitude. She hinted that her husband was so busy that he found no time for her. A hard fact of life, which cannot be denied is that some people in view of their occupation, or profession find very little time to devote to their family. Lawyers, professors, doctors, and perhaps judges share a common attitude to women and to them Manju's case should be an eye opener."

The judgment in Manju's case aroused a strong protest. Women all over Maharashtra organised protest demonstrations and public meetings. There was a spontaneous *bandh* in several towns and within 15 days 10,000 signatures were collected, demanding a review of the judgement. The Supreme Court rejected the review petition.

The setting up of Family Courts by the government also has many alarming implications which seem to have been overlooked by those who hail such courts as a step forward for women. The present law leaves it to the judges to decide whether or not a settlement is possible, and they can adjourn the proceedings for any length of time. This can cause a great hardship to a wife needing a speedy divorce or payment of maintenance allowance or custody of her child. When a case is adjourned for a long time, usually it is the woman who suffers more because, in Indian society, the man is generally in a stronger economic and social position and the woman may have to return to her husband even under humiliating conditions. Then there is this basic question : if neither the husband nor the wife desires a settlement, why should the judge have the power to adjourn the proceedings simply because he or she thinks that a settlement is possible?

The basic purpose of the Act concerning the Family Courts is to introduce changes, but it may make matters worse, since it gives more arbitrary powers to judges, who will be the same people who control the legal profession in other courts which have been so ineffective in giving justice to women in the past. To expect them to suddenly become pro-women could be a folly.

The economic independence of woman is the most important condition for enabling her to defend her self-respect as an individual. The government should make concerted efforts in this direction rather than speeding up the legal process in matrimonial cases alone. Turning a law court into a marriage counselling center can serve only a limited purpose and the Act itself can simply enable a few more women to take recourse to the legal process to claim their rights. In a way, the Act may even make it more difficult for women to do so, for it exhorts women to remain silent in the best interest of "the family," which, of course, means, those who control it.

Social norms constitute the value system of a society, and women's position and participation in society are largely determined by this system. Article 44 of the Indian Constitution states that "the state shall endeavour to secure for the citizens a uniform code throughout the country." However, such a code has not yet been formulated even after 40 years of independence. The various personal laws, which accept discrimination between men and women, violate the fundamental rights, and their continuance is "against the spirit of national integration and secularism." The disadvantages of not having a uniform civil code in the country has long been evident to many enlightened citizens. M.R. Masani, Hansa Mehta, and Amrit Kaur wanted a uniform civil code because they believed that one of the factors that has held India back from advancing to nationhood has been existence of personal laws based on religion.

The government moved with great zeal to reform Hindu laws but has not dared to touch the Muslim Personal Law. Electoral politics has influenced Government's behaviour. In 1941 the Hindu Law Committee was set up. On the basis of the Committee's recommendations, the Hindu Code Bill was introduced in Parliament in 1948. Ironically, on the eve of the first elections in 1951, the bill was dropped, for Prime Minister Nehru felt that there was too much opposition to it.[11]

The Muslims continue to have their own personal law which allows them not only four wives but also "divine sanction" to discriminate against women. The entire country is governed by one criminal law, and there is the same law for everyone who wishes to establish an industry or wants to go into the export business; but there is no one civil code for the women in the country. A Hindu woman is governed by the Hindu Law : a Muslim woman by the Muslim Law : and the Parsis, the Christians, and the tribals have their own personal laws which determine the position of women in these communities.[12] A common civil code was not made when the Constitution was framed because it was felt that it would interfere with the religious rights of various communities.

In two recent cases, *Ms. Jorden Diengdeh vs. S.S. Chopra (1985)* and *Mohammed Ahmed Khan v. Shah Bano Begum (1985)*, the Supreme Court has drawn attention to the need for a common civil code for national integration. Underlining this need, the Bench of five judges in the Shah Bano case also noted the difficulties involved in bringing persons of different faiths and persuasions to a common viewpoint. It observed that, "It is a matter of regret that Article 44 of our Constitution has remained a dead letter. A common civil code will help the cause of national integration by removing disparate loyalties to laws which make conflicting ideologies."

The problems of working women and the question of their liberty were also seemingly taken care of by the Constitution. Article 19 (1) (g) guarantees every citizen the right to carry on his or her occupation. Whenever a woman has decided to work—and it has meant that she has had to live away from her husband—the courts have held that she does not have the right to work on an equal right with her husband to decide where they will live after marriage. The courts had done this by granting the husband a decree for the restitution of conjugal rights. The overwhelming majority of such cases in Indian High Courts have been decided in favour of the husband, even when the wife was better educated than the husband and was contributing a valuable service to society (*Gaya Prasad vs. Bhagwati*, Madhya Pradesh, 1966). A few cases decided in favour of the wife were on the ground that the husband was not earning enough to support her (*Radhakrishan vs. Dhanalakshmi*, Madras, 1975).

Regarding the questions of whether or not a woman also has a right to file a suit for the restitution of conjugal rights, the Indian High Court held the view that such a step was a violation of the right to personal liberty. In *T. Sareetha vs. T. Venkata Subbaiah* (1983), Justice P.A. Choudhary said : "The remedy of restitution of conjugal rights ... is a savage and barbarous remedy violating the right to privacy and human dignity guaranteed by Article 21 of the Constitution." But within a few months the Supreme Court overruled this judgment in *Smt. Saroj Rani vs. Sudarshan Kumar Chadha,* (1984). According to the Honourable Justice, it "serves a social purpose as an aid to the prevention of break up of marriage."

Paradoxically, not only society but the laws also have double standards of morality. The most glaring example of this paradox is the law on prostitution contained in the Suppression of Immoral Traffic in Women and Girls Act, 1956. The Act does not seek to ban prostitution as such. It forbids trafficking in women by those who live off the earnings of prostitutes and disallows prostitution near public places. The victim is viewed as a guilty party and is punished, but there is no provision to punish the male patron. Significantly, the Sixty-Fourth Law Commission declared that prostitution cannot be banned and the law must "regulate it so that it may be kept within its legitimate bounds without unduly impinging upon the institution of marriage and family." The Commission considered the question of whether a "person who hires a prostitute be punished" and it decided that the patron could not be punished. The decision was based on the idea that man is something more than a partner in an immoral act; he discharges important social and business functions and is a father or brother responsible for the maintenance of others. Therefore he cannot be imprisoned without damaging society. A woman prostitute, on the other hand, can be brought to book without disturbing the natural course of society. Most of the prostitutes take up their profession to support themselves and their families. Locking up a prostitute means depriving her children of their source of livelihood. The law is blind to this fact.

Economic exigencies and the spread of education among women have led to more and more women taking up jobs in offices, industries, and other establishments. In order to protect their interests, the government has enacted several laws and adopted welfare measures. The laws containing welfare and protective provisions for women are of two kinds. The first are those statutory enactments such as the Equal Remuneration Act, 1976, and the Maternity Benefit Act, 1961, which are exclusively meant for women; and the second category consists of the general laws which govern the conditions of work in some industries and contain special provisions for the welfare of women. However, because of political and cultural differences, these enactments have not yet brought about any significant change in the status of women in India.

Today India is witnessing economic modernization without fully destroying the social and ideological elements of feudalism. The average Indian, particularly the educated one, is caught in the middle of two conflicting pulls: the modern urge to be rational, humanist, and democratic, and the feudal instinct to be egocentric and self-righteous. The sense of shame induced by an emerging modern outlook leads to the mouthing of good words about women, but the submerged feudal self prevents the hand from striking at those barriers which block the way of women. The laws in India reflect this conflict. A more informed and assertive public opinion, enlightened legislative and bureaucratic leadership, and a constructive role for women themselves could help in expediting these changes.

NOTES

1. Altekar, A.S., *The Position of Women in Hindu Civilization*, Delhi : Motilal Banarsidas, 1962, p.1.

2. The custom of levirate was quite common during ancient times in several civilizations.

3. It came to be believed that a man was saddled with a threefold debt, the most important of which was the debt to the forefathers which could be paid only by the birth of a son.

4. *Upanayana*, a ritual necessary for endowing women with proper Aryan status.

5. *Vasishtha Dharmasutra*, XVIII, 17 and *Vishnu*, ch. 26.

6. Altekar, A.S., *op. cit.*, p.346.

7. When King Ranjit Singh died, his four queens and seven concubines ascended the funeral pyre.

8. A report by the Indian Education Commission, 1882, on the Madras Province shows that in 1826 A.D. only 1,023 girls were attending school as against 157,664 boys.

9. Quoted from Haksar, Nandita, *Demystification of Law for Women*, New Delhi : Lancer Press, 1986, p.84.

10. *India Today*, 30 June 1986. The total figures for the country are astounding : 990 for 1985 and 1, 319 for 1971. Surprisingly, the practice is spreading to new areas of the country. Its southwards spread has been much more dramatic. In Andhra Pradesh the cases of bride burning have risen six-fold, from 13 in 1985 to 79 in 1986. By July 1987, the number

had leapt to 166. In Tamil Nadu, the number of such cases was 12 in 1985 and 38 in 1986. These are government figures and they might be on the lower side.

11. The then Law Minister, Dr. Ambedkar, resigned on this issue and openly accused the government of giving stepmotherly treatment to the Hindu Code. In his long and strong letter giving a detailed explanation of the Hindu Code Bill, he says : "It has been said that the Bill had to be dropped because the opposition was strong. How strong was the opposition? This Bill has been discussed several times in the party and was carried to division by the opponents. Every time the opponents were routed. The last time, when the bill was taken up in the party meeting, out of 120 only 20 were found against it. When the Bill was taken up in the party for discussion, 44 clauses were passed in about three and a half hours' time. This shows how much opposition there was to the Bill within the party. In the house itself there have been divisions on three clauses of the Bill, 2, 3 and 4. Every time there has been an overwhelming majority in favour, even on clause 4, which is the soul of the Hindu Code."

12. Hakser, Nandita, *op. cit.* p.37.

7

DHIRENDRA VAJPEYI

FREEDOM OF THE PRESS, COURTS AND THE INDIAN CONSTITUTION

I

"A popular Government without a popular information or the means of acquiring it, is a prologue to a farce or a tragedy; or perhaps both. Knowledge will for ever govern ignorance. And a people who mean to be their own Governors, must arm themselves with the power which knowledge gives them."

James Madison, August 14, 1822.

The nature of the relationship between the state and the press has attracted its fair share of debate and controversy. Oftentimes this adversarial relationship between the power holders (legislative, executive) and the press is part of a broader and more important issue as to who shall exercise the powers of the state, and who has the legitimate authority or right to speak for the people of the land. To put it differently, the problem is one "of organization of the state and of distribution of power amongst the various authorities... It is the problem of relationship between the state and the individual." (Sen 1986:1) The following three models of this relationship prevail:

1. Total and absolute control of the state is exercised over the press and other media. The Soviet Union, Communist China, and other totalitarian states fall into this category.
2. State regulated media. The state through a public corporation regulates certain aspects of the electronic and print media. Usually the press is free within some statutory limits, i.e., India.
3. Free press. Under constitutional arrangements, the press and other media enjoy almost total freedom, e.g. the American press.

My paper analyzes the relationship between the press and the state in India in general, and the press during Rajiv Gandhi's tenure as Prime Minister, in particular. The paper briefly traces the press-state relationship since independence, role of the Indian Courts, Constitutional and parliamentary provisions and then takes up developments in the last twelve months of this relationship. In recent months the state has taken a very aggressive stance in its attempt to suppress the freedom of the press in India. The massive country-wide raids against the *Indian Express* and the attempt to pass the Defamation Bill in the Parliament point toward these trends. The lively and relatively free press in India is under siege. The *Indian Express*, one of the most influential English language daily newspaper with a circulation of 583,647, and the most powerful cutting edge of the opposition to Rajiv Gandhi's government stands accused of evading customs duties and violating the Foreign Exchange Regulation Act (FERA). The *Indian Express* has become a symbol of press freedom and democracy in India. On August 29th, 1988 Prime Minister Rajiv Gandhi's government introduced a bill in Parliament with the ostensible purpose of reforming the law against defamation. India's defamation laws, modeled on British law of the mid-19th century, have always been severe. In the Indian Penal

Code, defamation is defined in the broadest possible terms to include anything that "lowers a person in the estimation of others", or "causes it to be believed that the body of that person is in a loathsome state." The bill, which was withdrawn on September 22, 1988 under intense public pressure, had stipulated that journalists and publishers, if convicted of defamation, could he imprisoned for two years and also face a five-year prison term for a second offense. The bill, if passed, would have made it an offense to alleged criminal wrongdoing by anyone, but in a significant departure from legal practice, it would have required the accused to prove his innocence, rather than have the prosecution prove gilt. The bill also contained provisions for summary and secret trials for a new offense that it called 'criminal imputation'. The provisions in the bill would have made it extremely difficult to make even general statements critical of a class of persons, or of institutions such as the police, the political parties, the corporate sector or trade unions. The bill was strongly criticized and was opposed by all-India strikes, supported by such diverse groups as Indian Journalists, the London-based Commonwealth Press Union (CPU), opposition political parties, lawyers and jurists, and even some elements of Rajiv Gandhi's own political party—the Congress. The bill was branded as a "threat to press freedom in India". As a result the Government succumbed to the intense public pressure and withdrew the bill on September 22, 1988. "Never before in India's parliamentary history has legislation passed by the Lok Sabha been withdrawn under public pressure". (*India Today* Oct. 15, 1988:15)

In conclusion, I have attempted to discuss the responsibility of the free press in a transitional society such as India with "a democratic government structure but mired in medievalism, a pliant press pretending to be a force but in the main mirroring the awe and undue respect of the average Indian for the 'mai baap Sarkar'." (Karnad 1988 : 19)

II

"Information is power. Officials struggle to control it, and in that struggle the citizen - critic needs constitutional support."

- **Anthony Lewis**

The leaders of India's freedom movements attached a great deal of importance to the freedoms of speech, expression, and the freedom of the press. After independence they had not forgotten the repressive measure taken during the colonial British rule to curb these freedoms and deny them the right to speak out in support of independence and against British exploitation. They were very well aware of the crucial role these freedoms played in a free and democratic political system, however, freedom of the press itself was not included in the Indian Constitution under Fundamental Rights. (It should be noted that the Constitution of the United States of America expressly includes it in its Bill of Rights). During the debates of the Indian Constituent Assembly the incorporation of freedom of the press as one of the Fundamental Rights was strongly advocated. B. N. Rau, the Constitutional Adviser, felt that it was hardly necessary to provide separately for it. Dr. Ambedkar shared this view and observed that "no special mention is necessary of the freedom of the press at all." Freedom of speech and expression have been universally construed as including freedom of the press or in other words the right to express and disseminate ideas and opinions through publications, whether periodicals or otherwise. Later, in a series of decisions, the Supreme Court of India has held the constitutional guarantee embodied in Article 19 (1) of the Constitution includes freedom of the press. The freedom of the press is only an element of freedom of speech and expression.

Various judgements of the Indian Supreme Court have maintained that the word "expression" is not qualified and embraces every form and manner of expression. Even demonstrations fall within the ambit of freedom of expression.

In *Kameshwar vs. State of Bihar* (1962) the Indian Supreme Court maintained that a "demonstration is an outward exhibition of feeling or an exhibition of opinion on political or other questions... It is, in effect, a form of expression." It does not, however, confer any special rights or privileges. The Supreme Court has held that freedom of the press is "the most cherished and valued freedom in a democracy", "one of the pillars of democracy", "the Ark of the Covenant of democracy", "(*Romeh Thappar v. State of Madras*, 1950; *Brij Bhushan v. State of Delhi*, 150). In the Brij Bhushan case an order issued under the East Punjab Safety Act, 1949, had imposed pre-censorship on an English weekly on the ground that this was necessary for public order and safety. The majority judgement held that pre-censorship was a restraint on freedom of speech and stuck to the decision in the Romesh Thappar case. The battle for turf between the Parliament and the Judiciary began in earnest. First, Amendment to Article 19 was provoked by the above Supreme Court decisions. Thus, even in the very early stages of constitutional development, parliament strove successfully to meet what it regarded as a challenge to its authority. This tussle between parliamentary sovereignty and the Supreme Court's claim to be the guardian and guarantor of constitutional rights will continue. In 1967, in the famous *Golak Nath* case, the Supreme Court by a majority of six to five ruled that parliament had no power to take away or abridge, by the process of constitutional amendment, any of the Fundamental Rights guaranteed by the Constitution. "These rights are given a transcendental position and kept beyond the reach of Parliamentary legislation". The parliament retaliated. The twenty-fourth amendment of the Indian Constitution gave parliament the right to modify chapter III of the Constitution. On November 30, 1971 H.R. Gokhale, the Indian Law Minister, observed that "the intention in inserting Article 31 (c) was to give primacy to Directive Principles and limit property rights in such a manner that the vested interests may not be able to take shelter under Fundamental Rights and block progressive legislation". He maintained that the judiciary would no longer be called upon to sit in judgement over political issues. By the twenty-ninth amendment the Indian Parliament overruled the

Golaknath case. The Indian Constitution does not give any preferred position to any Fundamental Right as does the United States Constitution. The Indian Supreme Court has categorically observed that no Fundamental Right is superior or preferred to another, and that Article 19 of the Constitution does not have a hierarchy of rights. Also, every constitution system maintains that fundamental rights are not absolute or unqualified rights. The seven freedoms guaranteed by Article 19 of the Indian Constitution are no exception. As regards freedom of speech and expression, clause (2) clearly authorizes the legislature to impose reasonable restrictions in the interest of national security, friendly relation with foreign states, public order, (*Superintendent, Central Prison v. Ram Manohar Lohia* (1960). decency or morality (*buon custume*) or in relation to contempt of court, defamation, or incitement to an offence. The clause also preserves the validity of any existing law which lays down reasonable restrictions on any of the specified grounds. (Sen 1966: 457). The Indian Supreme Court has attempted to defend the phrase "reasonable restrictions", in several of its judicial pronouncements. In *Motilal v. Uttar Pradesh Government* (1951) Justice Malik observed that reasonable restriction cannot mean a total stoppage is not sound. The words in the Article are not 'regulation' but are 'reasonable restriction". The founding fathers of the Constitution were aware and conscious of the distinction between the power to regulate and the power to restrict. It will be apparent from a scrutiny of sub-clause (a) of clause (2) of Article 25 where the words 'regulating' and 'restricting' occur in juxtaposition thereby indicating unmistakably that the framers of the Constitution intended to convey two different meanings by the two words. It is to be noted that Article 19 and consequently the expression 'restriction' in Article 19 (6) cannot be held to be synonymous with regulation. Restriction may be complete or partial and where it is complete it would imply absolute prohibition. (Sen 1966: 458). In *State of Madras v. V. G. Row* (1952) Chief Justice Patanjali Sastri spoke of reasonable restrictions. "The test of reasonableness, wherever prescribed, should be applied to each individual statute impinged, and no abstract standard, or general pattern applicable to all cases." The judgement in Virendra v. State of Punjab (1957) supported

Patanjali Sastri. At times the issue of the freedom of press got caught in middle of a turf-tussle between the Parliament and the Indian Judicial System as to who has the supreme authority over the validity of the laws. Two famous examples are: *His Holiness Keshavanand Bharati v. State of Kerala*, and *Golaknath*. However, despite these implicit, unwritten guarantees in the Constitution and repeated assurances by the Indian Supreme Court of its desire to safeguard freedom of the press, the Indian press remains one of the most pliant and weak, and largely toes the official line to please those in power. Also those in power—from the first prime minister, Nehru (1947 - 1964), to the present one—have very carefully and successfully clipped the free press whenever it became too critical of their policies and behavior. Many arguments from patriotic and national security to the role of a responsible press in a democracy have been presented. A critic of Indian power wielders even suggests that the exclusion of the freedom of the press from the list of fundamental rights was intentional and political. "Our constitution makers had from the beginning the Machiavellian intent to hogtie the press and prevent its developing into an independent agency whose activities are protected by a constitutional writ and which could ensure a government accountable to the people." (Karnad 1988 : 20). Let us review them briefly.

Nehru

At the time of independence most of the influential English newspapers were owned by private capitalists, and there were very few national Hindi newspapers. A few were even owned by the British. Most of them were not very favourably inclined towards Nehru's socialist policies and non-alignment. Nehru was not very fond of some of these publications but was too popular and powerful to be hurt by them. "The relationship between the so-called big papers and the government was in reality ambivalent. Nehru criticized them but did not do anything to seriously hurt them." (Jain 1988 : 14). In public and private, Nehru championed the cause of freedom of expression and speech. But it was Nehru who steered the First Amendment

Act, 1951 which severely limited freedom of speech and of expression. The amending Act gave cart blanche to government to further restrict this freedom in the interest "of national security, friendly relations with foreign states, public order, decency, or morality, or in relation to contempt of court, defamation, or incitement to an offence." Nehru observed that the First amendment Act was no more than an effort to correct "errors in drafting or in possible interpretations to be put on what we had drafted." In short, freedom of the press and the individual's rights are all very well but expendable in the interest of the state, or, depending on the scruples of the leader,the interests of his party of even solely of himself... "unwilling to accept Constitutional constraints on governmental power and on the power of the Parliament to sweep aside rights and freedoms contained in the Constitution, Nehru set the authoritarian stamp on Indian politics and press. (Karnad 1988: 21).

Shastri

Shastri's tenure as prime minister was so short (1964-1966) it is hard to make a meaningful analysis. There existed a kind of truce between the press and the government. Shastri was faced with so many domestic problems—language riots in the south and foreign-war with Pakistan and his own image that he did not have time to do much.

Indira Gandhi

The first two and a half years (1966-1969) of Indira Gandhi as prime minister were uneventful in terms of government and press relationship. The split in the Congress party in 1969, Indira Gandhi's populist policies, and her determined efforts to manipulate institutions—government and non-government—to enhance her political power, glorify the Nehru name and continue her dynasty brought her into in conflict with the Indian press and the intelligentsia. The proclamation of Emergency on June 25th, 1975 launched the most virulent attack on press freedom. A host of repressive measure

Freedom of The Press, Courts and The Indian Constitution

were introduced. For the first time in free India, pre-censorship was imposed by promulgating a Censorship Order on June 26, 1975. It prohibited the publication of "words, signs, or visible representation" which "bring into hatred or contempt or excite disaffection towards the government established by law in India or in any state thereof and thereby cause or tend to cause public disorder". The government was also empowered to demand cash bonds from printers, publishers, and editors who published material other than "prescribed" material. The government could also close down the press that printed material considered 'prejudicial'. The Press Council of India, a body of journalists and newspapers to protect the freedom of the press, was dissolved and the accrediation of more than forty newspaper correspondents was withdrawn (Nayar 1978 : 109-110). Later, other guidelines and instructions were issued to the press. All of them were executive orders. One of the instructions read, "Nothing is to be published that is likely to convey the impression of a protest or disapproval of a government measure." No criticism, however mild, of the government was allowed. Even quotations from Mahatma Gandhi and Tagore were banned. The reaction of the Indian press was shameful. For the first two or three days, blank editorial pages appeared as a gesture of protest but official threats, conveyed unofficially, took care of such gestures. Leading newspapers and their editors fully realized both the absurdity and the unconstitutionality of law. Fortunately, there were a few brave editors, lawyers, and leading private citizens who challenged the government's draconian actions. *The Indian Express*, and *The Statesman* were two such English dailies. Most of the publications, particularly small ones, succumbed because of their almost total reliance on government advertisements. Many newspapers virtually became government gazettes or sycophantic supporters of Mrs. Gandhi. Tremendous pressure was brought upon a few newspapers like *The Indian Express*, and *The Statesman* which showed guts and refused to be cowed down. The proprietor of the *Indian Express*, Ram Nath Goenka was forced to reorganize the Board of Directors of the *Indian Express* to accommodate government's nominees on it. K.K. Birla, a staunch supporter of Sanjay Gandhi, became the

Chairman of the newly-constituted Board (Nayer 1977:87). Commenting on Mrs. Indira Gandhi's efforts to muzzle the freedom of the press in India during the Emergency, columnist Loren Jenkins observed that, "In ten years of covering the world from Franco's Spain to Mao's China, I have never encountered such stringent and all encompassing censorship." (Nayer 1977 : 49)

The Janata Government

The Janata party in its election Manifesto issued in March 1977 promised to repeal the Prevention of Publication of Objectionable Matter Act. Once in power it withdrew all the restrictions which were imposed by Mrs.Gandhi on the freedom of speech and expression. The Janata interlude was too brief (1977-1979) and was spent in factional fights and scandal mongering. The return of Mrs. Gandhi to power in January 1980 did not improve her attitude towards the press of her relationship with it.

Rajiv Gandhi

Rajiv Gandhi came to power in 1985 in most unusual circumstances. The assassination of his mother, Mrs. Gandhi, and the terrorism in the Punjab united most of the country and it gave him overwhelming support. The absence of any good or bad political baggage, his promise to wipe out corruption and inefficiency in the government kindled a new hope in the Indian electorate. He was ushered in as 'Mr. Super Clean'. All sections of Indian society expected him to break away from the past political mess and start afresh. In the early months of his office, Rajiv Gandhi seemed to stand for a repudiation not only of Indira Gandhi's politics and style but even of Jawaharlal Nehru's. His relationship with the media was quite cozy, very much like President Reagan and the American media. Rajiv could not do anything wrong. But by the beginning of 1987, this relationship started to change. There were several reasons for it. V.P. Singh as finance minister ran away with the 'Mr. Super Clean' image, his transfer from finance to defence lent credence to rumors that he had uncovered evidence incriminating two of Rajiv Gandhi's close friends, Amitabh Bacchan and Ajitabh Bacchan, for violating the Foreign Exchange Regulations Act, and in the process the Prime Minster himself. V.P. Singh's decision as defence minister to order an inquiry into the West German submarine deal and his subsequent resignation further confirmed the growing impression that Rajiv Gandhi had a lot to hide; President Zail Singh challenged the Prime Minister's claim that the latter had kept the former informed on matters of national importance; the *Indian Express* campaign against Reliance Industries developed into one on the Fairfax affair and subsequently against Rajiv Gandhi personally; the government handled the Bofors matter most ineptly. Serious charges of huge commissions paid by foreign defence contractors to Rajiv Gandhi personally and his political party were highlighted in the press in general, and the *Indian Express* in particular. Behind it all lay the issue of public morality. Rajiv Gandhi was on trial, and he was incensed. And so began the story of Rajiv Gandhi and the *Indian "Express*. The *Indian Express* became a symbol—a veritable bastion—of press freedom in India.

The Saga of the *Indian Express*

The interesting saga of Rajiv Gandhi and the *Indian Express* began on March 13, 1987 when the newspaper's morning editions published the text of a letter from India's President Zail Singh to Rajiv Gandhi. The letter merely confirmed the capital gossip that the President and the Prime Minister were at loggerheads and something big was up. The avalanche of moves aimed at punishment of the *Indian Express* came within a short span of time. By the evening of the same day, around 7.30 p.m., fourteen men from the Central Bureau of Intelligence swooped upon Ramnath Goenka's (the owner of the newspaper) residence in New Delhi. They searched the building till late into the night and then, in a dramatic pre-dawn arrest, they picked up the newspaper's financial adviser, S. Gurumurthy, in Madras (South India) and took him in for some intensive interrogation. The reaction of the paper was sharp, and in a editorial on March 15 Arun Shourie observed that "instead of wasting its energies on taming the press, the government will be well advised to direct them at answering charges that the President has levelled. No President of India had sent this kind of letter to a Prime Minister. Nor are the issues that arise from it a private affair between Zail Singh and Rajiv Gandhi." The government decided to retaliate. It proceeded to launch a series of intensive inspections of the newspaper's affairs under the Indian Company and Income Tax laws, and also started putting on the financial pressure by quietly persuading government-owned banks to be more careful and prudent in granting credits to the paper. The paper felt the squeeze but instead of buckling under it decided to confront the government in pursuit of a principle—freedom of expression and the press. Rajiv Gandhi could not have picked a worse time to 'punish' the *Indian Express* editor Arun Shourie—a tough journalist with a "milk-mannered exterior but a belly full of fire", whose "speech is soft but it is laden with barely controlled outrage. Against the system. Against political leaders who lose their hearing. Yet, Arun Shourie is a man of immense faith in Buddha. And in the creative mind of Mahatma Gandhi who dared to march to the sound of a distant drummer." (Badhwar 1987 : 16). March 1987 was the beginning of bad times for the Rajiv government. The first details on the West German Submarines and Swedish gun deal began surfacing. The *Indian Express* decided that it had no choice but to expose government corruption. Some believe that it perhaps went a little too far in the front page editorial on April 13. It said that, "Two things, therefore, need to be done. First, Mr. V. P. Singh must disclose in Parliament all he has found out about the deal (HDW Submarines) as well as what had transpired in the last months of his tenure at the Finance Ministry. Nor should he stop at a statement in Parliament. This is not time for good men to betray the cause and rest at home... Secondly, the President must act. The defence of the country is involved. There is the paramount need to cleanse our public life. Substantial funds have been siphoned from the country and the question is being asked whether the Prime Minister and his associates have been privy to the loot." The President did not act and V.P. Singh acted in a wishy-washy uncertain sort of way but the *Indian Express* continued its frontal assault. It wrote on the Bofors and related matters; wrote exposes of Bacchans' assets abroad, the Fairfax involvement and about industrialist Ram Jethmalani. The paper pointed out the corruption in the Prime Minister's innermost circle and implied guilt by association. "One particular newspaper" was the phrase Prime Minister Rajiv Gandhi used to point out the source of his government's problems with the press. In public statements he tried to ridicule and taunt the paper. In private the government seethed and started to build up its case against the newspaper until it finally took its next step in what was now an open war. Intolerance of the press started to reach down even to lower levels of administration. The Editors' Guild documented a case in July 1987 of the wives of district magistrate, superintendent of police, and other local officials buying saris in a town of Uttar Pradesh but not making full payments. The resultant "hartal" (strike) by shopkeepers was reported by several newsmen which led to their harassment and repression. One journalist's property tax was raised by 800 percent with a retrospective five year effect. The district magistrate was eventually transferred. (*Amrit Bazar Patrika*, July 30, 1987). But as a microcosm of the assaults and built-in constraints under which correspondents in outlying areas beyond the national and state capitals and the small town press function, the problem resulted in more serious manifestations all over the country.

The legislative and judicial branches of the government in Congress-ruled states also struck at the press. In Madhya Pradesh, the Nagpur bench of the Bombay High Court convicted on a contempt charge the resident editor of *Nagpur Times* for his article on alleged malpractices in the district judiciary. He refused to pay the fine of Rs. 1000 (about $ 85) and chose imprisonment. In Tamilnadu, the Speaker of the State Legislative Assembly sent an editor to jail for a cartoon considered to belittle the dignity of state cabinet ministers and legislators. A public outcry helped the editor's early release.

On September 1, 1987 a convenient 24 hours after the monsoon session of parliament came to an end, the Rajiv Gandhi government decided to act. All over India the offices of the *Indian Express* were raided by the Directorate of Revenue and Intelligence (DRI). The scene at the newspaper's New Delhi headquarters was hardly that of an ordinary raid. It was a veritable armed siege, replete with guns and uniforms. Two Central Reserve Police Force (CRPF) armed companies, scores of Delhi policemen and plainclothesmen from the DRI, customs and revenue service, invaded the building, including the editorial offices. The ostensible purpose was to find proof in support of a government case which had been under investigation for a year, that the *Express* had evaded customs duties and violated foreign exchange regulations in the purchase of Rs. 120 crore machinery (Badhwar and Chawla, 1987: 12-20). The newspaper's lawyers in a writ petition to the Supreme Court stated that the raid was the largest ever (600 officials) on a single organization. They also pointed out that even before the raid was complete, the DRI began issuing press statements charging the newspaper management with various crimes and misdemeanors. These allegations were also prominently aired on government-owned All India Radio, and Doordarshan (TV).

The *Indian Express* refused to be cowed down. In a defiant editorial "*This Won't Work Either*" it challenged and questioned government action as "an act of desperation against a paper that has contributed to changing the tone of debate in this country."

The general reaction of the Indian press was critical of the government action. It saw government action as vindictive and heavy with political rather than economic considerations. The raids made it to the cover of both *India Today*, and *Sunday*.

It said that "a government in paralysis suddenly went into a paroxysm of pressure against the press— without quite being able to sell its side of the story. The massive country-wide raids against the *Indian Express* empire were worrying overtones, signalling, as it decidedly did, a stentorian warning to the government's ever expanding circle of critics. The excessive, and armed force employed in the crackdown indicated that democracy may not be in danger, but it is increasingly under siege." Nobody quite believed Rajiv Gandhi's statement that he was out of Delhi and therefore knew nothing about the raid. However, the Rajiv government also had its 'loyalist' papers and supporters who stood up for the government. M. J. Akbar, editor of *The Telegraph*, and a respected journalist, observed that "there is a difference between investigative journalism and allegation journalism. Either you treat a man as innocent until proved guilty or as guilty until proved innocent." (*India Today*, September 30, 1987: 15). Kamal Nath, a member of the Indian Parliament, and supporter of Rajiv Gandhi said "The Express kind of journalism is sensationalism and very close to movie magazines." (*India Today*, September 30, 1987: 15).

In addition, the government came under heavy criticism from several national and international press and civil rights organizations. Among them were the Indian and Eastern Newspaper Society, the Indian Federation of Small and Medium Newspaper, the Delhi Lawyers Association, the people's Union For Civil Liberties, and the World Press Freedom Committee.

It became an explosive political issue. Political parties from left and right came out against the government's action. The Communist Party of India said that the raids smacked of "Political intimidation and an attempt to muzzle the voice of the press for daring to expose the sins of omissions and commissions of the government." The Bhartiya Janata Party echoed the sentiments by observing that "the raids ... immediately after the adjournment of the Parliament session were a planned assault on the freedom of the press." The government was not deterred by these criticisms and, in fact, intensified its efforts against the *Indian Express*. The Customs Department decided to delay the clearance of equipment worth Rs. 45 crores purchased by the *Indian Express* to expand the paper from thirteen to nineteen editions. The paper was blamed for not paying sufficient duty on the imported machinery. The

Customs also threatened to auction the newspaper's supply of imported newsprint unless the additional duty was immediately paid. The government-owned banks also moved in for the kill, and decided to financially hurt the operations of the *Indian Express* by denying it sufficient credits. On October 15th, 1987 came the worker's strike which closed down the newspaper's crucial Delhi edition for six weeks during parliament's session. The Congress (I) inspired strike began with a demand for a bonus. According to the management, the strike could have been averted even before it started. A settlement was near on the night of October 14 when "two of the representatives of the Worker's Union, obviously under the influence of outside elements, walked out of the meeting. Immediately after the walkout these elements began spreading disinformation about the management's stand to the effect that the management had not agreed to anything."

Press and public sympathy remained with the *Express*. Even those people who might have not agreed with the *Express's* freewheeling and unconventional style of journalism nevertheless agreed that the *Express* had become a symbol of press freedom in India.

The Rajiv Gandhi government seemed more determined than ever to teach a befitting lesson to the newspaper. On November 15, 1987 the *Times of India* carried a story saying that the *Express* lease was terminated by the government for alleged violation of lease provisions. The government accused the paper of subletting its building, (something that nearly every other newspaper did). The government moved on despite the fact that a legal case was in the Supreme Court, and the Court had ordered the government not to "take any action" in this regard. Once again the government's credibility was questioned. The *Indian Express* is still under siege and the case will be tied down in Indian courts for a long time to come. In the meantime, government is defiantly moving on to curb the freedom of the press in India. The latest shot was the introduction of the controversial Defamation bill in the Indian Parliament. Given the absolute majority of Rajiv Gandhi's party in Parliament, the only hope to stop it was public outcry and a determined and united opposition by important segments of Indian society. "But the stark reality is that if a government is successful in stifling the voice of the *Express*, it will have silenced a major critic and dissenter and thereby created a chilling effect on the rest of the press. It will also have silenced those voiceless millions who find their voice through the columns of the *Express*, for the battle today is not just between the Government and the *Express* but between a significant section of public opinion and the Government." (Badhwar and Chawla 1987: 20) - This time it was the government which buckled under intense public pressure. Whether the withdrawal of the Bill was tactical retreat or a sincere change of heart is anybody's guess. The case of the *Indian Express* and earlier attempts of the Indian government to suppress and regulate freedom of speech and expression raises the crucial question of the role of a free and responsible press in a transitional society. Is it possible to have a free and responsible press in a society where the process of political development is still incomplete, and the traditions of coexistence between power holders and their critics are tenuous at best? Also in a country like India "where the mass of people cannot even afford one square meal a day, leave alone a newspaper, the fight for press freedom is an unequal confrontation between a predatory government and a sliver of the intelligentsia. A majority of the press does not care one way or the other whether the government strengthens its hold on the institution." (Karnad 1988: 23). In such a situation is it even desirable or worth an attempt to fight for a free press?

The answers will depend not on the state of the laws on the provisions of the Constitution but on the integrity of the press, and the extent of development of the culture of an independent press. Walter Lippman had rightly warned that the real danger to the press springs not so much from the pressures and intimidation to which it may be subject but from the sad fact that journalists can be captured and captivated by the company they keep, their constant exposure to the subtleties of power. Judicial protection is certainly helpful that is not all that is needed. Freedom cannot be preserved for an inert people by the Constitution or the courts. That lesson was bitterly brought home during the Emergency in India in 1975. It is trite to say that civil liberties do not defend themselves. This is true of freedom of the press also. In the context of the Indian press, it has been observed that "much of English language journalism had taken a new turn which was irreversible. It discussed persons rather than issues. Inevitably, it lacked a sense of history and perspective. Journalism had got divorced from history and the larger society; poor imitation of the U.S. press had become the order of the day. Its language was either racy, which sought to sweep the reader along and not allow his critical faculties to come into play, or hectoring which sought to overwhelm the reader with 'facts' which he had no capacity to check for himself..." and that "new journalism was, in a fundamental sense, an expression of the decline in the appeal of old style nationalism and Marxism among upper-crust Indians. This decline by itself calls for a thorough discussion." (Jain 1988: 16-17). An imitative press cannot provide meaning and soul to the content to be conveyed in a different society. A responsible press must, therefore, provide "a truthful, comprehensive, and intelligent account of the day's events in a context which gives them meaning; a forum for the exchange of comment and criticism, a means of projecting the opinions and attitudes of the groups in the society to one another, a method of presenting and clarifying the goals and values of the society, and a way of reaching every member of the society by the currents of information, thought, and feeling which the press supplies." (1947: 20-19). Only then can it be free.

In the ultimate analysis, the reality of press freedom can only be realized by the will and determination of its champions and defenders to assert their rights and defend this precious freedom. As observed by Benjamin Franklin, "they who would give up essential liberty to purchase a little temporary safety deserve neither liberty nor safety." One can only hope that both Indian political elites and the Indian people will be farsighted enough not to "purchase a little temporary safety" by sacrificing the principles of democracy and justice—

principles which inspired and provided moral strength not only to the framers of the Constitution but also to valiant freedom fighters for Indian independence from British colonialism.

REFERENCES

Badhwar, Inderjit, and Prabhu Chawla 1987. "Indian Express on the Firing Line," *India Today*, Sept. 30.

Badhwar, Inderjit 1987, "You Cannot Afford to Let Go," *India Today*, Sept. 30.

Jain, Girilal 1988, "The New Journalism," *Seminar*, March.

Karnad, Bharat 1988, "Roots of a Feeble Press," *Seminar*, March.

Nayar, Kuldip 1977, "*The Judgement: Inside Story of the Emergency in India*," New Delhi: Vikas.

Sen, Dhirendra 1966, "*A Comparative Study of the Indian Constitution*," Calcutta: Orient Longmans.

"A Free and Responsible Press," 1947, *The Commission on Freedom of the Press*, Chicago, University of Chicago Press.

8

VELCHERU NARAYANA RAO

COURTS AND LAWYERS IN INDIA

Images from Literature and Folklore

One of the outstanding features of colonial rule in India was its judicial administration. The system remained as an integral part of Indian administration, even after independence. It is well-known that during the struggle for independence, the leadership of the Congress party, including its leader Mahatma Gandhi, fought against the legal system. They spoke critically of the judiciary, courts, and the legal profession and vowed to change the system in favor of a more Indian kind of judicial administration after independence. Independent India, however, has found that such a change is neither possible nor even desirable.

The British style of justice in India is administered by courts presided over by judges who are assisted by lawyers arguing on behalf of their clients. The courts are organized hierarchically with the lowest at the district level and the highest, the supreme court, at the national level. Most of the judicial administration is conducted in a foreign language, English, intelligible only to about two percent of India's population. Laws are written in English, advocates argue in English, and judgements are pronounced in English. Only evidence and cross-examination are conducted in a regional language, if the situation demands it.

The most impressive feature of the system is the lawyer. His presence in the Indian society is powerful indeed. A significant number of English-educated men of India have chosen to be lawyers (Law and Society, 1968-69). The impact of legal education on the Indian intellectual class may be measured by the fact that nearly every important leader of the national movement against the British was a lawyer trained either in England or in one of the prestigious law schools in India. Even the greatest leader, Mahatma Gandhi, received legal training in Britain. Lawyers were not only political leaders; they were prominent in social reform, and literature. Some of the best writers and scholars were lawyers In fact, free India's constitution was made by lawyers. Its chief draftsman was B.R.Ambedkar whose expertise in constitutional law was a strong enough qualification to override the complaint that he did not represent the majority of Indian people. All the members of the constitution-drafting committee were lawyers, some of whom did not even have a role in the national movement. The trust that India put in its lawyers was enormous indeed.

Students of the history of India's struggle for independence know well that a popular part of the movement was court boycott. National leaders, among whom were some of the most successful lawyers of the time, advocated and participated in rejecting the British courts. Yet it is this same leadership that accepted the British legal system as desirable after independence.

The conditions that led to the acceptance of and even respect for the British legal institutions after independence are well known. Extensive scholarly work is available to show that the traditional Hindu law before the British was not uniform. (Galanter, 1968: 66-9 provides a summary of Hindu law before the British) and many localities and groups exercised some degree of autonomy in legal administration. What happened to the indigenous law after the foundation of the uniform legal system? Galanter states (Galanter 1968: 69) succinctly:

> First, its administration moved from informal tribunals into the government's courts; second, applicability of indigenous law was curtailed; third, the indigenous law was transformed in the course of being administered by the government's courts.

In the centuries of British style administration, the legal system has apparently adjusted to the needs and aspirations of the country. The presence of a huge body of lawyers (second only to the number of lawyers in the U.S.) and extremely active litigation (Galanter, 1968-9: 201-17, Schmithenner, 1968-69: 337-82) is evidence of the stability of the system. Efforts to provide any kind of indigenous legal system have not succeeded. The classical legal texts, the Dharma Sastras, are no longer living sources of law. The social reformers from Raja Rammohun Roy onwards have found the British courts useful institutions of social reform and modernization. Local communities have even found new uses in the courts as means for achieving upward social nobility. The higher courts, and especially the Supreme Court, are seen as protectors of fundamental rights and even as agents of national integration (Dhavan, 1979.) The legal system is clearly irreversible and has come to stay.

The discomfort in adapting to a foreign legal system, however, seems to be continuing. The purpose of this paper is to present evidence to show that the concepts of justice as reflected in folklore, popular literature, and popular movies represent an opposition to and criticism of the established form of British style, modern justice in India and especially of the institution of lawyers. I shall also suggest that the leaders of the Congress

Party reflected the popular/folk perception of justice when they appealed to the masses during the freedom movement. Later in the paper, I shall indicate that folklore among city lawyers presents lawyers as better than the judges, while the village view of lawyers is positive only when the lawyer is learned, charitable, and merciful—qualities one would associate with a good judge.

Data for ths paper were gathered largely from one area of India, the Telugu-speaking state of Andhra Pradesh. In 1982, Bapu, a well-known Telugu film director, produced a movie, "Edi Dharmam? Edi Nyayam?" (What is Justice? What is Law?). The story of the movie is based on the theme that courts do not deliver justice and that the law protects the rich and the clever (Ramana, 1982.)

> Bharati, a young and beautiful woman, is elected as beauty queen. A rich industrialist patron of the arts, Prasad, who served as a judge at the beauty competition, invites himself to her house on the pretext of showing her the photographs of the ceremony, then rapes her. In the court case which follows, Dharma Rao, a brilliant advocate, presents the case as a sexual intercourse planned and coveted by Bharati with the motive of enticing the rich man in order to gain favors from him. Dharma Rao's competent conduct of the trial succeeds and the judge dismisses the case. Bharati, who has lost respect in society because of the adverse publicity from the rape case, finds a small job as a typist in a gun shop. Prasad, who grows proud of his success, repeats his criminal conduct and rapes Bharati's sister, Bharani, who unknowingly walks into his office in search of a job. Enraged at this atrocity, Bharati picks up a pistol and shoots Prasad dead. Advocate Dharma Rao, who is now the public prosecutor (a position similar in the Indian judiciary to the American district attorney), appears in court for the prosecution, accusing Bharati of murder. Bharati makes an impassioned speech accusing the judge, the advocate, and the entire system for their failure to protect her and her sister from a rapist. The judge,

convinced by her arguments, acquits her, admits his failure to deliver justice, and resigns from his position.

Let me compare this to a situation depicted in a medieval South Indian literary epic *Cilappatikaram*. The story of the epic, (Elder 1982) is as follows:

> The faithful wife of Kovalan discovers that Kovalan has been executed by the king on the false accusation that Kovalan had stolen the Queen's jeweled anklet. The enraged wife stands before the King's throne and announces that she is the widow of the executed man. The King replies: "... there is no injustice in putting a robber to death. Do you not know that it is the duty of a king?" To which Kovalan's widow responds, "King of Korkai, you went astray from the path of duty..." When the King breaks open the ostensibly stolen anklet and sees gems rather than pearls, he recognizes that he has, indeed, gone astray from the path of duty. The anklet in question is not the Queen's. Had the King inspected the anklet, as he should have while Kovalan was still alive, Kovalan would never have been executed! Recognizing his blame, the King cries out: "For the first time I have failed in my duty as protector of the southern kingdom. No way is left open to me save to give up my life." So saying, the King collapses in a fatal swoon.

In both stories there is a miscarriage of justice. In other words, the system failed to protect the honest person. In the Hindu tradition, the victim in such a context acquires a powerful ability to speak against the authority for its failure in its responsibility of representing *dharma*. The wife in *Cilappatikaram* and Bharati in the Telugu movie are representing a similar *dharmic* power. The voice with which they speak is the voice of *dharma*. In *Cilappatikaram* the King dies; in the movie the judge resigns. The mode of representing has changed, but the concept of justice remains the same. The judge in the modern movie is filling the same role in the system of *dharma* as the King in the medieval story. The movie does not recognize the principles of the modern legal system. What it does, rather, is to transform the modern system by restructuring it using the categories of traditional *dharma*.

Telugu literature has a number of writers who have used the court theme to depict social injustice and to advocate radical social and political reform. Kandukuri Viresalingam, a nineteenth century social reformer and writer, in 1879 wrote a play, "*Vyavahara-dharmabodhini*" (Primer of Social Law) (Viresalingam, 1969:73-144) Despite its scholarly, textbook-like title, the play was popular on stage and, due to its appeal to common audiences, acquired the nickname, "Plidaru Natakam (Play about Lawyers"). It depicts the story of an illiterate peasant, Virayya, who quarrels with his brother about a small piece of land. Virayya is advised by a tout to go to a city lawyer. In the ensuing court case, he and his brother get so deeply entangled that in the end both of them are totally ruined by the unscrupulous lawyers, their touts, court clerks, and even the judges. In the end, Virayya is even jailed on a false criminal charge. Throughout the case, the lawyers encourage him to tell lies. He is advised to testify that he and his brother are not really brothers. They forge documents for him. One of the lawyers even stocks old legal stationary on which documents are forged with old ink back-dating them by several decades. At every stage they make Virayya pay and force him to give gifts to them.

Racadonda Visvanatha Sastri, himself a lawyer in private life, is a well-known writer. He makes rich use of the court theme in many of his short stories, plays, and novels. One short story with a court theme is "Kortukirani Saksulu" (Witnesses Who Failed to Show Up at the Court). Briefly stated the story is as follows (Sastri 1969);

> A certain rich man has a mistress. When the mistress becomes pregnant, he decides to get rid of her. As a legal way to do so, he pays a man to go to the court claiming that the woman is his wife. According to the claim, the woman is legally married to him but now refuses to live with him.

The lawsuit prays for restitution of his conjugal rights. An impressive series of witnesses are brought to testify that they were present at the wedding. Even a priest testifies that he performed the ritual. The innocent woman, who does not even know who this man is, fails to understand the point of the case. The woman says that she was never married. But the evidence is heavily against her, and the court decrees that she should go to live with the person who is legally married to her. The man who was paid to pretend as her husband leaves soon after the case is decided in his favor and is never seen again. The rich man legally gets rid of his mistress.

The story presents a court scene with great detail and realism. The message of the story is clear: the court defends the rich and the system of justice serves those who can manipulate it to their advantage.

In his play, *Nijam* (Truth), Visvanatha Sastri portrays a rich, middle-aged man who has a clandestine sexual relationship with his maidservant. The maidservant falls in love with a young man and wants to leave the protective patronage of the middle-aged man in order to marry the man she loves. Meanwhile, the rich man's son is involved in a drunken brawl and accidentally kills one of his friends by hitting him with a whiskey bottle. The rich man, who controls the police as well as the local magistrate, gets his son cleared from the case by implicating his mistress's lover in the murder. A case is framed against the young man, who is now tried for a murder he did not commit. Due to the skill of the prosecution lawyer, the young man is convicted.

The message of the play reinforces the already popular notion: lawyers save the rich and dishonest people. The lawyer in Telugu literature is always described in unflattering terms. A stereotypical image for a lawyer, in literature as well as popular speech, is the prostitute. In Visvanatha Sastri's short story, "Maya" (The Illusion), a senior lawyer advises his junior in the following words (Sastri, 1981).

Prostitutes hang around the doors. Foxes stick to the burial grounds. Cranes tend the river banks. It is not a good analogy, but that's what we have got to do... We have to attract the parties to the court. That is professional ethics. What can we do?

A similar analogy is found in a book on the evils of prostitution published in 1926. In this interesting work, *The Pen Pictures of the Dancing Girl: With a Sidelight on the Legal Profession*, its author G.S. Mani gives, in a four-page chart, a detailed description of the similarities between prostitutes and lawyers (Mani, 1926:1-5). Typically a lawyer is depicted, in both literature and folklore, as one who encourages his client to tell lies, who even trains the client who may not be smart enough to skillfully tell lies. An important message that is driven home, either in literature or in the movies which involve lawyers, is that there is an ethical dividing line between real life and the court. A person, even if he is truthful, should still tell some lies in court in order to have his case accepted as truthful. Novels and movies frequently show situations where a person losses because he or she innocently speaks the truth in the court. It is a belief held in rural Andhra that approaching a lawyer is something an honest man should never do. Just as you do not go to the doctor unless you are sick, you do not go to an advocate unless you are untruthfull. A Sanskrit word, *nyayavadi*, is used as an equivalent for the lawyer in formal Telugu. Folk speech refers to him as *plidaru*, slightly altering the pronunciation of the English word 'pleader'. Ordinary people believe, as a folk epigram about the lawyers says, that he can make a *nandi* (the sacred bull) into a *pandi* (the pig) and vice versa if you pay him enough money.

A 1981 documentary film produced by Joseph W. Elder, "Courts and Councils: Dispute Settlement in India" presents this point forcefully. A scene from a caste Panchayat of Nadiwallas, a nomadic tribe of bull-trainers of Maharashtra, has the following conversation between the headman of the tribe and one of his fellowmen. (Elder, Hayden 1981):

> Which court is better—this court or the State courts?
>
> I haven't stepped into those courts, so I don t know...
>
> But they can make truth into falsehood.
>
> And if you go to a lawyer and give enough money—falsehood can be made into truth.
>
> Do we have enough money to step onto those premises?
>
> Here, if someone commits an offense, we fine him.
>
> Do not quarrel and do not go to the courts.

A lawyer has agents mediating between him and his clients. The folk analogy describes them as pimps in continuation of the description of lawyers as prostitutes. Since the entire legal procedure is conducted in an alien language, the ordinary client does not know what is happening in his own case. The tout, who serves as a go-between for the lawyer and the client, interprets the procedures for the client and also advises him as to how to please the lawyer in order to make sure that the latter will argue his case with his skill.

The lawyer, described by Viresalingam in the play mentioned above, has a mistress in whose house he stays until late morning. The clients are expected to wait for him in his office until he comes from his mistress's house. The clients are also encouraged to please the fancies of the lawyer in order to gain his attention.

Mahatma Gandhi (1938: 55-7), whose political and moral philosophies have had a great impact on the minds of the people, uses the same popular perspectives as were mentioned above in his opposition to the lawyers. He says:

The lawyers, therefore, will as a rule advance quarrels instead of repressing them. Moreover, men take up that profession, not in order to help others out of their miseries, but to enrich themselves... It is within my knowledge that they are glad when men have disputes. Petty pleaders actually manufacture them. Their touts, like so many leeches, suck blood of the poor people. Lawyers are men who have little to do; lazy people, in order to indulge in luxuries, take up such profession... If pleaders were to abandon their profession and consider it just as degrading as prostitution, English rule would break up in a day.

What is significantly absent in movies, literature, and folklore are stories of lawyers who stand out as heroes fighting for justice. India does not have hero characters like Perry Mason. There are no stories of skillful lawyers who work for innocent people in order to vindicate them. Neither is the image of law courts in popular literature and folklore respectable. A folk aphorism says that going to the court is like riding on a donkey. It is humiliating in itself, and in the end you get kicked by the animal. Whether you are fair or unfair, truthful or untruthfull, a court will kick you equally. It is the lawyers who ultimately get rich while parties on both sides lose their wealth. Another folk saying sarcastically quotes the statement of a litigant who says, "I may have lost all my estate, but I have learned every law on the statute book." Motilal Nehru, in an article advocating boycott of the courts quotes a similar proverb from Hindi, "*adalat men jo jita, so hara, jo hara, so mara*: "Success in courts is defeat; the defeat is death" (Mani, 1926: 118). A folk tale of two birds which went to a cat to have their dispute adjudicated is often quoted to dissuade people from going to court. In this tale, the cat eats both the birds, one after the other. The moral is that the parties who go to court will share the same fate. It is considered respectable to settle disputes outside the court and within the family. Family unity and caste identity are broken if members within the group seek settlement in a court of law.

Mahatma Gandhi gives a similar message (Gandhi, 1938: 56). He says:

> True men were less unmanly when they settled their disputes either by fighting or by asking their relatives to decide for them. They became more unmanly and cowardly when they resorted to the courts of law.

A respectable person is not expected to go to court even to give evidence in a matter which will help justice. A person who is seen around the court is called in Telugu a kortu paksi (court bird) meaning a bat which hangs around dark corners of old buildings, in this instance, court halls.

A court is a place where there is nothing sacred. One can tell a lie in a court of law without fear. A folk saying equates the court with a lavatory where urinating does not make it any more unclean than it already is. Motilal Nehru quotes another saying in the article referred to above:

> There can be no greater condemnation of the ordinary law court morality than what one often hears when litigants of this class approach each other for an amicable settlement. "We are not the court, why don't you tell the truth?" is not an uncommon form in which a fact alleged by one party is challenged by the other. (Mani: 1926, 118-119).

A folk joke, told among educated people in India reflects the same lack of confidence in the judicial system. A junior lawyer won his case and sent a telegram to his senior: "Justice is done". The senior advocates sent a telegram in return: "Appeal to the higher court" (Galanter, Personal Communication). A good contrast to the court is the temple. A temple is a pure place where even the worst of liars is not expected to tell a lie. It is positively insulated. If a person is known to have told a lie in the temple, the community will punish him by treating him as an outcaste. A person would typically challenge his opponent to speak the truth in the temple after blowing out a lamp lit in front of the deity. A very unreliable person is described in folk speech as one who can tell a lie after blowing out a lamp in front of the deity.

That religious oaths are part of dispute settlement in India in the medieval period may be seen from the following case reported by Derrett (Derrett: 1968: 218-19).

> There was a dispute over land and a commission was appointed to settle the matter. The date was 1241. The two parties were apprehended and both made a pratijna (oath?) and made their respective statements. One said he had paid the money to the female and a male and had received possession of the land. The other said he had received no money and had not delivered the parcel in question. The one party held the *divya* (object used in the ordeal) before the goddess Kali of Bandanike, while the others took with his head "hanging down". The first then was given his *jaya-patra*, or certificate of having won his case, and the circumstances were carved on stone so that the whole of that little world knew all about it forever.

Courts have adopted some of the symbolism of the temple. In Andhra a witness takes an oath in the name of God in the following words: *devuni eduta nilabadi nijam ceptanu; abaddham ceppanu* (Standing before the god, I shall speak the truth; I shall not speak lies). This statement is converted into a joke in folk speech by slightly lengthening the end vowels, thus converting it into a sarcastic question. The statement would now mean, Facing the god, do I speak the truth? Don't I speak lies.

The huge body of Sanskrit and regional language *dharma sastra* texts and their commentaries represent a very complex, codified, traditional Hindu law. There is, however, an equally complex law which was never written. It remained in oral tradition and was known to the elders of the local communities. Ludo Rocher (1968-69) reviews the literature related to lawyers and concludes that there is no clear evidence that there were professional lawyers in the traditional system. A folklorist would have no difficulty in agreeing with Professor

Rocher. The common sense of folk communities that anytime two people quarrel, the truth lies somewhere in the middle. A person who speaks for dharma is ideally one who can see that each of the parties is presenting a partial case. From this common sense perspective, a lawyer who represents one side is at least partially a liar. This, I suggest, is at the root of the general disrespect that the lawyer has earned in the folk/popular view in India.

In the movie mentioned above, What is Justice? What is Law? the following exchange takes place between Bharati and the prosecution lawyer:

Bharati: A good doctor knows the disease as soon as he feels the pulse of the patient, and a good lawyer knows the crime or innocence as soon as he sees the face of the accused. A skilled lawyer like you would know even without a trial who is a criminal and who is not. You know that Prasad raped me. Yet you argued his case with all your skill and helped him go free. Why did you do so? Why did you not do justice even though you knew everything? Answer me straight!

Advocate: Justice is what the judges do. My job is to serve my client. That's the professional duty of any lawyer. I did my job.

Bharati: And what did you get in return? You made money and got yourself promoted in your job for helping a criminal to go free. But have you thought of the consequences of what you did? The cruel animal allowed into the society could some day harm you, your children. Have you thought of that? This Prasad who raped me and my sister, might rape your sister tomorrow. Would you then talk of the niceties of evidence and proof?

The folk/popular view of justice does not recognize the role of lawyer as different from the judge's. If the lawyer is to speak for fairness, he should be speaking only on behalf of the fair side of the case. Any system which enshrines and rewards the skill of a lawyer who presents an unfair case with professional distinction, automatically glorifies injustice. A court, viewed as a place where lawyers are allowed to manipulate justice in this manner, for this reason acquires disrespect in the popular view.

In contrast, however, the judge is viewed with respect even when he fails to deliver justice. Popular movies and folklore do not usually present the judge in a bad light. Visvanatha Sastri and Viresalingam have not portrayed great judges, but the characters of judges in their works are not half as bad as their lawyer characters. Often a judge is portrayed as a weak person rather than as an immoral character. In one of the stories of Visvanatha Sastri, the judge goes crazy and is to be taken to a lunatic asylum, because he has not been able to stand the misery of life paraded before him day after day, as prostitutes, pimps, bootleggers, and destitutes are brought to his court by the police. In general the role of a judge is viewed as a respectable one, necessary for maintaining *dharma*. The reason for this seems to be that the judge's role fits into the categories of the traditional concept of justice whereas the role of the lawyer does not.

There is a different kind of "folklore" frequently circulated among the English-educated upper middle class urbanites. I Collected several interesting repartees attributed to famous lawyers of the past generation. The narrators of the incidents are members of clubs. Each major town in Andhra Pradesh has at least one club, in which the local lawyers, college teachers, and businessmen gather in the evenings for socializing and entertainment. Some of the anecdotes told here related to the wit and humour of well-known lawyers from the Madras high court, Bhashyam Ayyangar, Tanguturi, Prakasam Pantulu, and Duvvuri Narasaraju were often held up as the great luminaries of the bar. The persons were real and not fictitious; the anecdotes were told because the narrator believed them to be true. But in nature and function, they are folklore, and should be considered similar to the folk proverbs and joks earlier used in this paper. I shall call this variety of folklore lawyer-folklore, since most often the tellers of and listeners to these stories are either lawyers themselves or person of similar social status. Narla Venkatesvara Rao (Rao 1975: 217) uses some of them in an essay on repartee. I shall quote one of them here, especially because I heard it frequently told.

Bhashyam Ayyangar once went to see a judge at his house. The judge's pet dog began to bark at the sight of this stranger. The lawyer was rather frightened and stepped back. The judge joked: Why, Mr. Ayyangar! Haven't you heard that barking dogs won't bite? "Yes, My Lord," said Mr. Ayyangar still staying still staying away from the dog, "I have, but I don't know if the dog has."

Most of the anecdotes told among these circles relate to lawyers who outsmart their judges. An anecdote told about Bhashyam Ayyangar (Rao, 1975: 217) is as follows: the learned lawyer was arguing an intricate case. The judge who was impatient with him snapped, "There's no use arguing at length. Whatever you say, enters through one ear and goes out through the other." Bhashyam Ayyangar retorted, "Yes, My Lord, There is apparently nothing in between them."

One of the skills lawyers in India prided themselves on, is their ability to use English. Stories about famous lawyers tell how they spoke better English than their judges. Here is a story about Narasaraju, who was reputed to be very expressive in English. One day Narasaraju was arguing before a Telugu Judge, who was not especially known for his facility in English. Narasaraju had to quote the judge's own judgements to him to make a point. After having quoted several of his judgements, Narasarau moved on to quote from other judges. Before he did so, he paused and said, "My Lord, I will now cite some American judgements for a change". And added, "It will be refreshing to listen to some good English."

One of the functions of folklore is to express the suppressed side of life. Folklore compensates for the lack of opportunity to get even in real life situations. Lawyers who are almost always subordinated to the whims of the judges in their profession enjoy the harmless pleasure of glorifying their famous peers who outwitted the judges.

Lawyer folklore such as this often ridicules lawyers too, especially those small lawyers whose work is limited to taluk (country) level courts. The folk jokes about them make fun of their lack of English language skills. Smaller courts, where most of the litigation pertains to petty matters, and the litigants are mostly villagers, frequently use local language. Lawyers in such courts do not have occasion to perfect their English. They use a special dialect in which Telugu and English is creatively mixed. The town lawyers and their friends enjoy jokes at their expense.

One of the jokes of this type, told in Eluru, the district headquarters town in Andhra Pradesh, quotes a part of a small town lawyer's representation to the judge, as follows: "Your honor, the accused Virayya's bullocks ate *paccagaddi*, in Doddipatla *Munasabu's* garden, not only the *vankara kommula* one, but also the *niluvu kommula* too."

If stories about lawyers give the town lawyers a vicarious sense of superiority over their judges, stories about the village lawyers give them a real sense of confidence in their own skills.

What is significant, however, is that in the lawyer folklore, there are no stories degrading the morals of lawyers. All the stories I heard were about the professional charm of lawyers, or the lack of it: about lawyers who were better than their judges or, lawyers who were not good enough in their skills.

Not all stories about lawyers circulated among the ordinary people are negative. Appreciative statements about famous lawyers are heard in Andhra especially underscoring their ability to non-stop (*anargalamga*), vehemently (*gattiga*) and pounding on the tale as they spoke (*ballaguddi*). Perception of a great lawyer in rural areas also relates to the knowledge of the lawyer. The heavy, leather-bound books that are often displayed in glass book-cases in a lawyer's office indicate how much he knows and how complicated the law is. "He has got in his head everything written in those books. He doesn't really need them, these books. He keeps them so that he can show them to the judges," said one very learned traditional brahmin *purohita*, speaking to me appreciatively of his lawyer. This man was a family priest and he was considerably learned in Sanskrit ritual texts. He memorized all of them. While he was learned in Sanskrit, the priest did not know any English. He had a court case which lasted several years. He visited the city lawyer who was recommended to him by his fellow priests. The priest's concept of scholarship was heavily based on memorization. According to his tradition, one did not know a book until one had memorized it. A Sanskrit aphorism equates knowledge inside a book, (*pustakayam gatam vidya*), with money in another person's hand, (*parahasta gatam dhanam*). You cannot use either of them because they are not yours.

Lawyers are also praised for being kind and merciful. These qualities are emphasized in the case of lawyers who work for poorer clients without insisting on high fees. Statements like *'ayana dharmarajandi* (He is Dharmaraja), "*ayana devudandi*", (He is God) are heard describing such lawyers. Dharmaraja is a character from the *Mahabharata*. In folk speech, this is a description for a kind man, charitable and merciful. Devudu, also is used with the same meaning. The point, however, is that these are also the qualities a good judge is praised for. In this sense, the folk perception of a good lawyer appears to see him in the same way one would see a good judge.

In conclusion, it appears that the adversary system of justice, and the role of the lawyer in representing his client to win his case do not seem to have percolated into the consciousness of the ordinary people, nor into literature and movies.

In small communities, where everyone knows everyone else, the facts of a dispute or a crime are known to everyone. Telling a lie and winning a case by technically proving it as true through manipulating evidence or frustrating the opponent by endless litigation through the maze of court procedures and appeals to higher courts, is not possible in small communities. And from the folk perspective, this kind of legal victory bears no relation to the delivery of true justice. A popular proverb points to this attitude: *inta gelici racca geluvu.* "Win in the house before you win in the court." In other words, it is of no use to win your case in court, because it is your community which must consent to your winning the fruits of your success in court.

REFERENCES

Derett, J. Duncan, 1968. *Religion and Law in the State of India.* New York: The Free Press.

Dhavan, Rajeev, 1979. "The Supreme Court as an Agent of Integration in India" Paper presented in Indian History Seminar-Workshop, Madison Wisconsin. Mimeographed manuscript.

Elder, Joseph W and Robert Hayden, 1981. *Film Guide; Courts and Councils: Dispute Settlement in India.* The film is written and directed by Ron Hess.

Elder, Joseph W, 1982. "Hindu perspectives on the Individual and the Collectivity" Paper presented at Conference on Religion and Human Rights: Historical and Comparative Perspectives. Mount Kisco, N.Y.

Galanter, Marc., 1968. "The Displacement of Traditional Law in Modern India," *Journal of Social Issues..*

Galanter, Marc. 1968-9. "The Study of the Indian Legal Profession," *Law and Society Review* III, 2 and 3, November 1968- February 1969.

Gandhi, Mohandas Karamchand. 1938, reprint 1962). *Hind Swaraj or Indian Home Rule*. Ahmedabad: Navajivan Publishing House.

Ilankovatikal, 1965 *Shilappadikaram* (The Ankle Bracelet) by Prince Ilango Adigal, translated by A. Danielou, New York: New Directions.

Law and Society Vol. III, 2 and 3, November 1968-February 1969.

Mani, M.S., 1926. *The Pen Pictures of the Dancing Girl: With a Sidelight on the Legal Profession*. Salem: Srinivasa Printing Works.

Ramana, Sri*Edi Dharam? Edi Nyayam*? Film script of Bapu's film. Vijayawada: Sakshi Books. N.D.

Rao, Narla Venkatesvara. 1975, *Kotta: Pata*, Vijayawada: Navodaya Publishers.

Rocher, Ludo, "Lawyers in Classical Hindu Law," *Law and Society Review*, III-2 and 3, November 1968-February 1969, pp. 383-402.

Sastri, Visvanatha Racakonda, 1969 "Kortukirai Saksulu,"

Sastri, Visvanatha Racakonda. *Nijam*.

Sastri, Visvanatha Racakonda. "Maya."

Schmitthenner, Samuel 1968-9 "A Sketch of the Development of the Legal Profession in India," *Law and Society Review* III-2 and 3, November 1968-February 1969.

Viresalingam, Kandukuri, 1969. "Vyavaharadharmabodhini, in *Hasyasanjivani*, Madras: M. Seshachelam and Co.

9

JOHN J. PAUL

AUTHORITY AND PROFESSIONAL CONTROL OF THE SUBORDINATE LEGAL PROFESSION IN THE MADRAS PRESIDENCY DURING THE LATE NINETEENTH CENTURY

Introduction

The present judicial system in India owes much to the imagination and experiment of the British in the nineteenth century. How the early rulers of modern India, whether under the company or under the Crown, went about setting up this legal system with its elaborate structures involving regulations, codes, courts, rules of procedures, and functionaries, raises many questions that hold enormous promise for historians and social scientists alike. Does this system represent a "total replacement" of an indigenous system with one of "foreign origin"[1] or a more "subtle blending" of local (or native) and alien institutions ?[2] One could debate endless on such a mooted question as this.

What follows, then, is a discussion of the internal struggle for control between the High Court Judges and District Judges over the appointment of an amorphous body of "lawyers", known as pleaders ; in this test of the will, the High Court ultimately triumphed and was able to consolidate its total control over the administration of justice in the Presidency during the 1880s. Prior to 1862, when the High Court was established in Madras, the District Judges had powers, under the defunct Company rule, to appoint and dismiss pleaders at will; these judges naturally resisted any attempt by the High Court to wrest that power from them in order to establish its supreme authority. That the High Court at this time had no legal power to curb the resistance of the subordinate judiciary, usually the civilian judges (or the I.C.S.) and that bureaucratic redtapism often stood in the way of reform, exacerbated the frustrations of the Judges.

From the protracted correspondence that ensued between the High Court and various government agencies (the District Judges, the Government of Madras, the Board of Revenue, and the Government of Calcutta) one captures the undercurrents of the deep-seated antagonism within the judiciary. This professional discord forms the main focus of the following discussion. It will, moreover, highlight various aspects of the subordinate legal profession and the quality of individuals who practised law during the latter part of the nineteenth century.

Conflict and Consolidation of Authority

Two different options were available to an individual who chose a career in law before the founding of the High Court in 1862. One could enter the profession either by passing the law examination, introduced in 1856, by attending the law lectures at the Presidency College and obtaining the Bachelor of Law (B.L.) degree. The or graduates of the latter were often admitted to the *Sadr Adalat* (or Chief Court) of the East India Company; those with the certificates (*sanads*) practised

Subordinate Legal Profession in Madras Presidency

exclusively in the District and Munsif's courts. At this period, the terms *vakil* and pleader were often used inconsistently to describe anyone who practiced in the Sadr courts. However, the amalgamation of the Supreme Court and the *Sadr Adalat* and the creation of the High Court in their place led to certain distinctions between various branches of the legal profession. Three different groups of legal practitioners—advocate, attorneys, and vakils—practised before the High Court, while the subordinate court lawyers generally became known as pleaders.

Vakils of the High Court had to meet certain academic and practical requirements before their admission to practice; their professional activities must also conform to the standards established by the Judges. In contrast, the majority of the pleaders had only high school education (or whatever was comparable) and the certificate authorizing them to practise law. Naturally, their professional roles and social eminence were far from matching that of their colleagues, who were graduates (in arts and law), and who, therefore, dominated the *mufassal* bar. The pleaders were usually admitted on the stipulation that they should confine their activities within the specific courts to which they had been attached. They enjoyed neither recognition nor patronage from the government, nor were they subjected to a close surveillance by the Judges of the High Court. None of the rules of professional etiquette applicable to vakils was relevant to the pleaders. The power to include or exclude an individual from the local bar was vested primarily with the District Judge, who was a member of the I.C.S. Because he was frequently shunted between different districts, he cared little about the quality of the bar or the character of the men who constituted it. Moreover, no appeal lay against his decisions to the High Court since the local government held the reins of the authority to enquire into matters of abuses of power by the civilian judges. Therefore, between 1856 and 1882, the *mufassal* lawyers were left to themselves and to the mercy of the presiding judicial officer. The High Court played very little role in giving any direction to the development of this particular branch of the legal profession.

When the Government of India enacted legislation, Act XX of 1865 (also known as the Pleaders', Mookhtars' and Revenue Agents; Act), bringing out uniform qualification and treatment of pleaders in Bengal and the North-Western Provinces, the law contained provisions for its implementation in the rest of British India.[3] The same year the Madras Government sought the advice of the High Court on the feasibility of introducing this Act in the Presidency; the latter discouraged the government's initiatives on the grounds that it was "neither necessary nor desirable." In the letter, the Registrar noted:

> It is unnecessary, because the High Court already possess the power of prescribing rules for admission of Pleaders in the lower Courts, and the duties and liabilities of persons admitted to practice are already sufficiently defined. It is inexpedient because it is not advisable to fetter the discretion allowed to the High Court under existing regulations; because the present rules for the examination of candidates for the legal profession have been found already to operate beneficially; and because any measure which may tend to increase the prevalent disbelief in their permanency is much to be deprecated.[4]

In 1875, however, the High Court Judges had serious misgivings about their previous decision. This time the Court took the initiative by approaching the local government "on the question of expediency of extending the provisions of Act XX of 1865."[5] The Judges realized that indeed they had very limited powers in the matter of regulating the activities of lawyers in the subordinate courts; they now saw that in appointing, suspending, and dismissing pleaders," the practice of granting *sanad* was extensively abused. Obviously, some District Judges issued certificates not only to those who had passed the prescribed examinations but also to those who merely styled themselves as "Private Vakils." Perched beneath the Second Grade Pleaders within the professional hierarchy, they, as a separate body, almost always appeared before the Sub-Magistrate and Assistant Magistrate Courts located at *taluk* head-quarters.[6] For example, in 1879, the Chief Secretary to the Government of Madras, C.G. Masters, ordered the Acting District Judges of Godavari, J. Wallace, to withdraw *all* certificates issued to unqualified men under his jurisdiction. The Judge obeyed the order immediately and later reported that matters were "restored to their former position."[7] Similar orders were issued to other judges as well.[8]

On receipt of the letter from the High Court, the Government of Madras referred the subject to the Board of Revenue because Act XX of 1865 also dealt with those agents who primarily appeared in Revenue Courts. The Board, after obtaining the opinions of Collectors from Nellore, Bellary, North and South Arcot, Madurai, and Coimbatore, eventually responded on May 14, 1875; loath to make any changes in the existing practice, the board wrote in unequivocal terms that there was no "practical necessity for the introduction of the Act as far as the Revenue Department [was] concerned, and they [were] averse to its being brought into force."[9] The government agreed with the Board and wondered whether or not an amendment to Regulation XIV of 1816 would improve the difficulties recognized by the High Court.

One further bureaucratic snag stood in the way before Act XX of 1865 could be extended to the Madras Presidency. At this time, the provincial governments had no power to tamper with any of the legislation enacted by the Governor General. The local government realized that if the Act were to be extended to Madras, "it must be as a whole."[10] But, in view of the strong opinions expressed by the Board against its introduction, that was now seen as undesirable. Thus, the local government on the basis of the recommendation from the Board turned down the request of the High Court.

The Judges realized that they had run into a dead end and decided to adopt a different strategy altogether. Between June

7, 1875 and November 25, 1876 the Registrar continued to address the government on this subject. During this time, the High Court also took extra-ordinary pains to ascertain the opinions of several Collectors and magistrates "regarding the number, status, and qualifications generally of the persons (other than those duly qualified by law) who [had] ordinarily [appeared and practised] in the Magisterial and Revenue Courts of the district."[11] The finding was startling. The High Court concluded from the evidence that "a large class of men ignorant, uninstructed, and too frequently unprincipled, whose object [was] to promote and foster litigation [was] let loose upon the community and [was] subjected to *no control*, either from the Legislature or the superior Judicial authorities."[12] As far as amending Regulation XIV of 1816, the Registrar pointed out to the government that most of the sections of the Regulation had become obsolete. Indeed, more than fifty years had elapsed since the enactment of that particular legislation; it generally applied only to the previous cadre of pleaders, who had commenced their practice with little or no preparation. Whatever sections had remained intact or had not become obsolete could be more appropriately replaced with the provision of Act XX of 1865. This was what the High Court desired "to see introduced" in the Presidency. The Registrar concluded the Court's plea with these remarks:

> As regards the difficulty arising from the circumstance that the Board of Revenue [was] opposed to the introduction of the Act in so far as it affect [ed] the Department under its control, and that there [was] no power to introduce the Act otherwise than in its entirety... the High Court [was] not so directly concerned with the working of the Revenue Courts as ... to urge the application of the provisions of the Act of 1865 to this class of Courts."[13]

An appeal was also made to the Governor to consider the possibilities of making recommendations to the Government of India to re-enact the relevant portions of Act XX of 1865, which dealt with pleaders. The Government of Madras took several months to decide what action should be taken on the letter from the Registrar. Persuaded by the arguments put forward by the High Court, Sir W. Robinson, one of the Members of the Governor's Council, strongly recommended the introduction of the Act in the Presidency. Yet he thought it might be appropriate to consult the Board of Revenue once again because the Board was one of the most powerful branches of government and its members carried much weight. Depending on the Board's reply, he had hoped to decide the question "whether the Judicial requirements of the country [were] to be further sacrificed in deference to the hesitation of the Board in regard to the application of the Act to Revenue Courts."[14] It is not clear what the Board had thought about the letter, but in view of the hesitation of the bureaucrats, which was tantamount to inaction on the part of the Government, the Council became polarized on this issue. On April 2, 1877 the Government sent a reply informing the Registrar that they had decided to "adhere to their previously expressed opinion that it [was] undesirable to extend the Act as a whole to the Presidency." [15]

While files containing the foregoing correspondence between the Government, the High Court, and the Board of Revenue were being exchanged in their usual, slow, secretive, and methodic fashion, the Press began to expose the scandalous treatment of pleaders by district judges. Advocating immediate reforms to raise the quality and dignity of pleaders, the *Madras Times* carried a rather long editorial on the "question of the admission and status of Pleaders and their relations to the Judges of the Court in which they practise."[16] Up till now, the High Court had mainly been concerned with exercising control over the activities of opportunistic individuals practising in magisterial and revenue courts; the men had taken such fancy titles as "agents," "law agents," and "private vakils." But now, *The Times* exposed the general humiliation of pleaders in many civil and criminal courts.

The Times pointed out that it was not so much by passing the prescribed examination that a candidate had access to the gates of courts as by his ability to get along with the presiding judge. So long as an individual remained subservient to the caprice of the "master," his position was secure. Furthermore, some judges arrogated to themselves the right in declaring who was and who was not to be permitted to practise before them and also had no scruples in using their "judicial" authority against pleaders who had incurred their wrath.[17] These "unwholesome" relations between Judges and pleaders had produced a duel effect. First "men of independence, intelligence, and education" had kept themselves away from the courts while individuals with marginal education and inferior character entered the profession. Second, as a result the judges themselves had been deprived of the services of efficient men and their duties had become onerous. In their anxiety "to get at the truth" the judges were often forced into taking sides with one party or another. *The Times* said, "We think it will be admitted by those who are in a position to judge, that the picture is by no means overdrawn."[18]

The Times then strongly urged the authorities to give effect to Act XX of 1865 by extending it to the Presidency. According to the provisions of this Act, pleaders would be brought under the jurisdiction of the High Court and would no longer be subjected to the "vexatious impositions of petty fines" by the district judges. It was hoped, moreover, that through the system of apprenticeship, similar to the one prevailing among vakils of the High Court, all pleaders, especially the new entrants, would learn both the civil and criminal law and procedure, and follow the examples of senior members; this would eventually enable them to develop a keen sense of dignity befitting the profession.[19] A few vernacular newspapers also voiced the same concerns over several issues related to pleaders, especially those who had practised in criminal courts.[20]

In light of these developments in the press, the High Court made a last ditch effort at persuading the Government of Madras to introduce Act XX of 1865. The Registrar argued that even though the government had concurred in principle on the expediency of introducing the Act in the entire Presidency, the Government's decision to defer the matter indefinitely had not improved the situation. On the contrary, the "evils and inconveniences" that had been pointed out previously by the Judges, in their letter dated November 25, 1876, had continued to increase; no proper provisions in law existed to check the abuses connected with the appointment of pleaders. Specifically, the High Court had no power to interfere with the actions of district judges; the judges freely exercised their power either by delaying the granting of the *sanads* or by revoking such certificates whenever they pleased. Certain judges had also permitted unqualified individuals to practise law in their courts because they alone had the power to decide who should or who should not be permitted to plead. In view of these "unhealthy" practices, it was deemed imperative that Act XX of 1865 be introduced and that the Government reconsider their previous decision to tolerate the prevailing practices (seen as "loopholes" in law).[21]

In his minutes, dated December 29, 1877, Sir. W. Robinson forcefully reiterated what he had previously expressed. He wrote, "the assent of Government should no longer be withheld. I would make and publish the requisite order under Section 47 of the Act at once and apply the Act in its entirety... I cannot, therefore, be a party to seeking... modification in any form or degree. I am prepared to give it effect at once."[22] Robinson obviously felt that the only course open to the Government, therefore, was to remove the bastions of resistance and accept the recommendations of the High Court. The Chief Secretary then contacted the Advocate General, P. O'Sullivan, soliciting his opinions as to "whether the first 18 sections of the Act can be re-enacted by the Madras Legislative Council as a local measure." On January 7, 1878 he advised the Government that a part of the Act alone cannot be introduced "without infringing on the spirit of Section 42 of the India Council Act, 1861." Only through an amendment by the Government of India to Act XX of 1865, authorizing the local governments to declare the whole or part of the Act as applicable, would such a measure be valid. In the end, the local government relented by addressing the Indian Government, enclosing copies of all relevant discussion and requesting that such an amendment be made so that other territories might benefit from the Act.[23]

Before discussing the nature of response to the letter from the Madras Government, it would be useful to observe that the present discussion on the condition and treatment of pleaders very much resembled a similar correspondence that had taken place between London, Calcutta, and Madras in 1848.[24] Although the issues in 1878 remained the same as they had been in 1848, the perceptions had now changed. Responding to an investigation on the treatment of pleaders by Judges in the districts, the Registrar of the *Sadr Adalat* wrote in 1848, that the judges had exercised their power to fine erring pleaders only "sparingly" and that some measure of "check and restraint' was necessary.[25] But, in 1878, the Judges of the High Court strongly asserted that the power to grant the *sanad* (and also to fine) had been abused to the extent that a thorough reorganization of the legal profession in the subordinate courts was necessary. They advocated that the power to regulate rules for the qualification and admission of pleaders and to punish the offenders must necessarily be within the High Court and not in the district courts. Thirty years ago, the *Sadr Adalat* had hoped that the introduction of Act I of 1846 and the advancement of time would bring "considerable advantage" to the institution of pleaders as whole; but, the High Court now pointed out the deterioration in the quality and character of pleaders, and cited instances of misuse of law. Against such abuses of law, the High Court possessed no corrective or punitive authority.

Before the letter from the Madras Government ever reached the Government of India in Calcutta, the latter had already begun to deliberate over the introduction of new legislation. Act XX of 1865 had been amended thrice before and the legislators felt diffident about amending it any further. They felt it would be beneficial for the whole of British India if the Act could be repealed altogether and a different Act introduced in its place, incorporating the various suggestions put forward by the High Court of Calcutta and Madras, and by the Chief Court in Punjab. Consequently, the Legal Practitioners' Act (Act XVIII of 1879), was enacted. It became effective on January 1, 1880.[26]

As R. Suntharalingam observed, "the Growth of the legal profession in South India was to a considerable degree influenced by British policies."[27] Thus, Act XVIII of 1879 removed every technical snag that had previously stood in the way of the Madras Government in applying the previous Act XX of 1865. It empowered local governments "to extend all or any of the provisions of the ... Act to the whole or any parts of the territories under [their] administration."[28] It also conferred a new status on pleaders. especially those who practised in the up-country; for the first time they were brought under the direct super-intendence of the High Court. As the highest judicial tribunal, the High Court, by granting certificates, recognized only those individuals proficient in English, who also had passed the prescribed examinations on select topics in law. The certificate issued by the High Court entitled them to practise in District, Subordinate, and Munsif Courts. Admission to practise law could no longer be refused to pleaders nor could judges subject them to arbitrary fines. The derogatory epithets such as pettifoggers, uneducated and unprincipled pleaders became inapplicable as they came to be known as "legal practitioners."[29]

The Act came into effect in Madras on April 1, 1882. Under the provisions of the Act, the High Court framed elaborate rules dealing with qualification, examination, admission, suspension or dismissal, and renumeration of pleaders; these rules were published in the Fort St. George Gazette as well as in local newspapers.[30] The new rules set forth two separate groups of individuals known as the First and Second Grade Pleaders. Whereas the former as a group were allowed to appear, act, and plead in any district court in which they had been enrolled or any of its subordinate courts (both in their civil and criminal jurisdictions), the latter were permitted to act, appear, and plead only in the Munsif courts. However, the Second Grade

Pleaders were permitted to appear in all criminal courts of the district except the Sessions Court of the Division.[31]

Candidates had to have a minimum education of F.A. (First Year in Arts) to qualify for the First Grade and matriculation for the Second Grade. Yet they both studied the same subjects and took the same examination; the only difference between them was the percentage of aggregate marks that they were expected to obtain: forty the twenty-five percent, respectively. Having completed the examination, a candidate applied for a certificate or license from the High Court through the District Court, with supporting documents on qualification and character, and proof of having paid the Stamp Fee. On receipt of his certificate, a pleader was then entitled to launch his legal career.[32]

A large number of candidates in the *mufassal* did not have the facility or the resources needed to attend the law lectures in the city. Most of them, therefore, read independently for the examinations. Although the textbooks prescribed for pleaders in 1882 were the same as those used by law students, pleader's understanding of the intricacies of law was naturally superficial. Yet it was remarkable that many First Grade Pleaders handled cases at their original instance with great skill and industry; often, they also advised vakils from the High Court on appeals. More numerous in number but inferior in legal knowledge and skill were the Second Grade Pleaders who exclusively practised in Munsif courts. The High Court Registrar once observed that there was neither honor nor profit in their profession and they had "only a familiar acquaintance" with the *Code of Civil Procedure*, the *Law of Evidence*, and the Hindu and Muslim law. Examinations in these subjects were held both in English and in the local vernaculars; many enthusiastically chose the vernacular examination.[33]

One of the most important concerns of the authorities in enacting Act XVIII of 1879 was to put an end to the notorious practice of giving commissions to law agents or touts. Neither the so-called "English" trained barrister or attorney, nor the

Indian vakil had been immune from the "corrupting" influence of this malady. Whatever provisions had previously existed, deprecating this "shameful practice," had been ignored with impunity; and the practice had become an accepted *mamool* (or custom) throughout India.[34] In order to stem the tide of this epidemic, the legislators introduced Section 36 of Act XVIII of 1879. This categorically stated that such practices were now "of a penal nature" and rules against them would be "precisely complied with."[35] The original Section read:

> Whoever, being a legal practitioner, tenders, gives, or consents to the retention of any [persons] for procuring, or having procured the employment in any legal business of himself, or any other legal practitioners shall be punished with simple imprisonment for a term which may extend to six months, or with fine, which may extend to five hundred rupees, or with both.[36]

The local press welcomed such bold measures. However, the measure proved ineffective in the long run, because the Amending Act IX of 1896 was primarily intended to tackle the growing menace of touts in public courts. In spite of such limitation, the Legal Practitioners' Act of 1879 proved to be beneficial in three respects.

First, it removed the uneasy tensions between the High Court and district judges stemming from the ill-defined rules about questions relating to the overall superintendence of pleaders. Now the High Court exercised this authority to grant or refuse certificates, prescribed and supervised examinations for pleaders, and dealt with the professional misconduct of pleaders. In short, the High Court finally had the power to regulate the control the subordinate legal profession and the pleaders were, from now on, responsible to the High Court.

Second, the office of a pleader was now looked upon with more respect than it had ever been before. Now graduates in Arts and Law entered the profession in the *mufassal*. Men like S. Subramania Iyer entered the profession under these provisions. Iyer started his practice in Madura but later moved

TABLE 1

Statement Showing the Amount of Admission and Stamp Fees Realized From the 1st April to 31st December 1882. By the Issue of Plead Certificates Under The Legal Practitioners Act, 1879.42

	Total No. of Certificates issued	First Grade	Second Grade	Amount of Admission Fee Realized. First Grade	Second Grade	Total	No. of Certificates issued after 30th Jan. i.e., Issued on Stamp of Half Value. First Grade	Second Grade	Amount of Stamp Fee Realized. First Grade	Second Grade	Total	Total of Stamp and Admission Fees.
Presidency Small Cause Court	10	10	...	70	...	70	2	...	225	...	225	295
Arcot (North)	101	24	77	168	385	552	2	8	575	2,095	1,670	2,223
Arcot (South)	92	25	67	175	335	510	3	4	587.5	975	1,562.5	2,072.5
Bellary	69	14	55	98	275	373	1	6	337.5	780	1,117.5	1,490.4
Canara (South)	163	27	136	189	680	860	...	4	675	2,010	2,685	3,554
Chinglepuc	80	25	55	175	275	450	3	6	587.5	780	1,367.5	1,317.5
Coimbatore	99	22	77	77	285	539	3	2	512.9	1,140	1,652.5	2,191.5
Cudapah	75	14	61	98	305	403	...	2	350	900	1,250	1,653
Ganjam	57	15	42	105	210	315	3	3	337.5	607.5	945	1,260
Godavari	191	36	155	252	775	1,027	1	11	887.5	2,242.5	3,130	4,157
Kistna	107	24	83	168	415	583	1	11	587.5	1,162.5	1,750	2,333
Kurnool	31	6	35	42	125	167	...	...	150	375	525	692
Madara	160	44	116	308	580	888	3	14	1,062.5	1,635	2,697.5	3,585.5

Subordinate Legal Profession in Madras Presidency

	Total No. of Certificates issued	First Grade	Second Grade	Amount of Admission Fee Realized First Grade	Second Grade	Total	No. of Certificates issued after 30th Jan. i.e., Issued on Stamp of Half Value. First Grade	Second Grade	Amount of Stamp Fee Realized. First Grade	Second Grade	Total	Total of Stamp and Admission Fees.
Maladar (North)	117	16	101	112	505	617	...	3	400	1,492.5	1,892.5	2,509.5
Malabar (South)	242	45	197	315	985	1,300	2	14	1,100	2,850	3,950	5,250
Nellore	67	14	53	98	265	363	1	5	337.5	757.5	1,095	1,458
Salem	93	20	73	140	365	505	...	8	500	1,035	1,535	2,040
Tanjore (North)	152	41	111	287	555	842	6	9	950	1,597.5	2,547.5	3,389.5
Tanjore (South)	184	54	130	378	650	1,028	3	6	1,312.5	1,905	3,217.5	4,245.5
Tinnevelly	145	27	118	189	590	779	6	4	600	1,740	2,340	3,119
Trichimopoly	96	24	72	168	360	525	3	9	562.5	1,012.5	1,575	2,103
Visagapacam	102	17	85	119	425	544	...	4	425	1,245	1,670	2,214
Total	2,433	544	1,889	3,808	9,445	13,253	43	133	13,062.5	27,337.5	40,400	53,653

to Madras; he became one of the two leading vakils of the High Court and Eventually found a place on the Bench.[37] Another such person was C. Rajagopalachari, who began his career in Salem and who rose to national prominence during India's struggle for freedom.[38] Examples like these abound.[39]

Third, the Act opened up "an entirely new source of revenue" for the coffers of the Government. Fees paid by candidates who desired to become pleaders amounted to a large sum, exceeding all the calculations of the authorities.[40] When the Act came into operation, the Government estimated that the sum collected from fees would be about 40,000 rupees for that year; but the total amount realized from granting new certificates was 53,653 rupees.[41] The following table provides the numerical breakdown of certificates issued to pleaders and the revenue raised through Stamp between April 1 and December 31, 1882.

Each year many more newcomers were added to the total number of 2,433 First and Second Grade Pleaders.

TABLE 2

Numerical Strength of Pleaders Between 1883 and 1897.[43]

	New Certificates		Renewed Certificates	
Years	First Grade	Second Grade	First Grade	Second Grade
1883	79	162	539	1801
1884	68	40	544	1795
1885	48	53	572	1725
1886	31	50	576	1658
1887	22	39	543	1527
1888	31	51	543	1582
1889	20	68	566	1572

Table 2 Cont.....

	New Certificates		Renewed Certificates	
Years	First Grade	Second Grade	First Grade	Second Grade
1890	20	54	549	1579
1891	36	87	558	1537
1892	30	132	555	1552
1893	34	94	549	1607
1894	48	226	552	1607
1895	41	75	563	1747
1896	16	23	574	1729
1897	33	34	568	1710

It is noteworthy that in 1883 only twelve and ten candidates appeared for the first and second grade pleaderships examination; but the total number of new certificates issued for the year was 79 for the first grade and 162 for the second grade.[44] This anomaly might have been due to the enrollment of service candidates with a B.L. degree or with pleadership certificates under the old rules. Second, while the renewal of licenses for the First Grade Pleadership varied only slightly each year, the number of certificates for Second Grade had begun to decrease gradually. The total number of renewed certificates issued in the 1890s never reached the original figure of 1801 in 1883. Many factors such as improvements in better education standards, failure to renew certificates because of little or no income, and even personal illness and death may have been the reasons for this decrease.

Glimpses of Pleaders in the Mufassal

The following is a brief discussion of the activities and conditions of these mufassal practitioners. These observations are based on the records of the Judicial Department of the Madras Government and local newspapers.

While a large proportion of individuals with higher educational attainments sought a livelihood through law practice, there were others for whom it was but an option. These persons usually held clerical positions in the government or taught in secondary schools.[45] With a smattering of English these "amateur lawyers" began their practice in the lower courts such as the Munsifs' and the Sub-Magistrates' Courts.

A small number of men entered the profession because members of their families had previously been involved in the judicial administration. For example, when V.O. Chidambaram Pillai was enrolled as a Second Grade Pleader in 1895, his "grandfather, uncle and father" had already been lawyers.[46] Chidambaram Pillai's father V. Olaganatha Pillai was the *samasthana vakil* (i.e., legal advisor in the court) for the Zamindar of Ettayapuram; he represented the Polygar warlord both in the collector's office and in the local court. In return for his "legal" services, he was paid both in cash and in kind, and was given free lands and timber. As legal advisor to the Zamindar, he was given a most prominent place in the *durbar*, next to that of the *diwan* (or tanapati).[47]

As vakils began to imitate the style of barristers in the High Court, and as vakils and barristers began to filter down into the districts, pleaders lost no time in superficially copying the High Court lawyers. Naturally, the Munsif Court pleaders looked up to the district court pleaders as their forensic mentors. Their bombastic and pretentious style has been captured and caricatured by S. Vedanayagam Pillai, a District Munsif, in a Tamil novel; he wrote

> As soon as a bad lawyer spotted a client, the lawyer says, 'it is only your good fortune that brought you to me. The moment you came to me then all your actions turned out to be virtuous...Whatever case you might have I will win it in the court for you. I will make your

opponent feel ashamed that he would never be able to appear in public. If he gains an upper hand by citing the law I will go beyond by pointing out the custom. If he cites the religio-legal texts in support, I will win by citing the English law. If he tries to use the French law, I will use the German law. If he darts at me the German law, I will assail him with Roman Law.'[48]

Vedanayagam Pillai was also an accomplished Tamil poet and has described the way some pleaders conducted their cases before him:

> Subbaiyar is a sack
> of lies; and Sundaraiyar's case
> has nine hundred
> holes; Appaiyar displays
> forged documents; and
> Anantaiyar builds castles
> in the air.[49]
>
> If these screaming,
> quarrelling vakils
> right next to me
> burst my skill,
>
> When will I
> mediate, O heart ?
> When will I
> meditate on the holy feet
> of the Lord
> O, heart?[50]

Despite the introduction of different Special Tests in 1866, and the consolidation of various rules for pleaders, a body of individuals had managed to elude these so-called reforms. Known as "Private Vakils," "Law Agents" or "Law Dubashees," they practised exclusively in the subordinate criminal courts. Two factors were conducive to their continued survival : first, the *Code of Criminal Procedure,* Section 342, was silent with respect to the special qualifications of a pleader, and, second, the Government of India was "not at all likely to open up [the] question [of private vakils] which would involve an amendment of the Criminal Procedure." These gave them unlimited freedom and opportunities to conduct criminal cases.[51] Pleaders who practised in civil courts complained furiously about the unrestricted freedom with which these private pleaders went about doing their business while they were subjected to various stringent rules of the High Court. A "Hopeful Lawyer," in his murmur against the existing rules, observed, "the law agents who [are] sarcastically called *Akkapore* [i.e., nuisance] or *Banniantree* pleaders, and who hang upon the tender mercies of Magistrates, need not be alarmed [by these rules]. The present Act [XVIII of 1879] and the rules do not in the least affect their position as agents...of accused persons."[52] This body of extra-legal practitioners continued to exist in criminal courts well beyond the first two decades of this century. Occasionally, they even sought recognition and legitimacy from the government and the High Court, but such attempts bore no fruit.[53]

There were mounting resentments between the civil court pleaders and private vakils against the later's encroachments in criminal courts. Pleaders frequently despatched petitions to their superiors protesting against loopholes in the law, against favoritism shown by some magistrates to private vakils, and against rules under which the civil court pleaders had been compelled to pay a fee for enrollment and renewal of certificates; they implored the government to intervene on their behalf. In addition to these disadvantages, the petitioners complained that the local bars were overcrowded and made a decent living difficult. One petitioner wrote :

[T]he profession has become *so cheap* that many needy circumstanced practitioners often hurt after engagements even for one tenth of the legal fees and thus spoil others by competing for lowest fees in every case... The Honorable High Court, who has insured stringent provisions to curtail the number when these were only 25 in 1879, has not now desired to amend their own rulings which has been the sole cause for the *annual swelling in the Mofussil Bar*.[54]

Conclusion

At the end of the nineteenth century, the High Court of Madras was the highest tribunal in the state apparatus for the administration of justice. Established under the Letters Patent, in 1862, it possessed enormous powers for dealing with every question of law, and for supervising the functions of numerous subordinate courts and the duties of a host of judicial officers. The High Court also had the statutory authority to frame rules for the regulation of the legal profession. From the outset, the Judges succeeded in prescribing specific rules for each of the three groups of lawyers—barristers, attorneys, and vakils—who practised before the High Court.

However, it did not have any authority over a vast number of individuals who practised law in the districts. From the beginning of the Company rule, the district judges exercised control over them under the old Regulation XIV of 1816. The High Court Judges, for reasons unknown, felt that they must leave the responsibility of granting certificates to the district judges who had enjoyed this power for many decades. But they soon felt that this power had been abused by some, who had allowed unqualified individuals to practise law. They wanted to assume the prerogative of regulating the legal profession in the subordinate courts as they had done in the High Court, but it was not easy. Proverbial bureaucratic "red-tapeism," constitutional limitations, conflict of interest between the judiciary and bureaucracy, and sheer innertia on the part of rulers in Madras and Calcutta impeded the process of consolidation of power and such delay prolonged the exasperation of the judges in gaining control over the pleaders.[55]

By the time, the Government of Madras was prepared to accept the recommendations of the High Court by extending Act XX of 1865 to the entire Presidency, the law had become obsolete. The Government of India had decided to abrogate this law altogether and enact a new statute, Act XVIII of 1879, known as the Legal Practitioners' Act, empowering the Judges of each High Court of formulate rules for the qualification and admission of pleaders. When the Act was introduced in the Madras Presidency on April 1, 1882, two different grades of pleaders, the First and the Second Grade, were constituted under the rules framed by the High Court. The rules stipulated that candidates for the situation of First Grade Pleaders should have a minimum education of F.A. (First Year in Arts), while the Second Grade candidates had to complete their matriculation. They both had to study a number of subjects in law and pass the examinations on those topics; the only difference between them was the total percentage of marks each was required to obtain : forty and twenty-five respectively. Candidates for the Second Grade Pleadership also had the option of appearing for the examinations conducted in the vernacular instead of English. Thus, an individual's basic educational attainments and percentage of marks he got in the examinations determined his avenue of practice : either in the District Court or in the Munsif's Court.

The results of the introduction of the Legal Practitioner' Act in the Madras Presidency were numerous and everyone concerned benefitted from them. First, the High Court had finally succeeded in consolidating its authority over the entire legal profession, and not just the High Court lawyers alone. Formulating the rules on the qualification and admission of pleaders aside, the Judges were able to pass a more general rule prohibiting both pleaders and vakils from participating in any "trade or business" without the prior sanction of the High Court. This measure was introduced to ensure that the practitioners did not get involved in any outside activities unworthy of their profession. Moreover, in an effort to bring about homogeneity within the profession in 1927, the Judges decided to abolish the group of Second Grade Pleaders altogether on the eve of implementing the Indian Bar Council Act of 1926.[56] That there were more unemployed law graduates at this time and that the bar as a whole was already "overcrowded" might also have been the reasons for this decisive measure that the Judges took.[57]

Second, the institution of pleaders, whether the First Grade or the Second Grade, acquired a new dignity that had either been absent or denied them before. After the implementation of the Act of 1879, pleaders generally had both an academic qualification and professional knowledge; they were now licensed by the highest judicial tribunal in the state and were no longer subjected to verbal insults or arbitrary fines by district judges. As pleaders came into contact with High Court Vakils, who frequented the district courts conducting trials or handling appeals arising from lower courts, they cultivated a network of relationships between the metropolitan and urban lawyers; from such encounters the pleaders also seem to have acquired a sense of solidarity and codes of ethics. When in 1920, for example, S. Srinivasa Iyengar, the Advocate General, organized the First Lawyers' Conference in Madras, pleaders showed much enthusiasm and participated in the meetings in the hundreds.[58]

This new sense of "dignity" also induced some pleaders to make such unrealistic claims as portrayed in the Tamil novel by Munsif Vedanayagam Pillai. It is instructive to note that in one of his poems on lawyers, the fictitious names given to pleaders were Brahmin names ! This might allude to the preponderance of Brahmins in every grade of the legal profession, except barristers and attorneys.

Relative freedom from the over-zealous officials and a new sense of dignity attached to their professional roles enabled many pleaders to take part in local politics and other activities that would not have been possible before. The life of V.O. Chidambaram Pillai serves as an example of the influence that a pleader could wield in the local society. His patriotism brought him not only wide acclaim but also a more permanent place in the pages of South Indian history.[59] During the second decade of this century, High Court vakils and pleaders played an important role in the development of the rural economy, particularly in the creation of numerous financial institutions that were spawned throughout South India. Known as Funds or Nidhis, these joint-stock companies rendered a valuable service by offering low-interest loans to local residents, farmers, and small-scale merchants. The Madras Government recognized the service that vakils and pleaders rendered as directors in the development of cooperative banks and it even persuaded the High Court to relax one of its own rules against such involvements.

With the introduction of provincial legislatures and district boards and municipalities in the late nineteenth century, the number of High Court lawyers and pleaders serving these bodies increased. Baker has shown that during the three elections held between 1920 and 1926, the number of lawyers elected to the Madras Legislative Council was far greater than that of any other professional group.[61] Testifying before the Select Committee of Parliament, Sir Alexander Cardew, a former civilian of Madras, noted:

> I do not know any class that will be able to compete with lawyers... There is no commercial class. There is no large business community. There is only this educated class of lawyers ; they are the only people that are known, and I doubt very much whether the local landowner, who is generally very little educated, will have any chance against a local vakil.[62]

The same pattern in the political ascendency of lawyers, whether vakils or pleaders, seems to have prevailed in other parts of India during the 1920s and 1930s. In a conversation with Sir Andrew H.L. Fraser, former Lieutenant Governor of Bengal, the maharajah of Dharbhanga declared :

> You have thrown all the power into the hands of the pleaders. They rule the courts; they have all the power of the local bodies; and they have a practical monopoly of the Legislative Councils. We cannot oppose them.[63]

Such was the legacy of Indian lawyers, who had risen from their servile position and ignorance of law in the nineteenth century to unenviable heights in national politics and social regeneration in the twentieth century. Their complete story is yet to be told by historians.

NOTES

1. Marc Galanter, "Study of the Indian Legal Profession," *Law and Society Review* 3 : 2-3 (November 1968-February 1969) : 214.

2. John J. Paul, "Vakils of Madras, 1802-1928 : The Rise of the Modern Legal Profession in South India," Ph.D. dissertation, University of Wisconsin-Madison, 1986.

3. This was Act No. XX of 1865, known as the Pleaders', Mookhtars' and Revenue Agents' Act. See, George S. Fogan, Comp., *The Unrepealed and Unexpired Acts of the Legislative Council in India. From 1834 to 1870*, 4 vols. (Calcutta : Central Press, 1871),

4. Letter from the Registrar to A.J. Arbuthnot, Chief Secretary, No. 575, dated April 1, 1865 : included in Government of Madras (GOM), Judicial Department, No. 261, dated February 6, 1878.

5. Letter from the Registrar to W. Hudleston, Chief Secretary, No. 749, dated April 2, 1875 ; included in GOM, Judicial Department, No. 261, dated February 6, 1878.

6. GOM. Judicial Department, No. 140, dated December 21, 1869.

7. GOM. Judicial Department, No. 274, dated March 31, 1879.

8. Orders were issued to several District Judges. See High Court of Madras, Administrative Records (HCAR), No. 91, dated January 22, 1879 (S. Malabar), GOM, Judicial Department, No. 412, dated February 27, 1879 (Nellore), and No. 2924, dated December 18, 1880 (Tanjore).

9. Proceedings of the Board of Revenue, No. 1295, dated May 14, 1875; *Ibid*.

10. *Ibid*.

11. Letter from the Acting Registrar to the Chief Secretary, No. 2739, dated November 25, 1876. Ibid.
12. *Ibid.*
13. *Ibid.*
14. Minute by Sir W. Robinson, dated March 29, 1877; *Ibid.*
15. *Ibid.*
16. *The Madras Times*, September 7, 1872.
17. *Ibid.*
18. *Ibid.*
19. *The Madras Times*, June 5, 1873. See, *The Madras Times*, November 5, 1873, and January 16, 1874 for further observations on the condition of pleaders and the various measures suggested to improve their character.
20. See, *Vivekavardhani*, December 16, 1878 ; *Kerala Patrika*, November 18, 1886 ; *Swadesamitran*, November 27, 1889.
21. Letter from the Registrar to the Chief Secretary, No. 2797, dated December 4, 1877.
22. *Ibid.*
23. *Ibid.*
24. Paul, "Vakils of Madras," Chapter I, pp. 61-63.
25. *Ibid.*
26. *Abstract of the Proceedings of the Council of the Governor General of India. 1879*, Vol. XVIII. (Calcutta; Government Printing, 1880), pp. 19, 218, 316-318.
27. R. Suntharalingam, *Politics and National Awakening in South India, 1852-1891* (Tuscon: University of Arizona Press, 1974), p. 136.
28. Tej Bahadur Sapru, Gen. Ed., *Encyclopaedia of the General Acts and Codes of India,* 10 vols. (Calcutta : Butterworth, 1938): 5 : 184.
29. Bisvesvar Mukherji, *The Leval Practitioners' Act* (Calcutta; R. Cambray, 1903), p. xxiv.
30. See, *Fort St. George Gazette*, 1881, Part , pp. 491 and 707; *The Madras Mail*, March 25 and 28, 1882.

31. Rules of the High Court, 5 and 6; *The Madras Mail,* March 25, 1882.

32. Rules of the High Court, 8 through 26; Ibid.

33. GOM. Judicial Department, No. 807, dated May 23, 1866 and No. 1003, dated June 27, 1866.

34. *Abstract of the Proceedings,* p. 212.

35. Sapru, *Encyclopaedia,* p. 212.

36. Act XVIII of 1879' Section 36 cited in *The Madras Mail,* November 17, 1879.

37. U. Ve. Caminataiyar, *Ninaivu Mancari* [Garland of Memories] 2 vols. (Madras : Kabeer Printing Works, 1957), 1 : 63-95 (in Tamil).

38. Rajmohan Gandhi, *The Rajaji Story,* 2 vols. (Madras : Bharatan, 1978).

39. S.P. Sen, ed., Dictionary of National Biography, 4 vols. (Calcutta : Institute of Historical Studies, 1975).

40. GOM, Judicial Department, No. 877, dated March 28, 1883.

41. *Ibid.*

42. *Ibid.*

43. *Report [s] on the Administration of Civil Justice in the Presidency of Madras, 1883-1897,* 15 vols. (Madras : Scottish Press, 1884-1898).

44. *Ibid.,* Report, 1883, p.12.

45. *The Madras Times,* June 5 and November 5, 1873.

46. M.P. Sivagnanam, *The Great patriot V.O. Chidambaram Pillai,* tanslated from Tamil by Soundara Mahadevan (Madras : Inba Nilayam, 1972), p. 10.

47. I am grateful to Mr. V.O.C. Subramaniam for his encouragements, hospitality and willingness to inform me about his ancestors ; personal interview was conducted on March 17, 1983.

48. Muncip Vetanayakam Pillai, *Piratapa mutaliyar carittiram* [The Story of Piratapa Mutaliyar] (Tirunelveli : The South India Saiva Siddhanta Works, Publishing Society, 1966), p. 286 (In Tamil).

49. Matu. Ca. Vimalanantam, *Tayakam tanta nayakam* [The Hero the Motherland Gave] (Cennai : Cekar patippakam, 1964), p. 83 (In Tamil).

50. Ibid., p. 88. See. *The Madras Times*, February 22, 1873.

51. Note by the Under Secretary on the petition of George Felix, a second grade pleader from Dindigul ; GOM, Judicial Department No. 411, dated February 14, 1884.

52. *The Madras Mail*, March 22, 1882.

53. See, HCAR. No. 8091, dated August 11, 1881; No. 5285, dated September 1, 1886 and No. 2775, dated October 12, 1886 ; GOM, Judicial Department No. 224, dated February, 1890 ; No. 1911, dated December 23, 1904 and GOM, Law General, Ordinary Series, No. 1591, dated may 13, 1925 and No. 2219, dated July 16, 1927, for a three-way correspondence and communication between private pleaders, the local government and the High Court on the matter of recognition of private vakils. Particularly, the 1904 document contains the names of all such practitioners throughout the Presidency and the amount of income tax each one had paid.

54. Petition from Caminadha Iyer, Tanjone Bar ; GOM, Judical Department, No. 4999, dated December 22, 1884. See also, No. 2484, dated September 26, 1879 and No. 411, dated February 14, 1884 for samples of similar petitions.

55. The correspondence that took place between the Madras Government and the High Court was one of the many instances where both the Executive and the Judiciary were at loggerheads. See, R. Suntharalingam, "The Salem Riots, 1882 : Judiciary versus Executive in the Mediation of a Communal Dispute," Modern Asian Studies 3 : 3 (1969) : 193-208.

56. See, *The Criminal rules of Practice (Moffusil)*, Third improved edition (Madras: V.S.N. Chari, 1933), pp. 111-114.

57. Bankey Bihari Misra, *The Indian Middle Classes: Their Growth in Modern Times* (London : Oxford University Press, 1961), p. 327; Unemployment Committee, *Report on the Question of Unemployment among the Educated Middle Classes* (Madras: 1927), and Unemployment Committee, United Provinces, *Report* (Allahabad: 1936). See, HCAR, No. 1027, December 30, 1937 for views of the Madras High Court Judges on the recommendations of the Unemployment Committee, United Provinces, headed by Tej Bahadur Sapru.

58. See, *Law Weekly- Journal Section* 10 (December 1919): 60-63; *Madras Law Journal-Journal Section* 38:1 (January 1920): 1-4, and *Madras Weekly Notes-Journal Section* II (February 1920): 19-25.

59. See, N. Rajendran, "Swadeshi Movement in Tamilnadu, 1905-1914," Ph.D. Thesis, Madras University, 1987. This is an important study dealing with the efforts that Chidambaram Pillai took in founding a steam navigation company with indigenous capital and management. As a result of fierce competition from the British India Steam Navigation Company, a British owned shipping firm, and on account of the imprisonment of Chidambaram Pillai, who provided the leadership, the Swadeshi Steam Navigation Company ultimately collapsed. No other South Indian undertook similar ventures until the independence of the country. See also, V.U. Chidambaram Pillai, *Va. U. Ci. Cuyacaritai* [V. U. C. autobiography], 6 patippu (Cennai : Pari Nilayam, 1979): Curata, ed. *Va. U. Citamparanar nurrantu malar, 1872-1972* [V.U.C. Hundredth Birth Centenary 1872-1972] (Cennai: Curata, [1972]; R.a. Padmanabhan, *V.O. Chidambaram Va. U. Ci. murpokku iyakkankalin munnoti* [V.U.C. : The Forerunner of Progressive Movements] (Cennai: Makkal Veliyitu, 1980).

60. See, John J. Paul, "New Frontiers in the Colonial Judicial Administration: Its Laws and Lawyers," Paper read at the Conference on "South Asia and World Capitalism," held at the Tufts University, Medford, MA, December, 12-14, 1986.

61. C.J. Baker, *The Politics of South India 1920-1937* (Cambridge: Cambridge University Press, 1976), p. 155, n. 267.

62. House of Commons, Cd. 203, Vol. IV of 1919, Paper No. 81. *Joint Select Committee on the Government of India Bill*, 3 vols. (London: His Majesty's Stationary Office, 1919), 2: 336

63. Andrew H. L. Fraser, *Among Indian Rajahs and Ryots* (Philadelphia: J.P. Lippincott, 1911), p. 58.

Index

Additional Judges 25, 26
Ahmed, Fakhruddin Ali 65
Akbar (Emperor) 158
Akbar, M.J. 191
Amardas 159
Ambani, Dhirubhai 74
Ambedkar, B.R. 112.5, 130
Antulay, A.R. 73
Arjun Singh 26, 44
Austin, Granville 5, 6
Ayer, S. Subramania 227
Ayyangar, Bhashyam 210

Baleanti, Ralph 1
Bachchans 187
Bahuguna, H.N. 69
Baxi, Upendra 34
Bhagwati P.N. 17
Bhatia, Krishan 67
Bhushan, Shanti 68
Bofors 75, 187, 188
Burke, Edmund 122

Campaign spending 55
Cardew, Alexander 238
Cases in arrears 33
Censorship 185
Cilappatikaram 200
Chagla, M.C. 18, 41, 57
Chandrachud, Y.V. 20, 36, 98
Charan Singh 58, 69
Communal Award 130, 131
Companies contributions 57
Cornwallis, Lord 122
Curzon, Lord 124

Dapthary, C.K. 42
Dayal, K.M. 28
Defections 61

Dey, N.C. 36
Directive Principles 5, 12, 161
Dowry Prohibition Act 167

Elder, Joseph W. 203
Electoral laws 55ff.
Emergency 22, 25, 41, 58, 69, 184, 185, 193
Equal Remuneration Act 175

Family courts 170-2
Farooque, M.B. 28
Foreign contributions 59, 76
Forest laws 143, 146
Fraser, Andrew H.L. 238

Galanter, Marc 113, 126-8
Gandhi, Indira 8, 12, 23, 58, 59, 63, 68, 70, 72, 75, 76, 78, 80, 184-94
Gandhi, Mahatma 77, 112, 127, 128, 130, 197, 198, 205, 207
Gandhi, Rajiv 59, 61, 77, 82, 179, 180, 186, 189, 190, 192
Gandhi, Sanjay 74, 75, 80, 185
'Garibi Hatao' 135
German Submarine deal 75
Goenka, Ram Nath 185, 187
Gokhle, H.R. 8, 181
Goloknath case 182, 183
Grant, Charles 123
Gurumurthy, S. 188
Guruswamy, Mohan 76, 77

Hegde, Ramkrishna 63
High Courts 17
Hindu Code Bill 120, 172
Hindustan Times 17, 75
Hobbes, Thomas 125

Humayun 158

Illegal donations 70
Indian Advocate, The 42
Indian Express 187, 193
Indian Rural Development Programme (IRDP) 142
India Today 42, 179, 190-1
Iyengar, S. Srinivasa 237
Janata government 22, 23, 41, 58, 186
Jha, Prem Shankar 71
Jones, Willian 96
Jardan Diengdeh case 172
Judges' transfers 22-33, 39
Judges' salaries 20-2, 39
Judges' vacancies 32-33

Kamal Nath 191
Keshavananda Bharti case 183
Khan, Mohammad Ahmad 89
Khanna, H.R. 35
Khare, R.S. 79
Kickbacks 74-76
Kissa Kursi Ka 26
Krishna Iyer, V.R. 25, 42
Kumaramangalam, Mohan 42

Lal, B.M. 25, 26
Lalit, H.R. 41
Law Commission 18, 30, 33
Lewis, Anthony 180
Lippman, Walter 193
Locke, John 53
Lowenstein, Karl 6

Macaulay, T.B. 123-5
Macpherson, C.B. 81
Madison, James 177
Madras Times 221-3
Malhotra, Inder 28
Mani, G.S. 203
Manju case 169-70

Masters, C.G. 219
Maternity Benefit Act. 162, 167
Mathura Case 168
Mill, J.S. 122, 132
Minimum Wages Act 139, 140, 146
Mishra, L.N. 69
Mody, Piloo 63, 73
Moynihan, Daniel 76
Mukerjee Pranab 62
Muslim League 129
Muslim Personal Law 91-94

Nagpur Times 189
Nandini Satpathy case 168
Narasaraju 210
National Rural Employment Programme (NREP) 142
Nayyar, Kuldip 28, 69
Nehru, B.K. 79
Nehru, Jawaharlal 5, 7, 36, 183
Nehru, Motilal 205, 206
Niyoga 155, 156
North, Lord 122

O'Sullivan, P. 223
Oza, G.L. 28

Panchayat Acts 141
Pandit, C.S. 69
Party Finances 64, 68
Pyne, R.N. 28
Pillai, S. Vedanayagam 232-33
Pillai, V.O. Chidambaram 232, 236
Pillai, V. Olaganatha 232
Poona Pact 130
Poverty 133 ff.
Press Freedom 185 ff.
Press Commission 186
Purdah 158, 160, 164

Rajagopalachari, C. 230
Rao, N.V. 210
Rau, B.N. 180

Index

Ray, A.N. 35
Robinson, W. 223
Rocher, Ludo 207, 208
Ross, Alexander 124
Roy, Raja Rammohan 119, 159, 198
Rozen, Lawrence 3, 4, 6
Rudolphs, Lloyd and Susanne 8

Sachar Committee 58
Sastri, Racadonda Viswanatha 201, 202, 209
Sati 155, 157, 160
Selznick 3
Seventh Amendment 24, 25
Shah Banu case 88 ff., 172
Shariah 95-6
Shsatri, Lal Bahadur 184
Shiv Shankar, P. 23, 34
Shore, John 123
Shourie, Arun 188, 189
Sikri, Justice 17, 42
Simon Commission 130
Singh, N.K. 27

Singh, V.P. 58, 76, 188-89
Spengler, Oswald 54
Seraljee, Soli J. 17
Statesman, the 20, 31, 185
Stephen, Fitzjames 123-5
Supreme Court 6, 7, 8, 13

Tarkunde, V.M. 19
Tewalia, D.S. 28
Times of India 39
Trubune 68
Trivedi, K. 71
Tutzapurkar, Justice 19, 29
Tyabji, Badruddin 98

Udham Singh case 169
Upanayana 155, 158
Urs, Devraj 74

Vajpayee, A.B. 62
Waqf 102
Weber, Max 78
Whiggism 122, 124

Zail Singh 187, 188